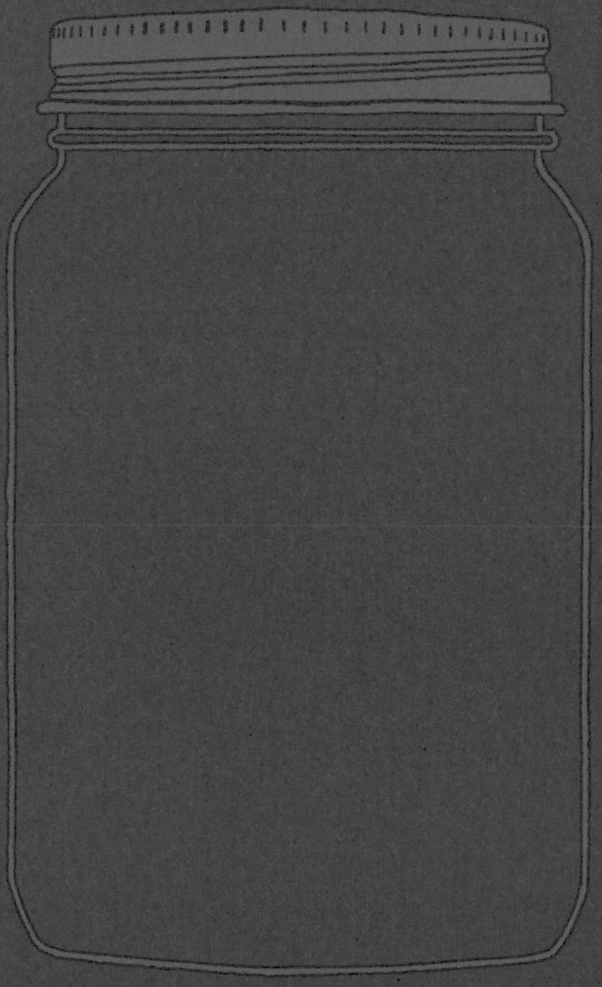

Ghostwriter

RAYCO PULIDO

Translated by Andrea Rosenberg

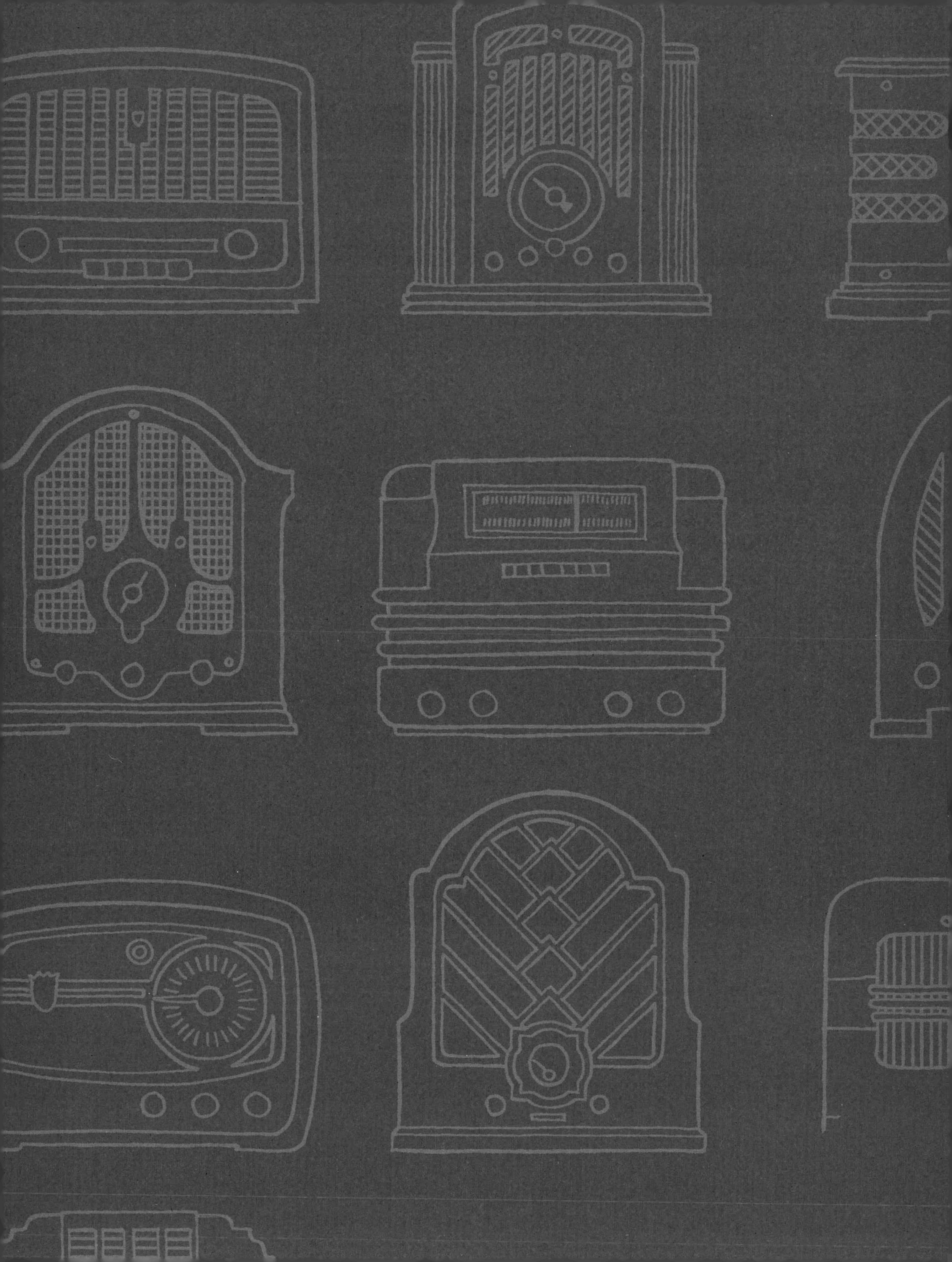

GHOST WRITER

Rayco Pulido

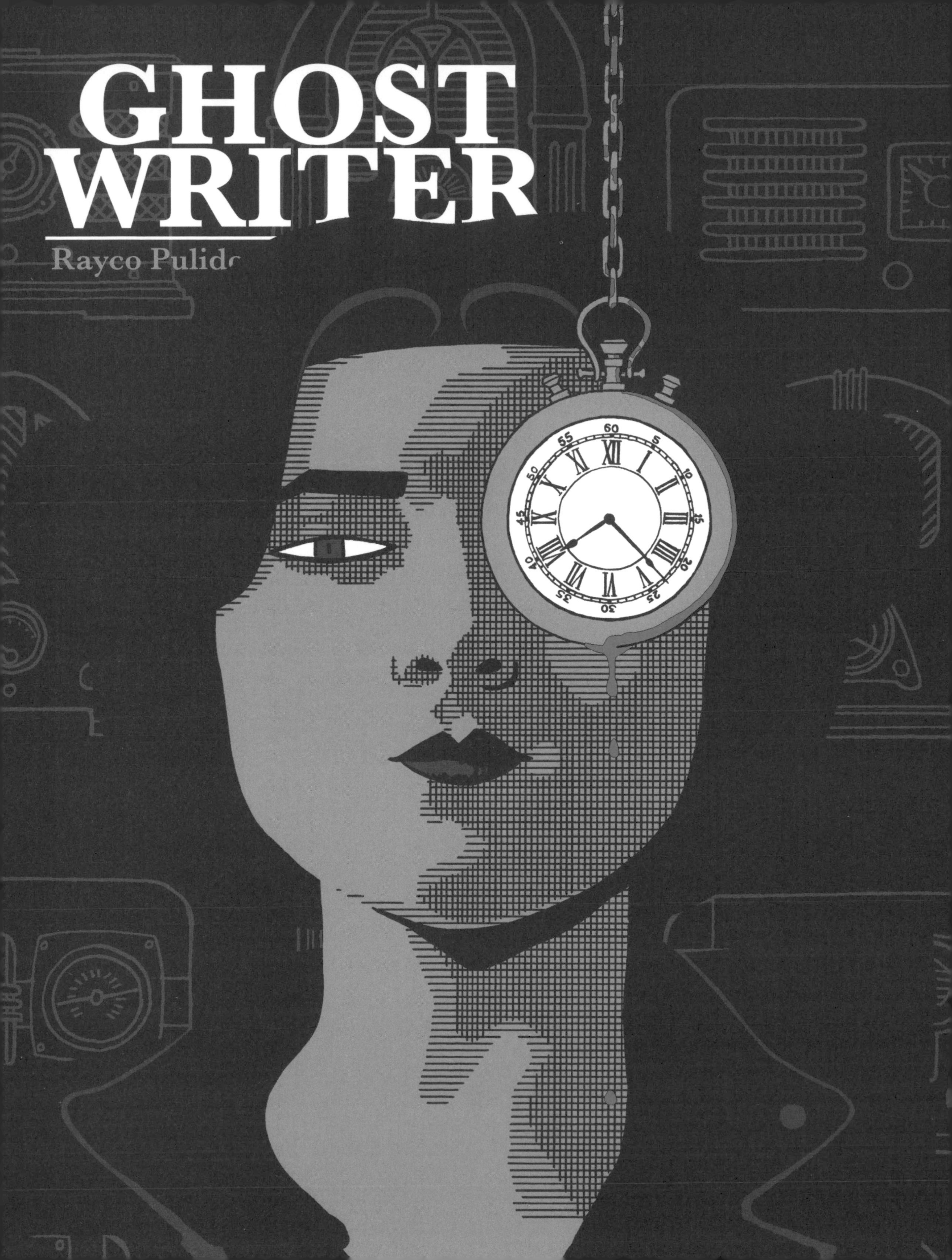

DESIGN: Rayco Pulido
EDITOR: Conrad Groth
PROOFREADER: Christina Hwang
PRODUCTION: Paul Baresh, Christina Hwang
ASSOCIATE PUBLISHER: Eric Reynolds
PUBLISHER: Gary Groth

FANTAGRAPHICS BOOKS, INC.
7563 Lake City Way NE
Seattle, WA 98115
www.fantagraphics.com
facebook.com/fantagraphics
@fantagraphics.com

ISBN: 978-1-68396-318-9 *LIBRARY OF CONGRESS CONTROL NUMBER:* 2019954462 *FIRST FANTAGRAPHICS BOOKS EDITION:* August 2020 *PRINTED IN:* Korea

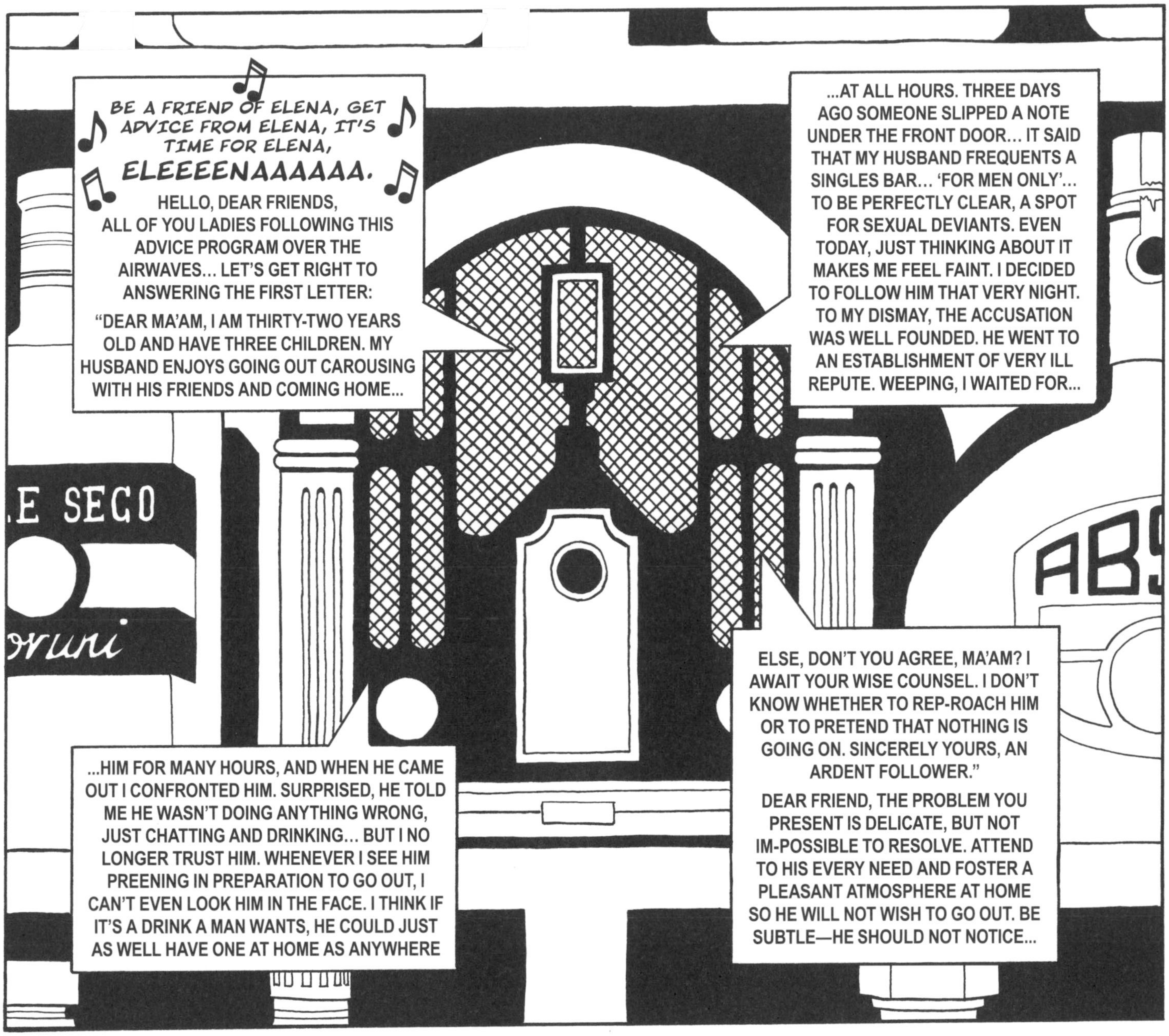
BE A FRIEND OF ELENA, GET ADVICE FROM ELENA, IT'S TIME FOR ELENA, ELEEEENAAAAAA.
HELLO, DEAR FRIENDS, ALL OF YOU LADIES FOLLOWING THIS ADVICE PROGRAM OVER THE AIRWAVES... LET'S GET RIGHT TO ANSWERING THE FIRST LETTER:
"DEAR MA'AM, I AM THIRTY-TWO YEARS OLD AND HAVE THREE CHILDREN. MY HUSBAND ENJOYS GOING OUT CAROUSING WITH HIS FRIENDS AND COMING HOME...
...AT ALL HOURS. THREE DAYS AGO SOMEONE SLIPPED A NOTE UNDER THE FRONT DOOR... IT SAID THAT MY HUSBAND FREQUENTS A SINGLES BAR... 'FOR MEN ONLY'... TO BE PERFECTLY CLEAR, A SPOT FOR SEXUAL DEVIANTS. EVEN TODAY, JUST THINKING ABOUT IT MAKES ME FEEL FAINT. I DECIDED TO FOLLOW HIM THAT VERY NIGHT. TO MY DISMAY, THE ACCUSATION WAS WELL FOUNDED. HE WENT TO AN ESTABLISHMENT OF VERY ILL REPUTE. WEEPING, I WAITED FOR...
...HIM FOR MANY HOURS, AND WHEN HE CAME OUT I CONFRONTED HIM. SURPRISED, HE TOLD ME HE WASN'T DOING ANYTHING WRONG, JUST CHATTING AND DRINKING... BUT I NO LONGER TRUST HIM. WHENEVER I SEE HIM PREENING IN PREPARATION TO GO OUT, I CAN'T EVEN LOOK HIM IN THE FACE. I THINK IF IT'S A DRINK A MAN WANTS, HE COULD JUST AS WELL HAVE ONE AT HOME AS ANYWHERE
ELSE, DON'T YOU AGREE, MA'AM? I AWAIT YOUR WISE COUNSEL. I DON'T KNOW WHETHER TO REP-ROACH HIM OR TO PRETEND THAT NOTHING IS GOING ON. SINCERELY YOURS, AN ARDENT FOLLOWER."
DEAR FRIEND, THE PROBLEM YOU PRESENT IS DELICATE, BUT NOT IM-POSSIBLE TO RESOLVE. ATTEND TO HIS EVERY NEED AND FOSTER A PLEASANT ATMOSPHERE AT HOME SO HE WILL NOT WISH TO GO OUT. BE SUBTLE—HE SHOULD NOT NOTICE...
.E SECO
ABS
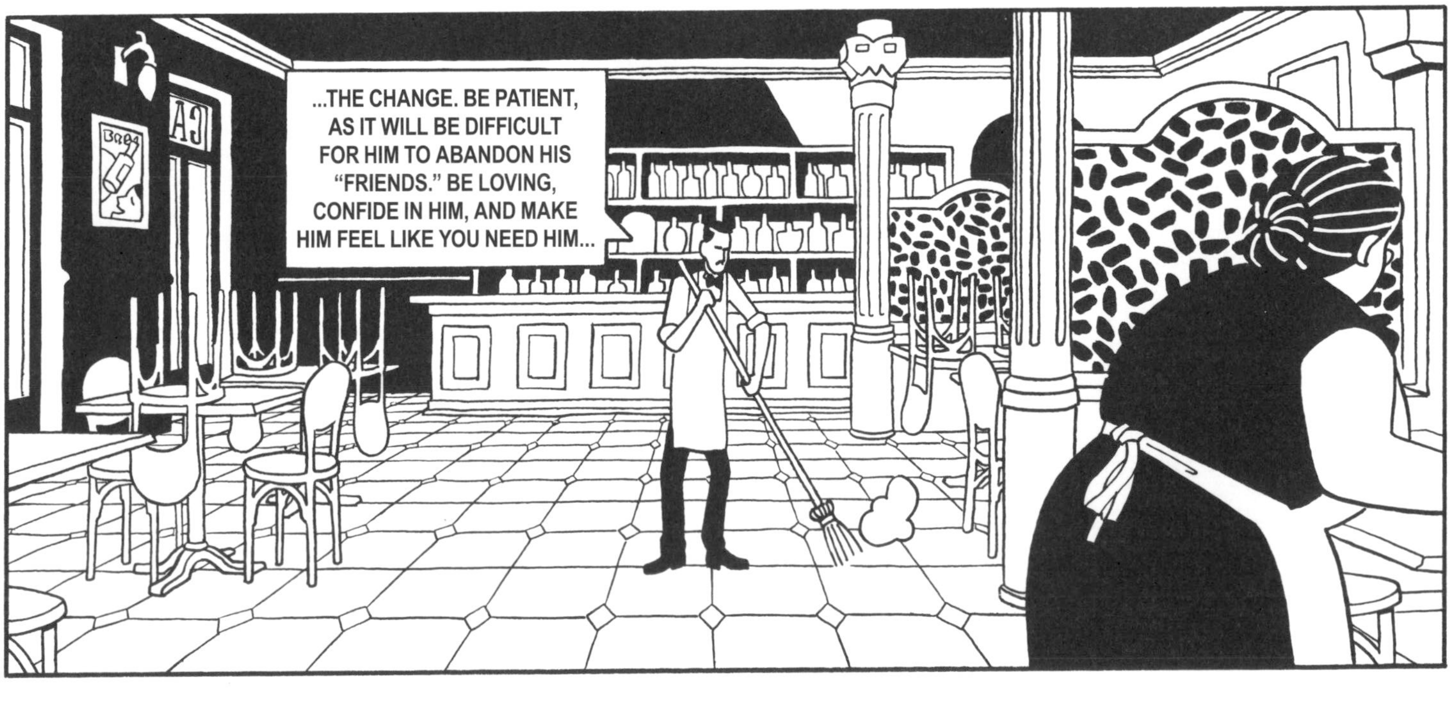
...THE CHANGE. BE PATIENT, AS IT WILL BE DIFFICULT FOR HIM TO ABANDON HIS "FRIENDS." BE LOVING, CONFIDE IN HIM, AND MAKE HIM FEEL LIKE YOU NEED HIM...

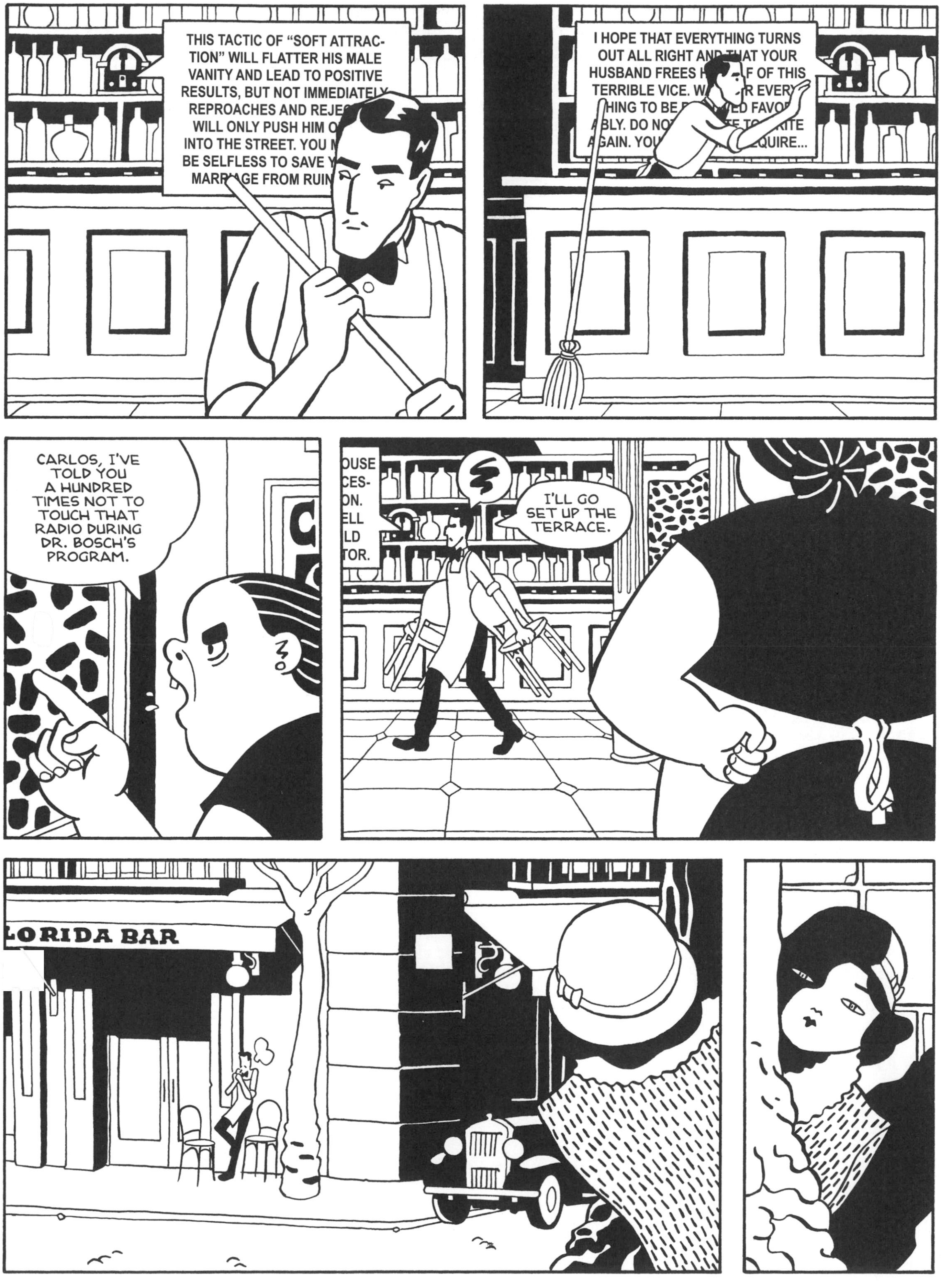
THIS TACTIC OF "SOFT ATTRACTION" WILL FLATTER HIS MALE VANITY AND LEAD TO POSITIVE RESULTS, BUT NOT IMMEDIATELY. REPROACHES AND REJE WILL ONLY PUSH HIM O INTO THE STREET. YOU M BE SELFLESS TO SAVE Y MARR AGE FROM RUIN
I HOPE THAT EVERYTHING TURNS OUT ALL RIGHT AND THAT YOUR HUSBAND FREES H F OF THIS TERRIBLE VICE. WE EVERY HING TO BE FAVOR ABLY. DO NOT TO RITE AGAIN. YOU QUIRE...
CARLOS, I'VE TOLD YOU A HUNDRED TIMES NOT TO TOUCH THAT RADIO DURING DR. BOSCH'S PROGRAM.
I'LL GO SET UP THE TERRACE.
LORIDA BAR

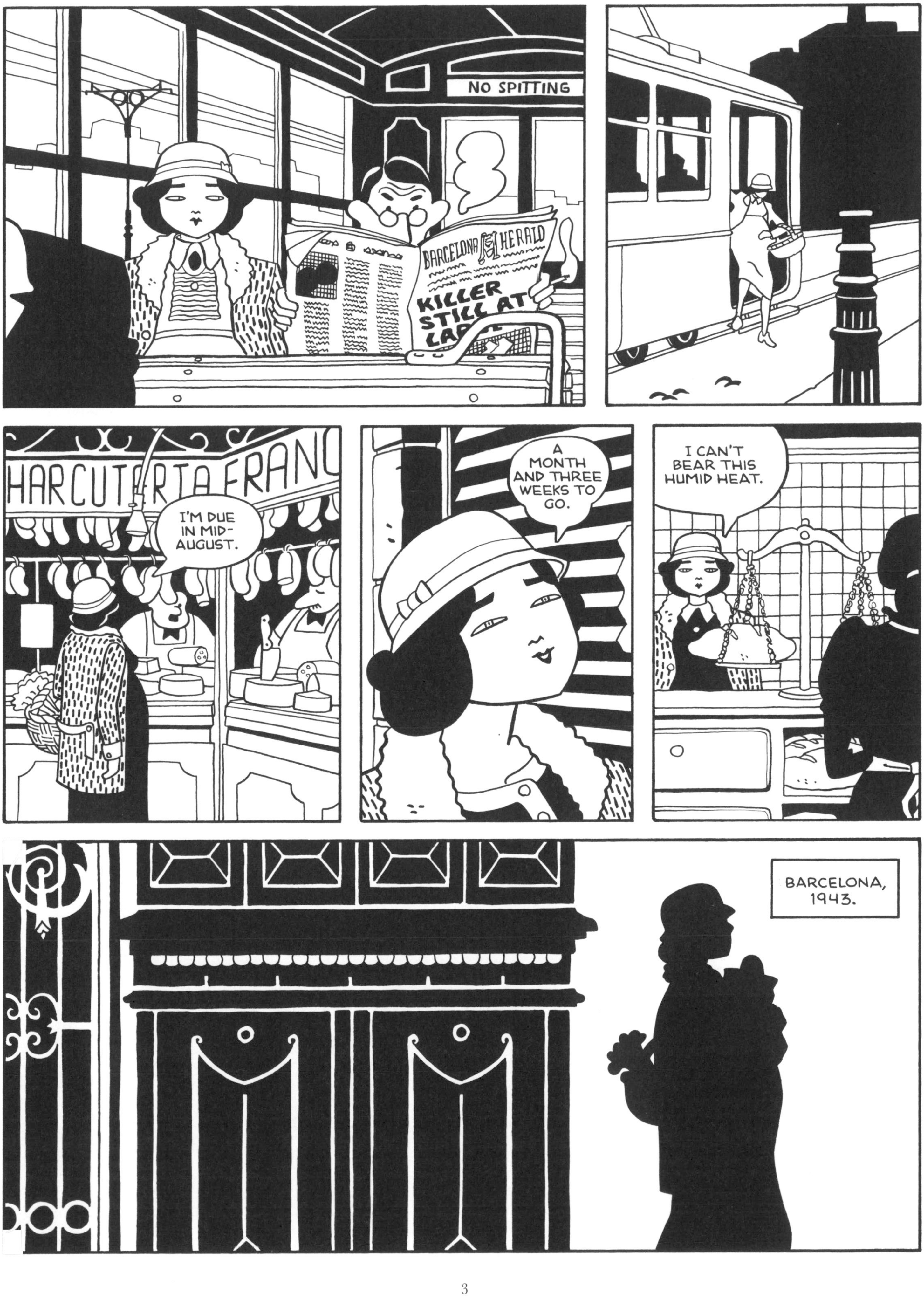
NO SPITTING
BARCELONA HERALD
KILLER STILL AT
HARCUTERIA FRANC
I'M DUE IN MID-AUGUST.
A MONTH AND THREE WEEKS TO GO.
I CAN'T BEAR THIS HUMID HEAT.
BARCELONA, 1943.

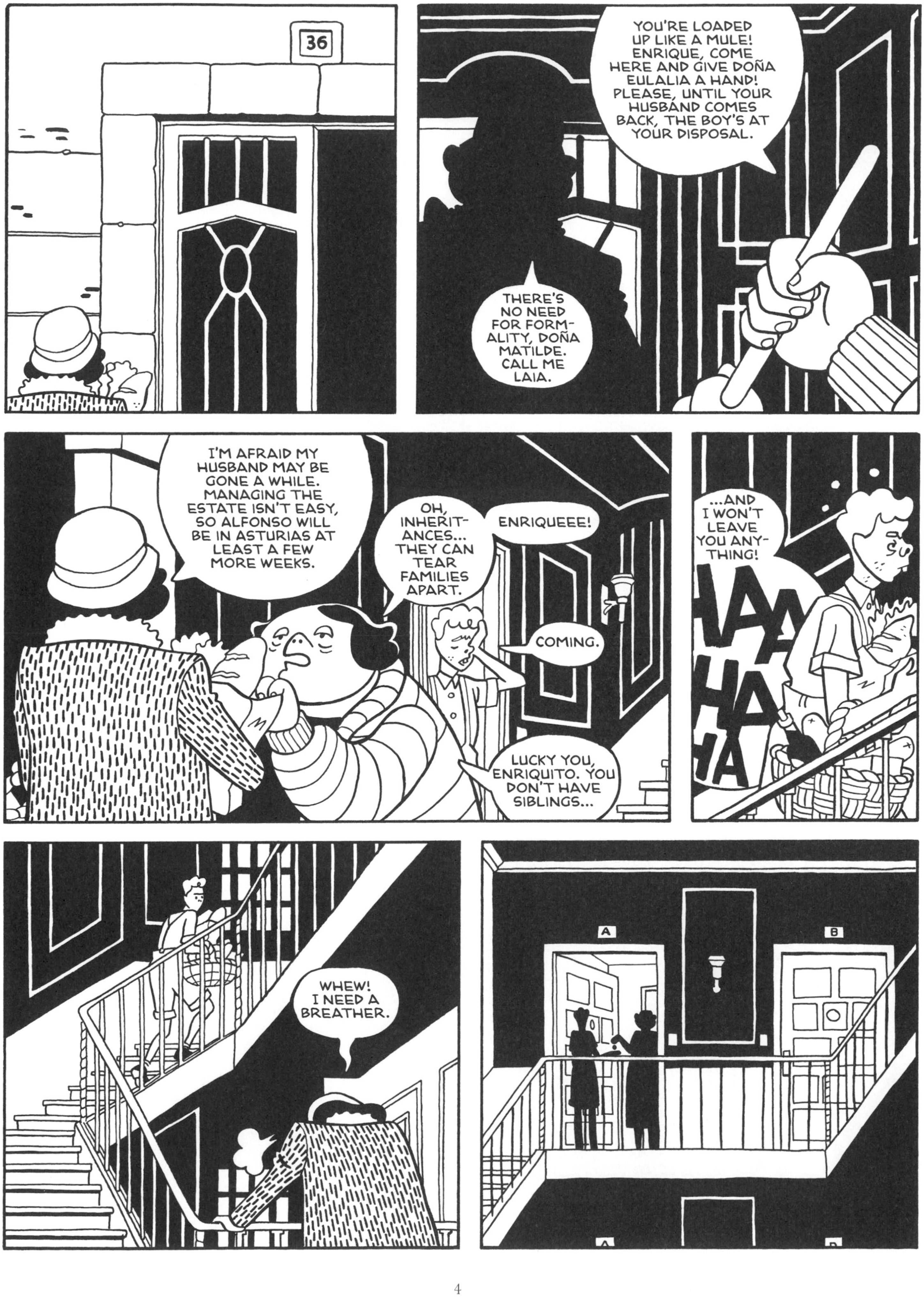
36
YOU'RE LOADED UP LIKE A MULE! ENRIQUE, COME HERE AND GIVE DOÑA EULALIA A HAND! PLEASE, UNTIL YOUR HUSBAND COMES BACK, THE BOY'S AT YOUR DISPOSAL.
THERE'S NO NEED FOR FORMALITY, DOÑA MATILDE. CALL ME LAIA.
I'M AFRAID MY HUSBAND MAY BE GONE A WHILE. MANAGING THE ESTATE ISN'T EASY, SO ALFONSO WILL BE IN ASTURIAS AT LEAST A FEW MORE WEEKS.
OH, INHERITANCES... THEY CAN TEAR FAMILIES APART.
ENRIQUEEE!
COMING.
LUCKY YOU, ENRIQUITO. YOU DON'T HAVE SIBLINGS...
...AND I WON'T LEAVE YOU ANYTHING!
HAA HA HA HA
WHEW! I NEED A BREATHER.
A
B

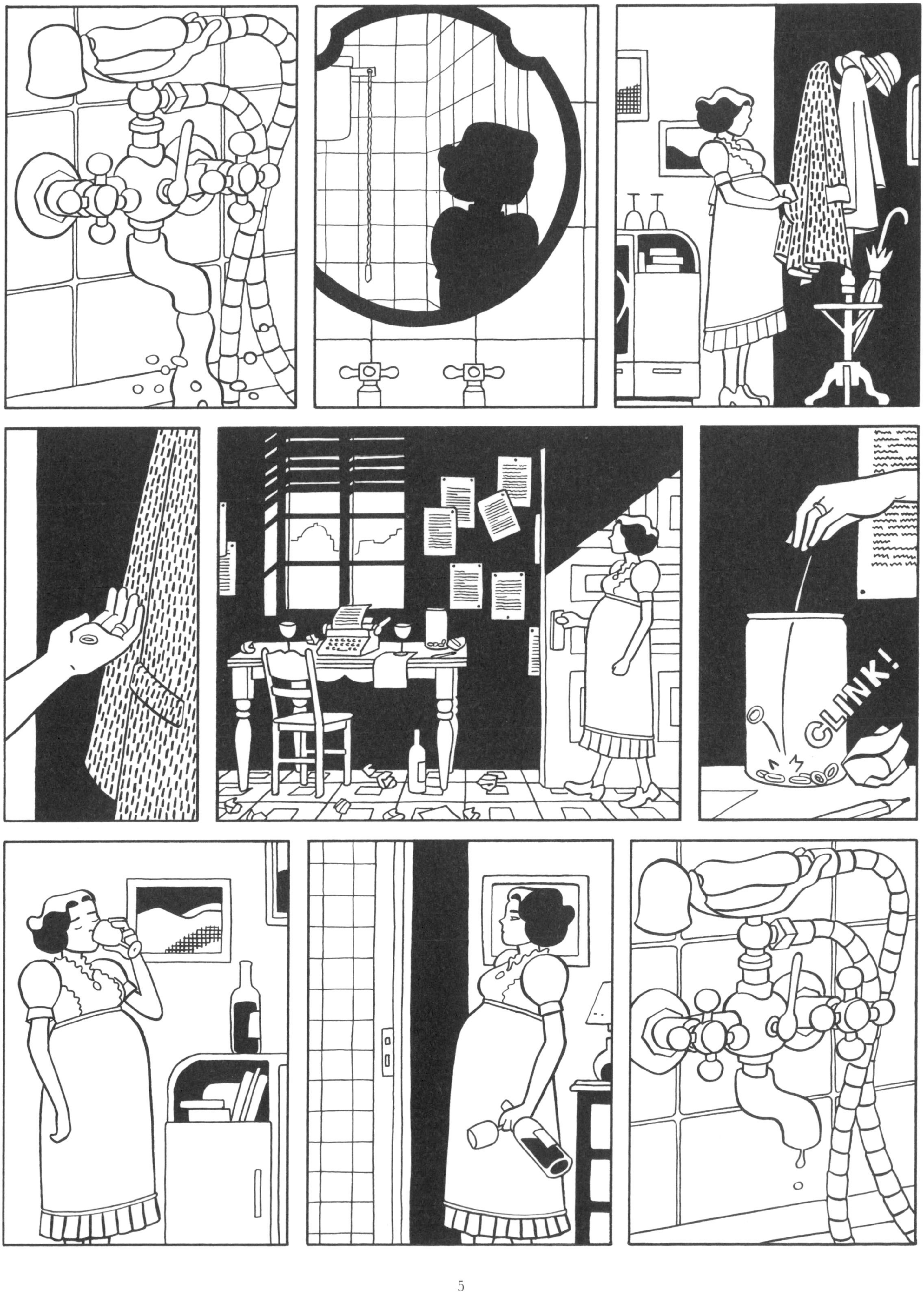
CLINK!

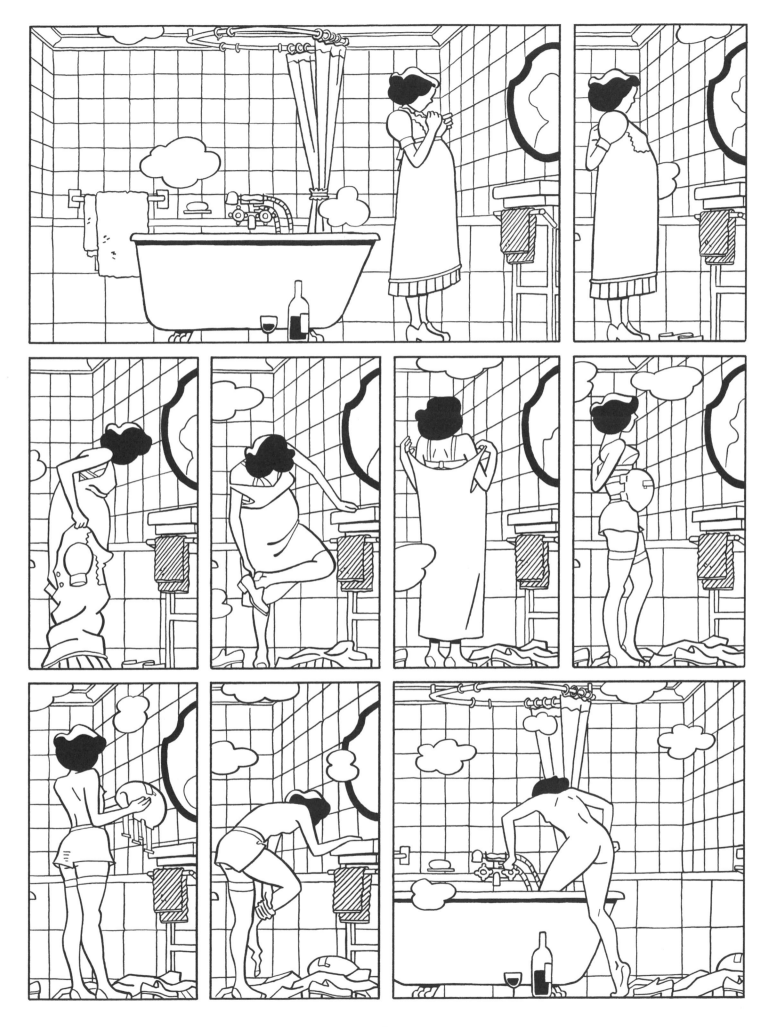

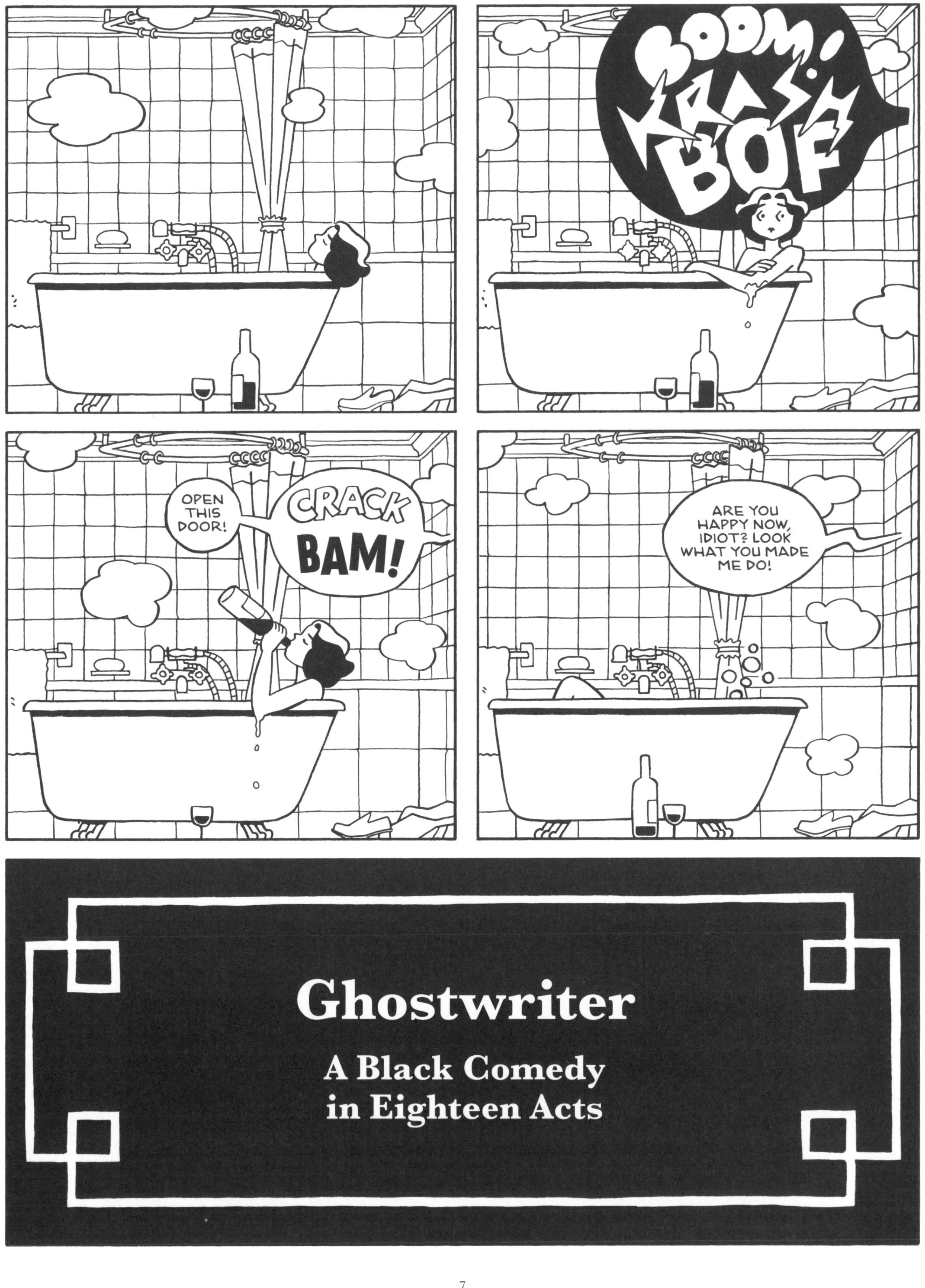
BOOM!
KRASH
BOF
OPEN THIS DOOR!
CRACK
BAM!
ARE YOU HAPPY NOW, IDIOT? LOOK WHAT YOU MADE ME DO!

Ghostwriter

A Black Comedy in Eighteen Acts

1

The Scriptwriter

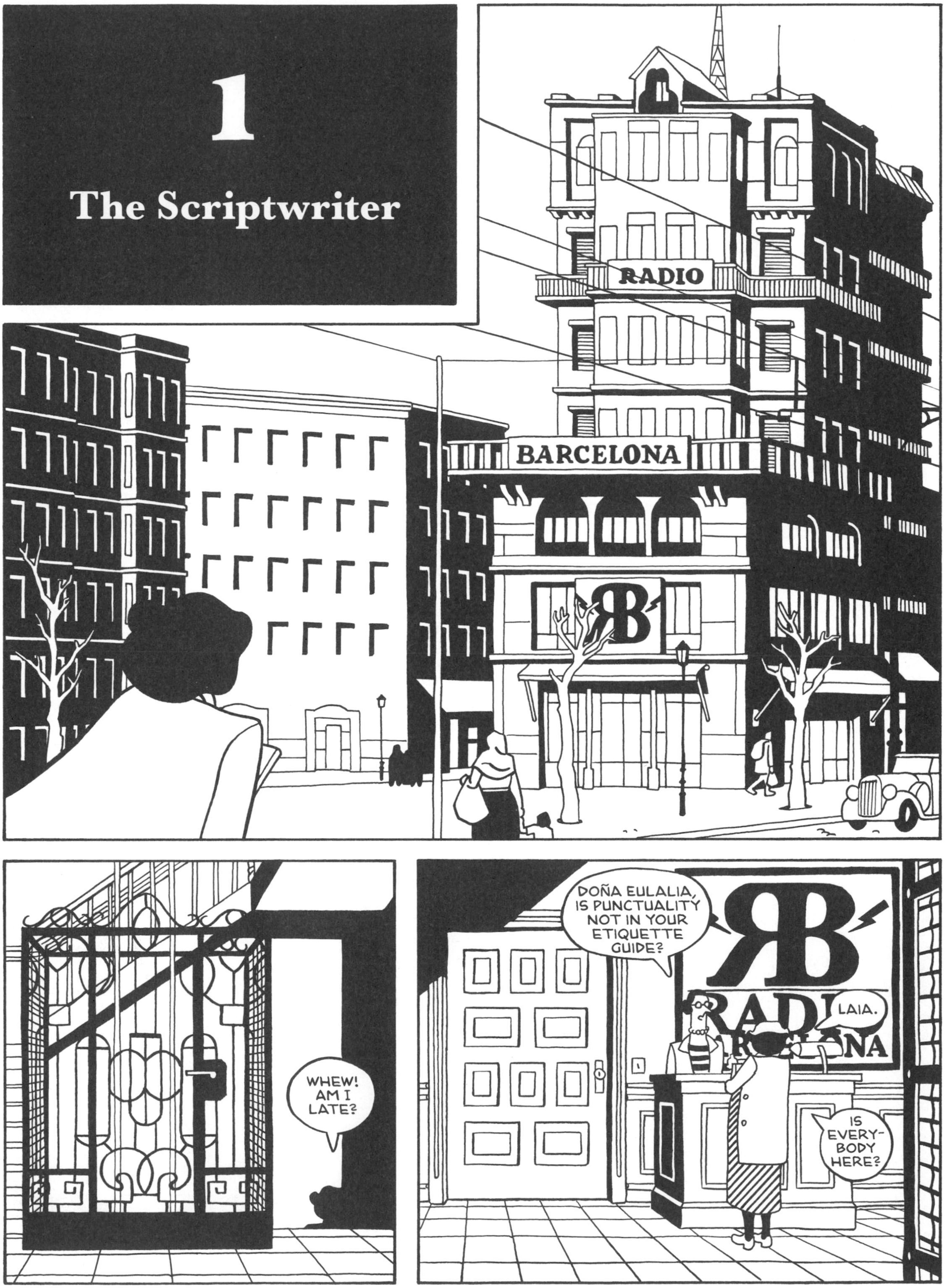

RADIO
BARCELONA
RB
WHEW! AM I LATE?
DOÑA EULALIA, IS PUNCTUALITY NOT IN YOUR ETIQUETTE GUIDE?
RB
LAIA.
IS EVERYBODY HERE?

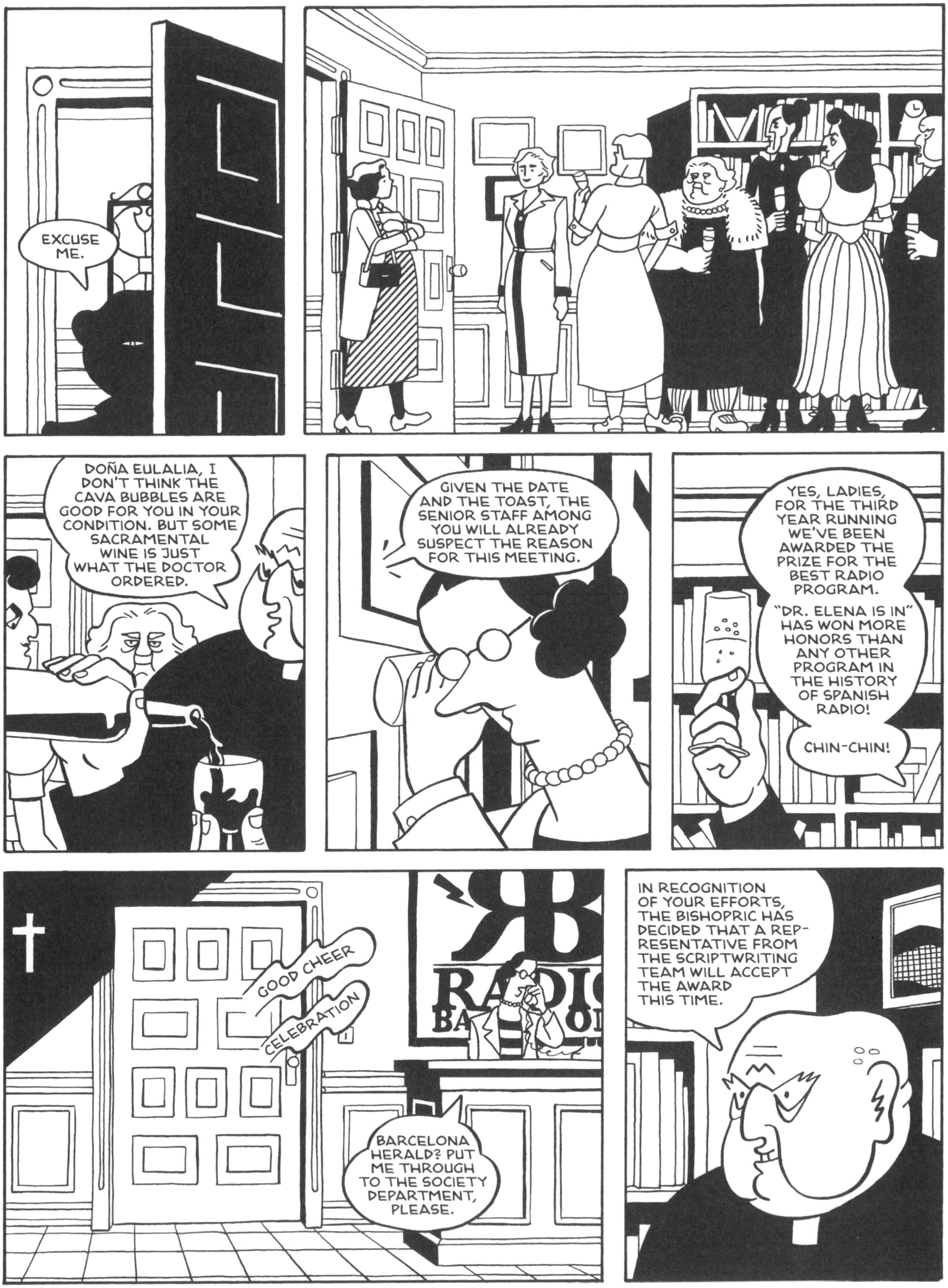
EXCUSE ME.
DOÑA EULALIA, I DON'T THINK THE CAVA BUBBLES ARE GOOD FOR YOU IN YOUR CONDITION. BUT SOME SACRAMENTAL WINE IS JUST WHAT THE DOCTOR ORDERED.
GIVEN THE DATE AND THE TOAST, THE SENIOR STAFF AMONG YOU WILL ALREADY SUSPECT THE REASON FOR THIS MEETING.
YES, LADIES, FOR THE THIRD YEAR RUNNING WE'VE BEEN AWARDED THE PRIZE FOR THE BEST RADIO PROGRAM.
"DR. ELENA IS IN" HAS WON MORE HONORS THAN ANY OTHER PROGRAM IN THE HISTORY OF SPANISH RADIO!
CHIN-CHIN!
GOOD CHEER
CELEBRATION
BARCELONA HERALD? PUT ME THROUGH TO THE SOCIETY DEPARTMENT, PLEASE.
IN RECOGNITION OF YOUR EFFORTS, THE BISHOPRIC HAS DECIDED THAT A REPRESENTATIVE FROM THE SCRIPTWRITING TEAM WILL ACCEPT THE AWARD THIS TIME.

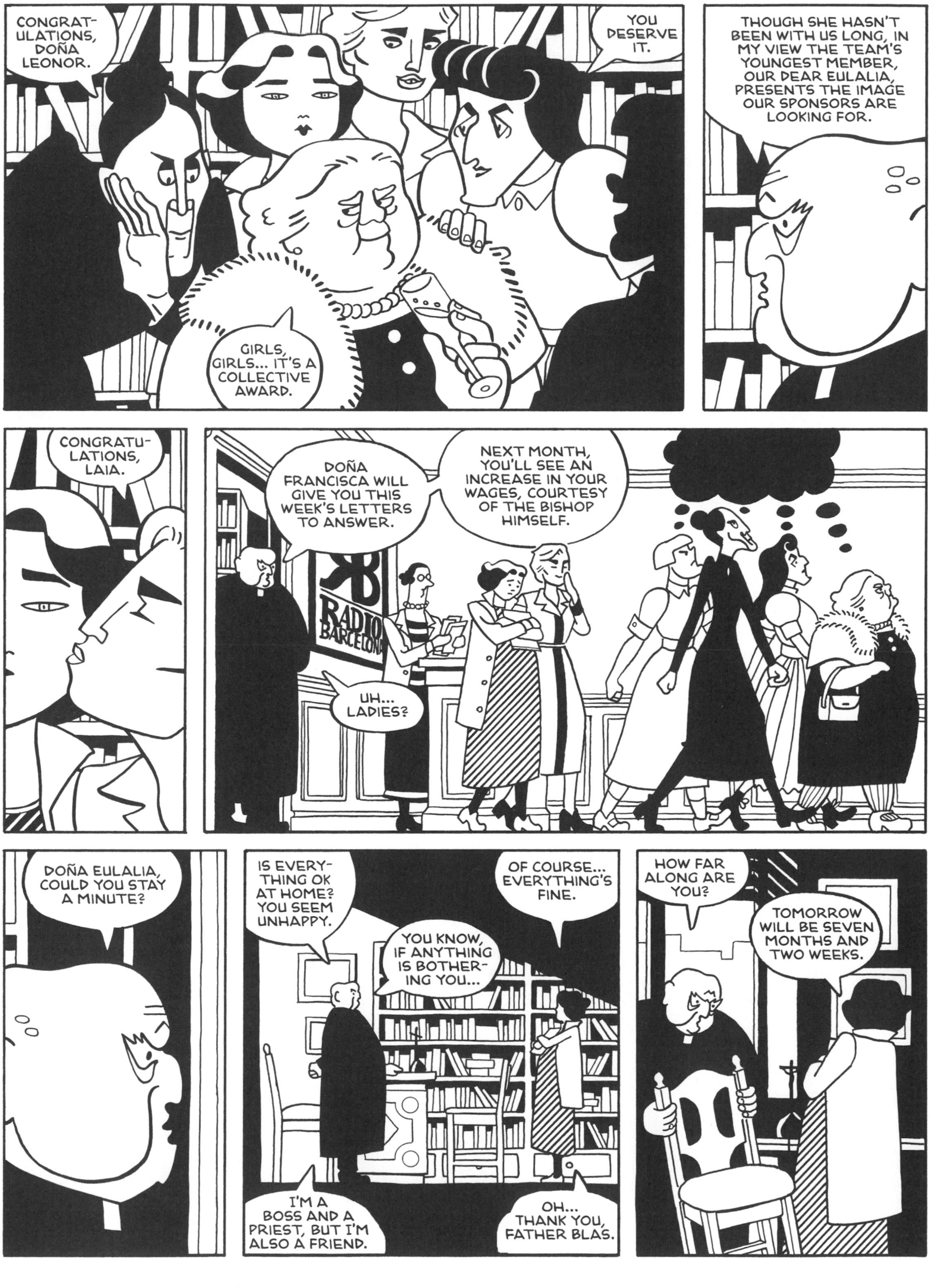
CONGRAT-ULATIONS, DOÑA LEONOR.
YOU DESERVE IT.
GIRLS, GIRLS... IT'S A COLLECTIVE AWARD.
THOUGH SHE HASN'T BEEN WITH US LONG, IN MY VIEW THE TEAM'S YOUNGEST MEMBER, OUR DEAR EULALIA, PRESENTS THE IMAGE OUR SPONSORS ARE LOOKING FOR.
CONGRATU-LATIONS, LAIA.
DOÑA FRANCISCA WILL GIVE YOU THIS WEEK'S LETTERS TO ANSWER.
NEXT MONTH, YOU'LL SEE AN INCREASE IN YOUR WAGES, COURTESY OF THE BISHOP HIMSELF.
RADIO BARCELONA
UH... LADIES?
DOÑA EULALIA, COULD YOU STAY A MINUTE?
IS EVERY-THING OK AT HOME? YOU SEEM UNHAPPY.
YOU KNOW, IF ANYTHING IS BOTHER-ING YOU...
I'M A BOSS AND A PRIEST, BUT I'M ALSO A FRIEND.
OF COURSE... EVERYTHING'S FINE.
OH... THANK YOU, FATHER BLAS.
HOW FAR ALONG ARE YOU?
TOMORROW WILL BE SEVEN MONTHS AND TWO WEEKS.

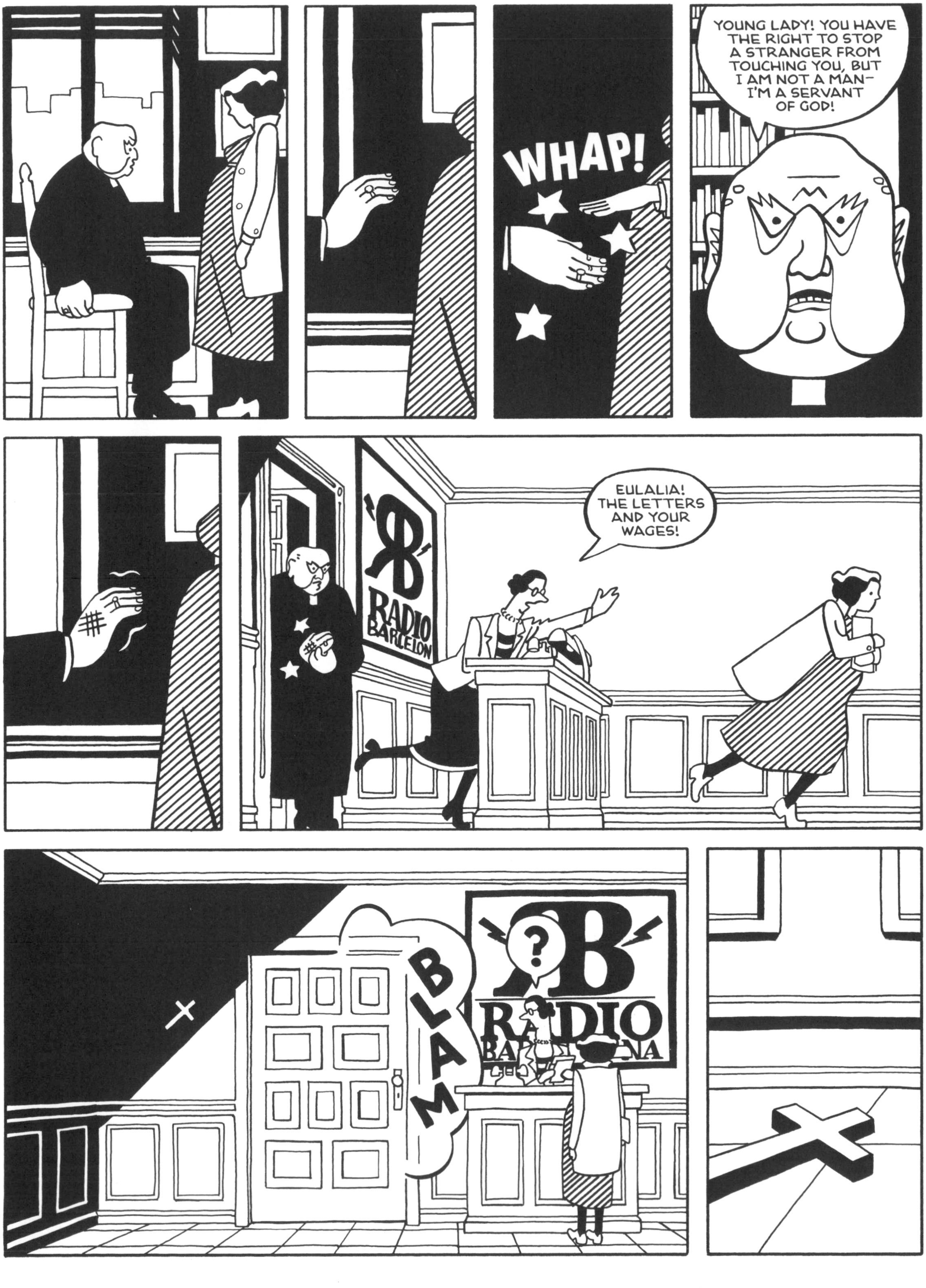
WHAP!
YOUNG LADY! YOU HAVE THE RIGHT TO STOP A STRANGER FROM TOUCHING YOU, BUT I AM NOT A MAN— I'M A SERVANT OF GOD!
RADIO BARCELON
EULALIA! THE LETTERS AND YOUR WAGES!
BLAM
?
RADIO

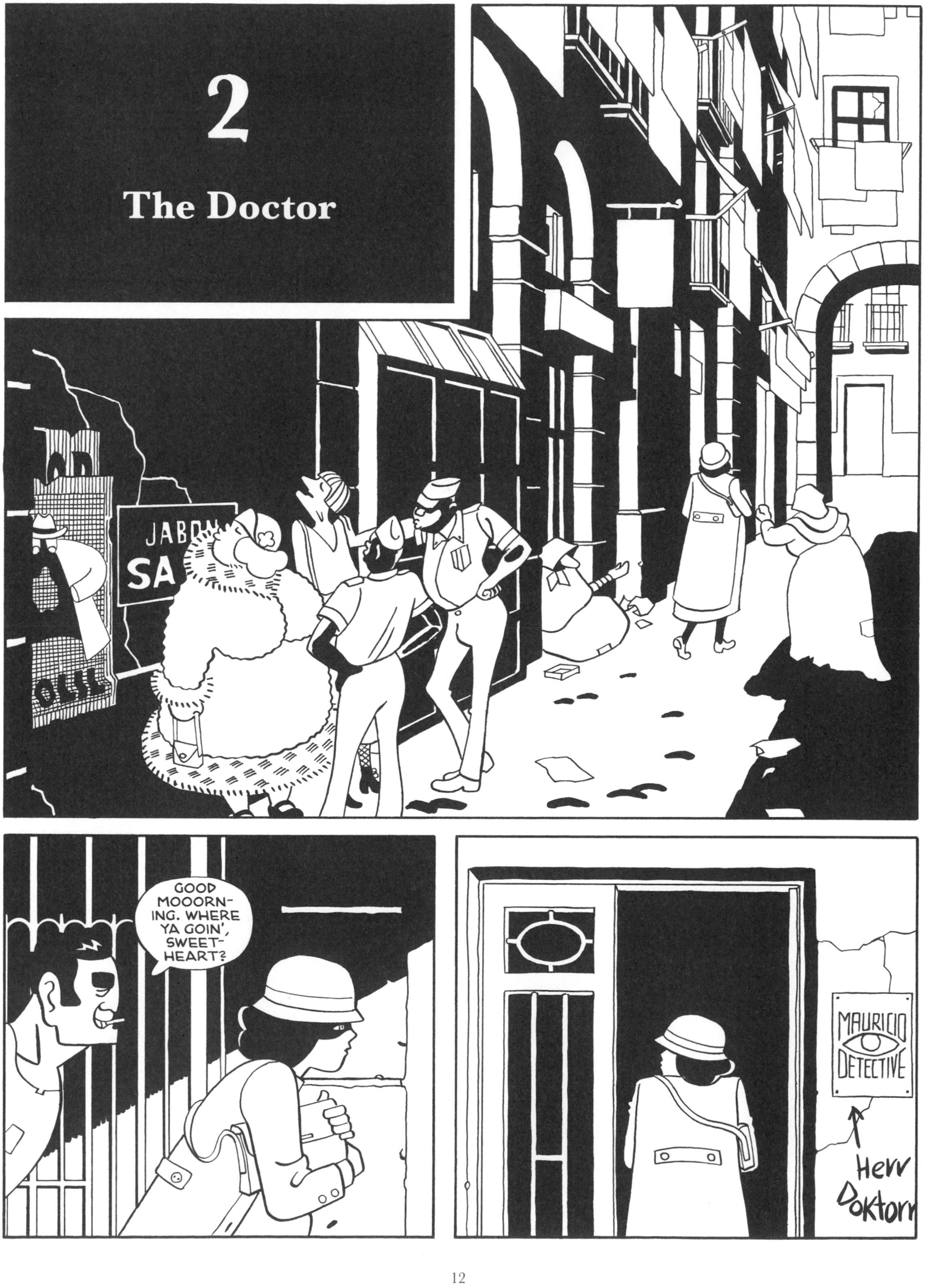
2
The Doctor
JABON
SA
GOOD MOOORN-ING. WHERE YA GOIN', SWEET-HEART?
MAURICIO DETECTIVE
Herr Doktorr

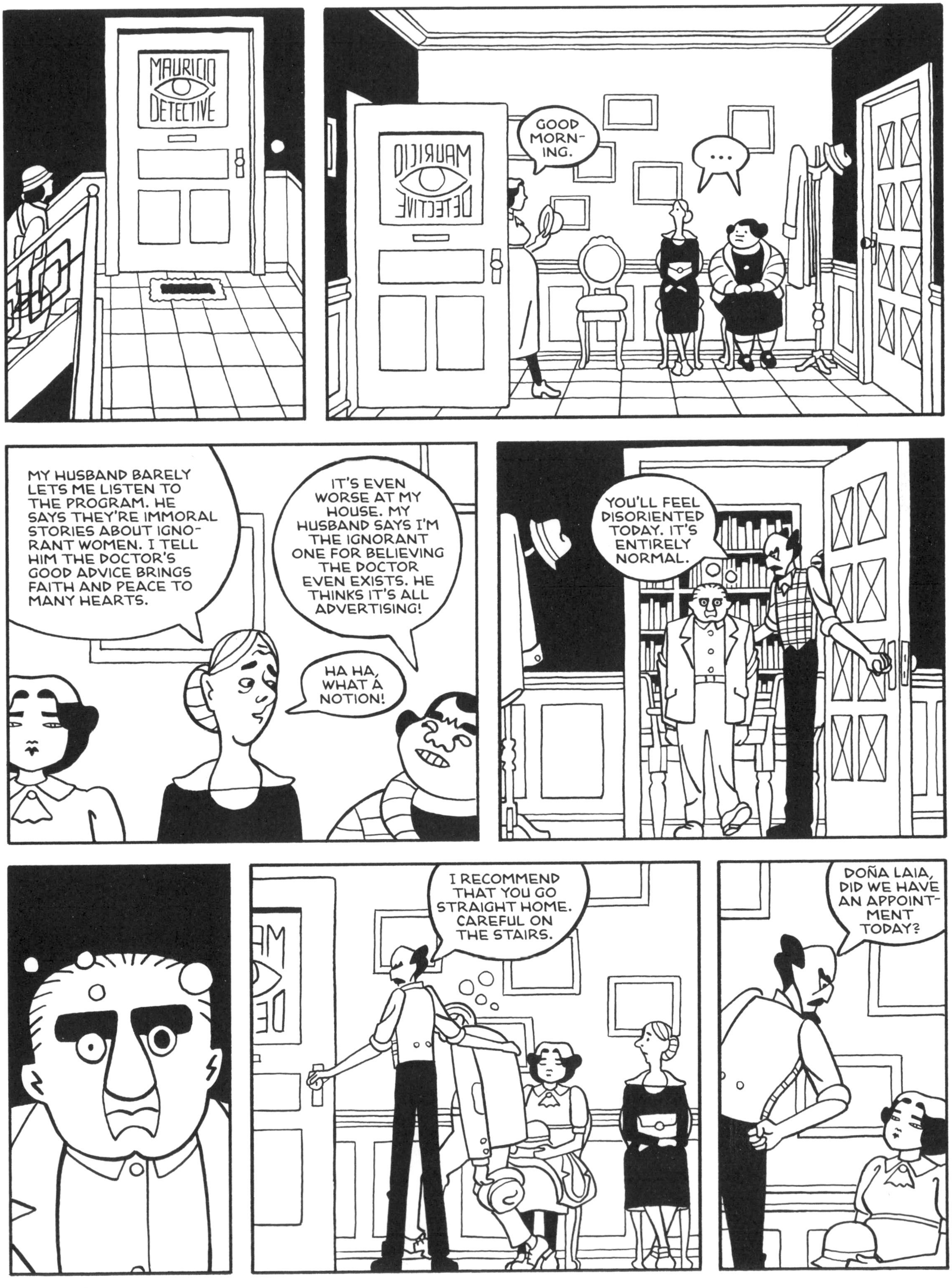

MAURICIO DETECTIVE
GOOD MORNING.
...
MY HUSBAND BARELY LETS ME LISTEN TO THE PROGRAM. HE SAYS THEY'RE IMMORAL STORIES ABOUT IGNORANT WOMEN. I TELL HIM THE DOCTOR'S GOOD ADVICE BRINGS FAITH AND PEACE TO MANY HEARTS.
IT'S EVEN WORSE AT MY HOUSE. MY HUSBAND SAYS I'M THE IGNORANT ONE FOR BELIEVING THE DOCTOR EVEN EXISTS. HE THINKS IT'S ALL ADVERTISING!
HA HA, WHAT A NOTION!
YOU'LL FEEL DISORIENTED TODAY. IT'S ENTIRELY NORMAL.
I RECOMMEND THAT YOU GO STRAIGHT HOME. CAREFUL ON THE STAIRS.
DOÑA LAIA, DID WE HAVE AN APPOINTMENT TODAY?

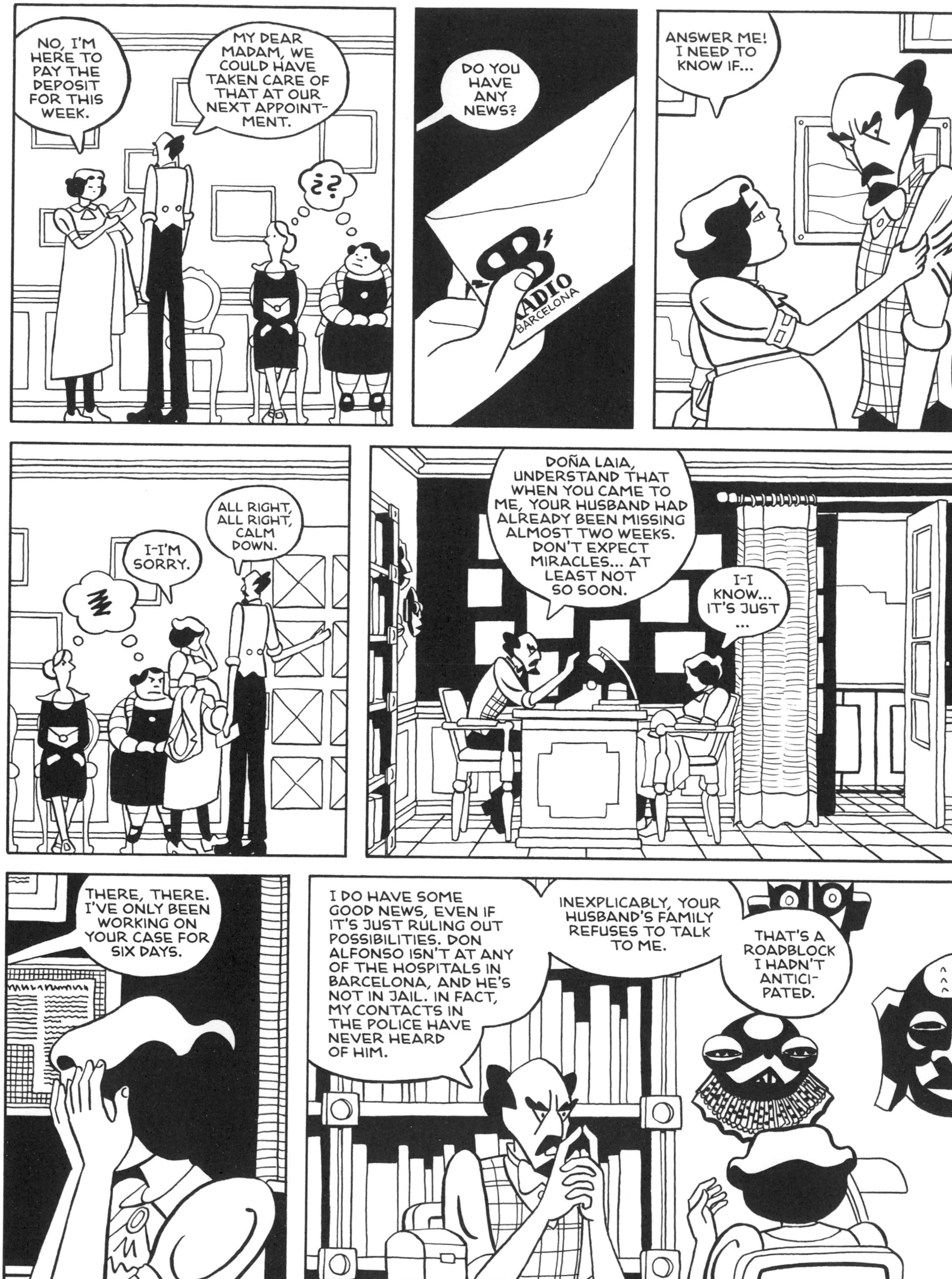
NO, I'M HERE TO PAY THE DEPOSIT FOR THIS WEEK.
MY DEAR MADAM, WE COULD HAVE TAKEN CARE OF THAT AT OUR NEXT APPOINT-MENT.
¿?
DO YOU HAVE ANY NEWS?
RADIO BARCELONA
ANSWER ME! I NEED TO KNOW IF...
I-I'M SORRY.
ALL RIGHT, ALL RIGHT, CALM DOWN.
DOÑA LAIA, UNDERSTAND THAT WHEN YOU CAME TO ME, YOUR HUSBAND HAD ALREADY BEEN MISSING ALMOST TWO WEEKS. DON'T EXPECT MIRACLES... AT LEAST NOT SO SOON.
I-I KNOW... IT'S JUST ...
THERE, THERE. I'VE ONLY BEEN WORKING ON YOUR CASE FOR SIX DAYS.
I DO HAVE SOME GOOD NEWS, EVEN IF IT'S JUST RULING OUT POSSIBILITIES. DON ALFONSO ISN'T AT ANY OF THE HOSPITALS IN BARCELONA, AND HE'S NOT IN JAIL. IN FACT, MY CONTACTS IN THE POLICE HAVE NEVER HEARD OF HIM.
INEXPLICABLY, YOUR HUSBAND'S FAMILY REFUSES TO TALK TO ME.
THAT'S A ROADBLOCK I HADN'T ANTICI-PATED.

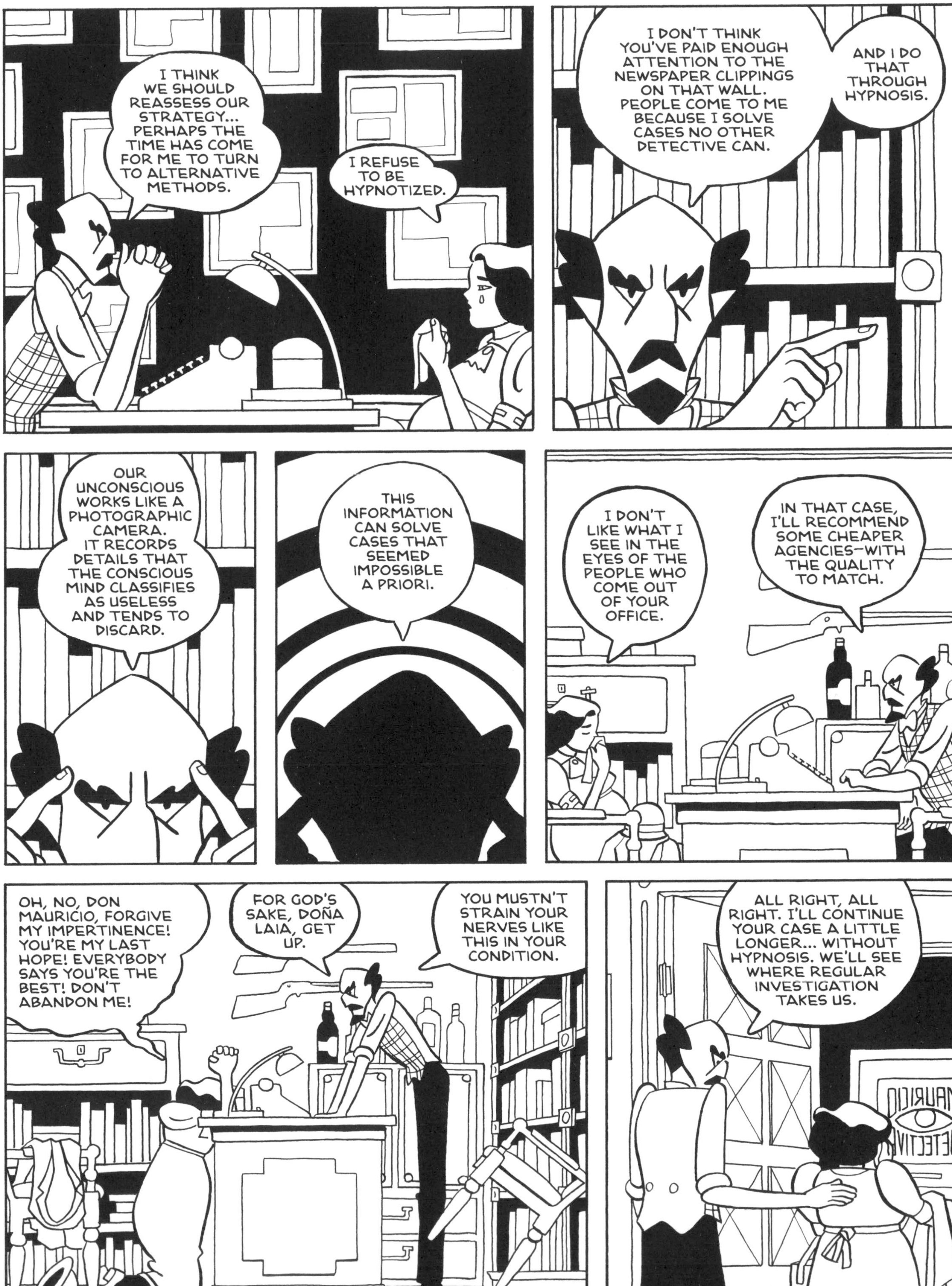
I THINK WE SHOULD REASSESS OUR STRATEGY... PERHAPS THE TIME HAS COME FOR ME TO TURN TO ALTERNATIVE METHODS.
I REFUSE TO BE HYPNOTIZED.
I DON'T THINK YOU'VE PAID ENOUGH ATTENTION TO THE NEWSPAPER CLIPPINGS ON THAT WALL. PEOPLE COME TO ME BECAUSE I SOLVE CASES NO OTHER DETECTIVE CAN.
AND I DO THAT THROUGH HYPNOSIS.
OUR UNCONSCIOUS WORKS LIKE A PHOTOGRAPHIC CAMERA. IT RECORDS DETAILS THAT THE CONSCIOUS MIND CLASSIFIES AS USELESS AND TENDS TO DISCARD.
THIS INFORMATION CAN SOLVE CASES THAT SEEMED IMPOSSIBLE A PRIORI.
I DON'T LIKE WHAT I SEE IN THE EYES OF THE PEOPLE WHO COME OUT OF YOUR OFFICE.
IN THAT CASE, I'LL RECOMMEND SOME CHEAPER AGENCIES—WITH THE QUALITY TO MATCH.
OH, NO, DON MAURICIO, FORGIVE MY IMPERTINENCE! YOU'RE MY LAST HOPE! EVERYBODY SAYS YOU'RE THE BEST! DON'T ABANDON ME!
FOR GOD'S SAKE, DOÑA LAIA, GET UP.
YOU MUSTN'T STRAIN YOUR NERVES LIKE THIS IN YOUR CONDITION.
ALL RIGHT, ALL RIGHT. I'LL CONTINUE YOUR CASE A LITTLE LONGER... WITHOUT HYPNOSIS. WE'LL SEE WHERE REGULAR INVESTIGATION TAKES US.

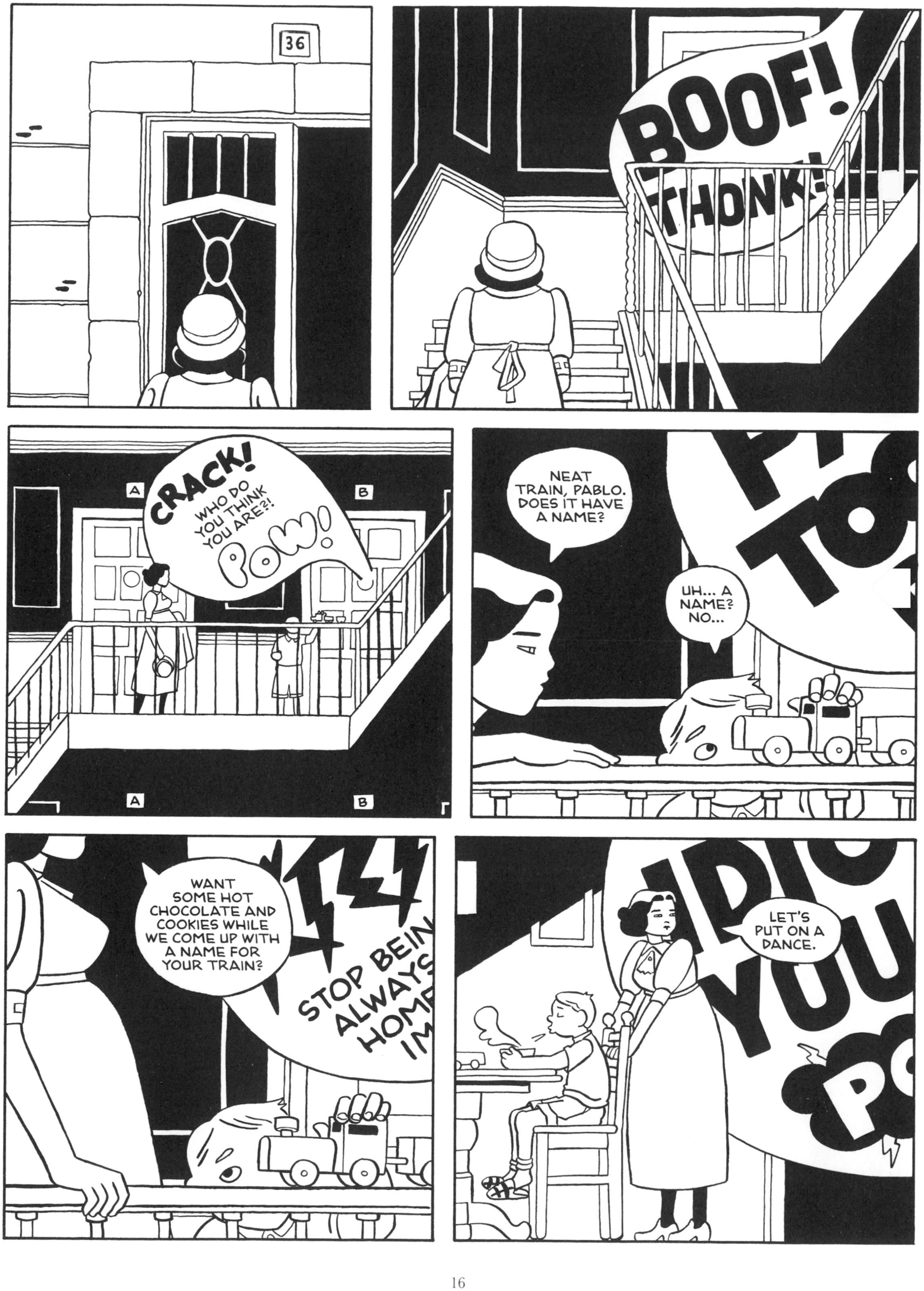
36
BOOF!
THONK!
A
B
CRACK! WHO DO YOU THINK YOU ARE?! POW!
A
B
NEAT TRAIN, PABLO. DOES IT HAVE A NAME?
UH... A NAME? NO...
WANT SOME HOT CHOCOLATE AND COOKIES WHILE WE COME UP WITH A NAME FOR YOUR TRAIN?
STOP BEIN
ALWAYS
LET'S PUT ON A DANCE.

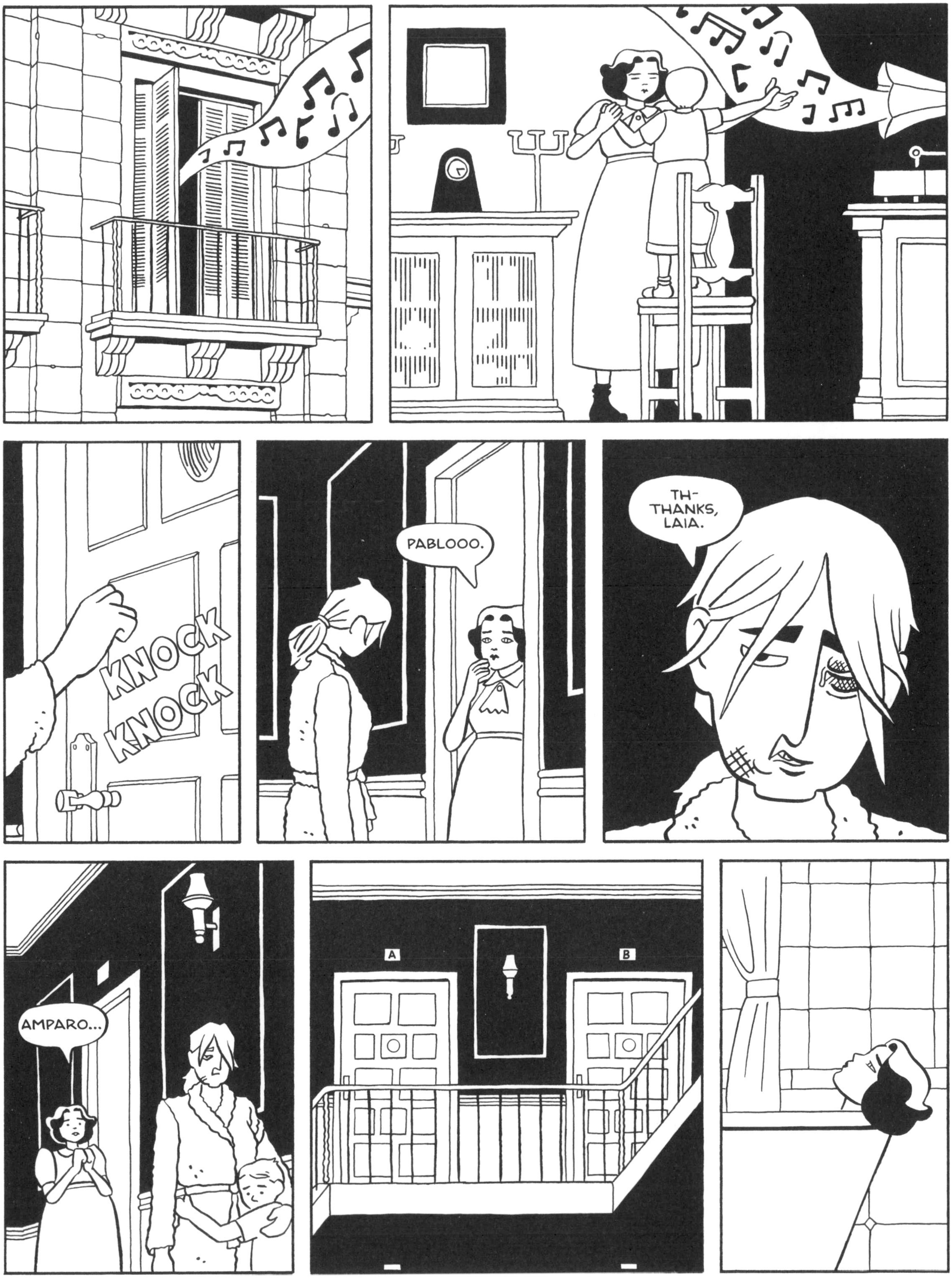
KNOCK KNOCK
PABLOOO.
TH-THANKS, LAIA.
AMPARO...

3
Write About What You Know

April 24, 1943

Most esteem Dr. Bosch:

I need your help, as I am grately upset. I have been married elven years. I can't say they've been happy ones, since only a month after our

weding my husband hit me. if I ask him for anything he yells at me and storms out of the house. I am 34 years old and I have brestfed my two children, offen going without food myself so he and my

children can eet, and I think I have acted as a good wife shood. But he has a very mean temper. Six years ago he struck my mother, who was holing my son in her arms,

CARRER D'ARIBAU

42

MONDAY

E LEAVES FOR WORK.
25. EMILIA TAKES THE
CHILDREN TO SCHOOL.
8:55 EMILIA COMES BACK.
9:15 EMILIA GOES TO HER
MOTHER'S HOU
12:10 EMIL   MES BACK
:22 H   RNS
   A PICKS UP THE
BACK TO THE FACT-
CHILDREN
A.

RMTE: EMILIA PÉREZ A.
C/ARIBAU Nº42. 1º2ª
0801 BARCELONA

18

in the belly. And a little while back he grabed my son to repriman him and walloped him in the spine, where he had a blod clot for a month.

Dispite everything he's done to me, I still love him... Do you know some way, save him falling ill, to soffen him toward me, the way he was before our marrage?

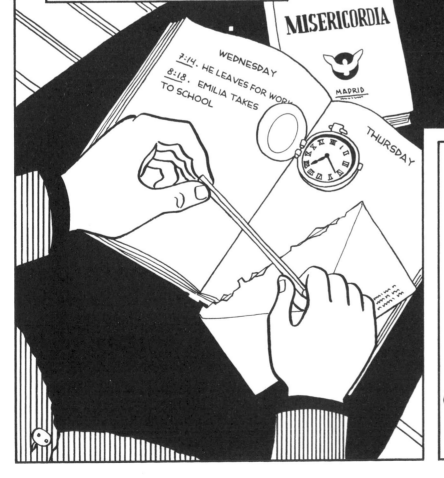

B. Pérez Galdós

MISERICORDIA

MADRID

WEDNESDAY
7:14. HE LEAVES FOR WORK
8:18. EMILIA TAKES TO SCHOOL

THURSDAY

Pleese respond by letter. if he heers this on the radio, I know my days will be numbered.

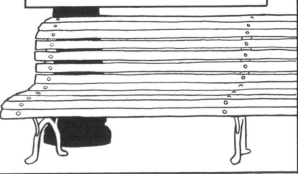

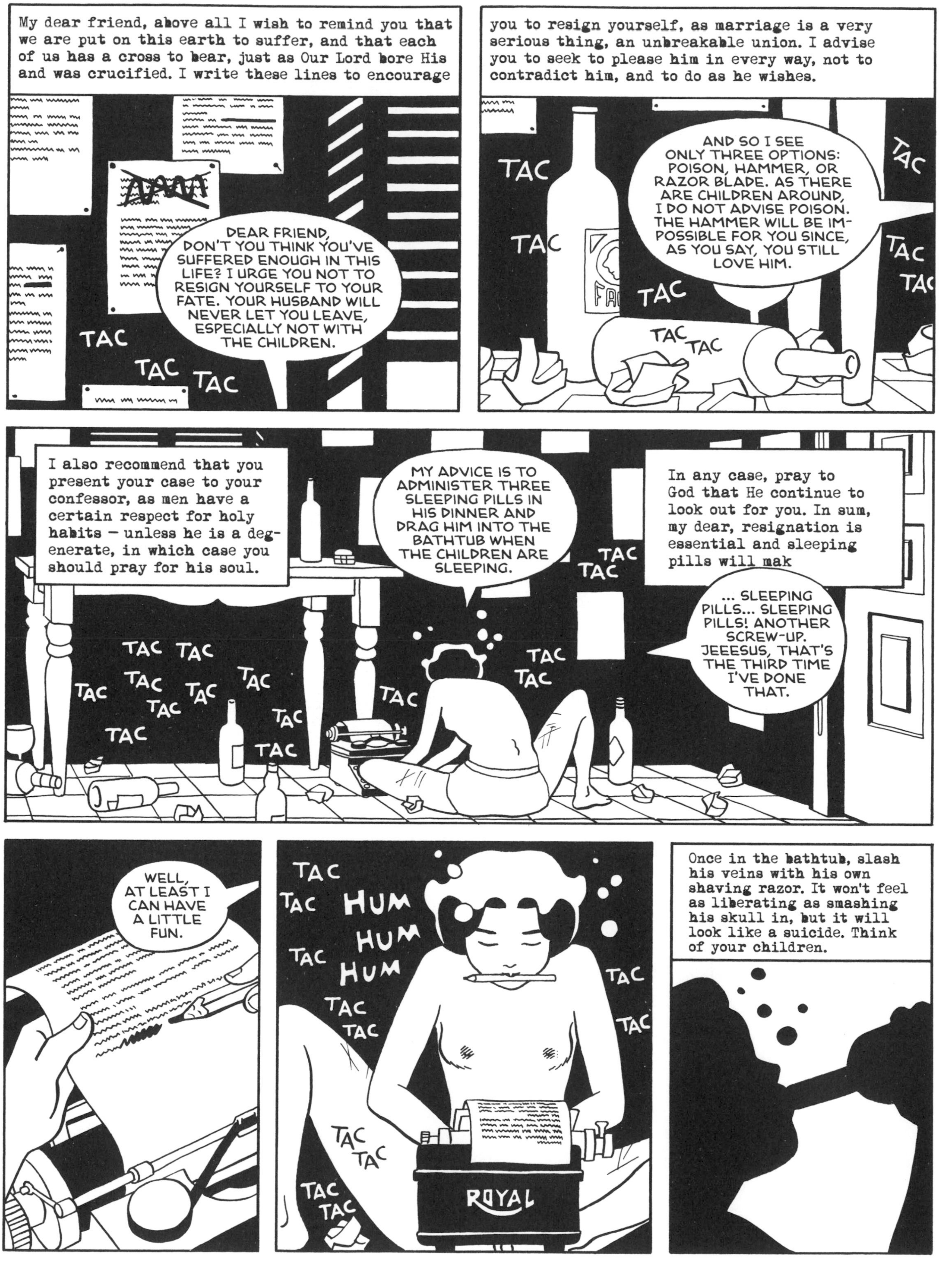

My dear friend, above all I wish to remind you that we are put on this earth to suffer, and that each of us has a cross to bear, just as Our Lord bore His and was crucified. I write these lines to encourage
DEAR FRIEND, DON'T YOU THINK YOU'VE SUFFERED ENOUGH IN THIS LIFE? I URGE YOU NOT TO RESIGN YOURSELF TO YOUR FATE. YOUR HUSBAND WILL NEVER LET YOU LEAVE, ESPECIALLY NOT WITH THE CHILDREN.
TAC TAC TAC
you to resign yourself, as marriage is a very serious thing, an unbreakable union. I advise you to seek to please him in every way, not to contradict him, and to do as he wishes.
AND SO I SEE ONLY THREE OPTIONS: POISON, HAMMER, OR RAZOR BLADE. AS THERE ARE CHILDREN AROUND, I DO NOT ADVISE POISON. THE HAMMER WILL BE IMPOSSIBLE FOR YOU SINCE, AS YOU SAY, YOU STILL LOVE HIM.
TAC TAC TAC TAC TAC TAC TAC
I also recommend that you present your case to your confessor, as men have a certain respect for holy habits — unless he is a degenerate, in which case you should pray for his soul.
MY ADVICE IS TO ADMINISTER THREE SLEEPING PILLS IN HIS DINNER AND DRAG HIM INTO THE BATHTUB WHEN THE CHILDREN ARE SLEEPING.
In any case, pray to God that He continue to look out for you. In sum, my dear, resignation is essential and sleeping pills will mak
... SLEEPING PILLS... SLEEPING PILLS! ANOTHER SCREW-UP. JEEESUS, THAT'S THE THIRD TIME I'VE DONE THAT.
TAC TAC TAC TAC TAC TAC TAC TAC TAC TAC TAC TAC TAC TAC TAC
WELL, AT LEAST I CAN HAVE A LITTLE FUN.
TAC TAC HUM HUM TAC HUM TAC TAC TAC TAC TAC TAC TAC TAC
ROYAL
Once in the bathtub, slash his veins with his own shaving razor. It won't feel as liberating as smashing his skull in, but it will look like a suicide. Think of your children.

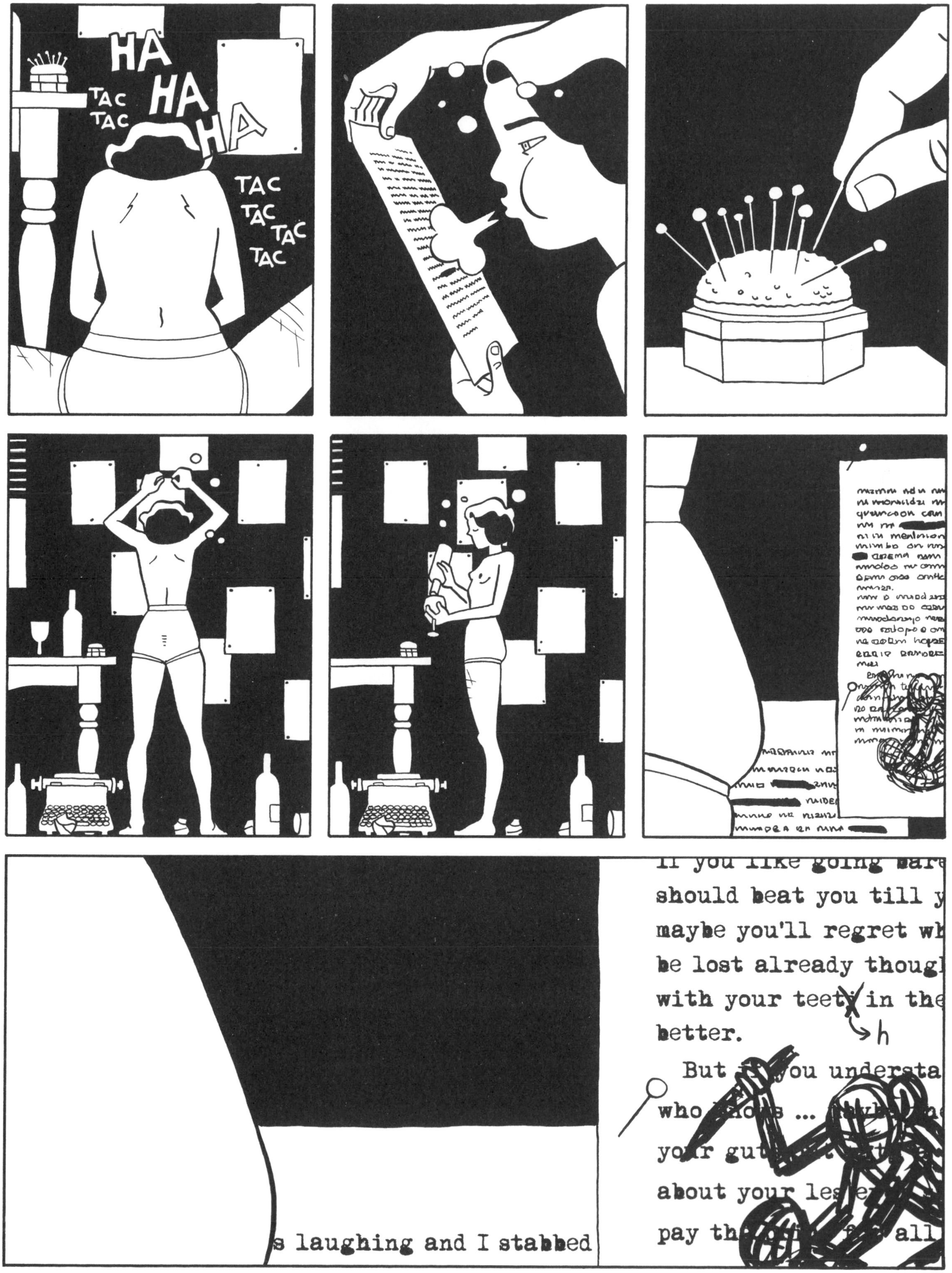
HA HA HA
TAC TAC
TAC TAC TAC TAC
should beat you till y
maybe you'll regret wh
be lost already thoug
with your teety in the
h
better.
But
who
about your
pay
s laughing and I stabbed

4

You Will Earn Your Bread By the Sweat of Your Brow

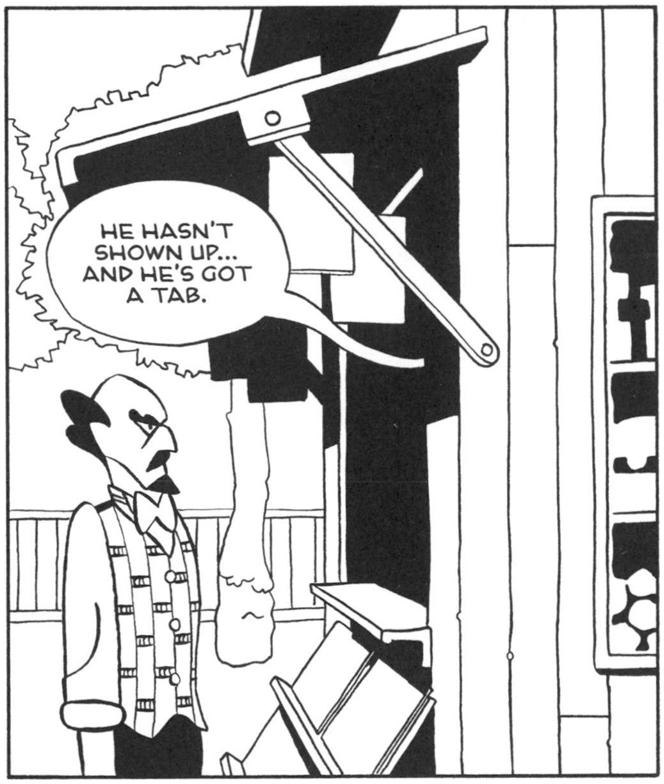
HE HASN'T SHOWN UP... AND HE'S GOT A TAB.

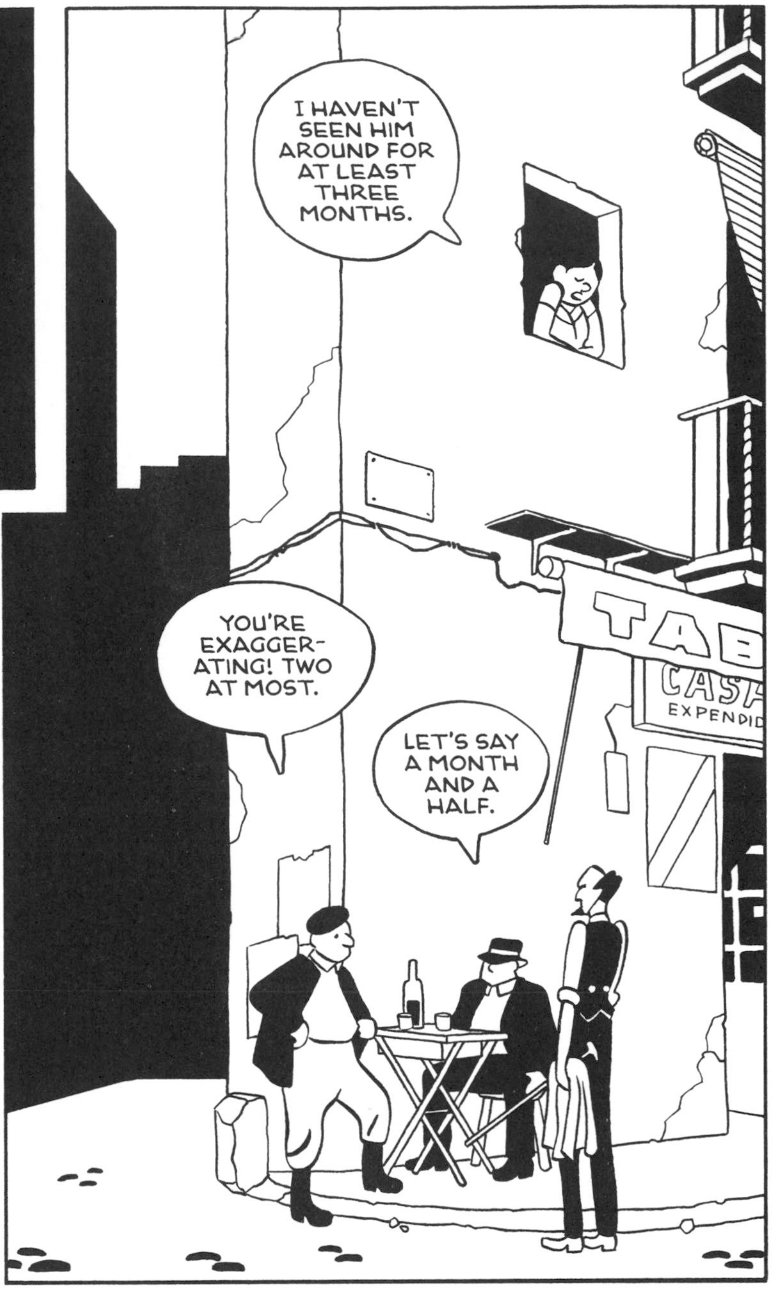
I HAVEN'T SEEN HIM AROUND FOR AT LEAST THREE MONTHS.
YOU'RE EXAGGER-ATING! TWO AT MOST.
LET'S SAY A MONTH AND A HALF.
TAB
CASA
EXPENDID

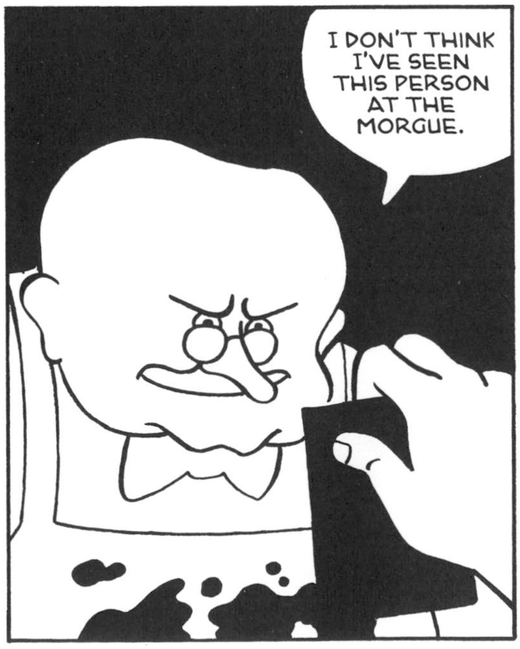
I DON'T THINK I'VE SEEN THIS PERSON AT THE MORGUE.

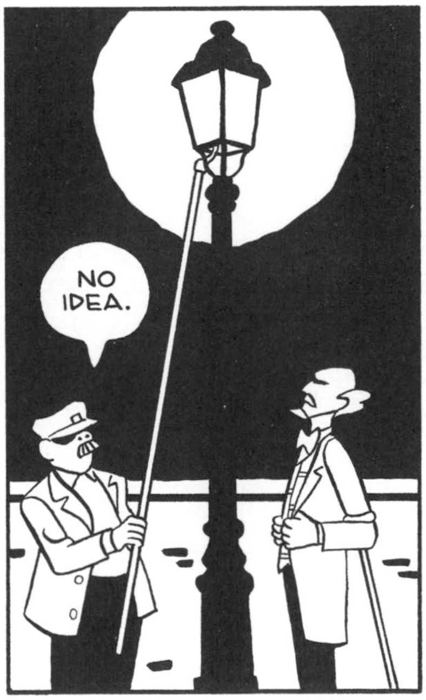
NO IDEA.

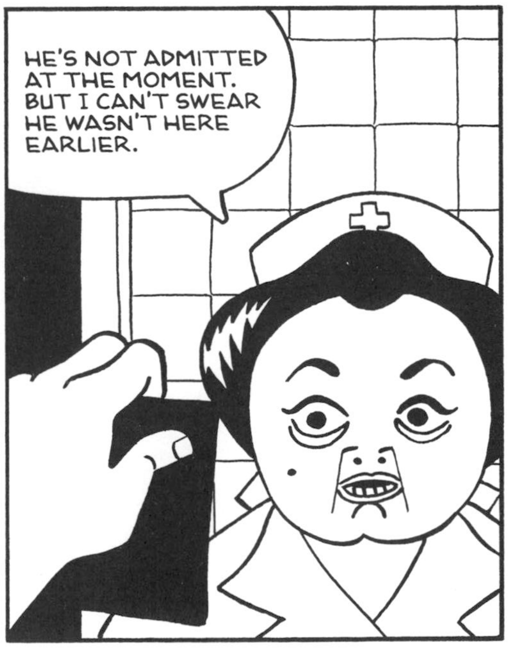
HE'S NOT ADMITTED AT THE MOMENT. BUT I CAN'T SWEAR HE WASN'T HERE EARLIER.

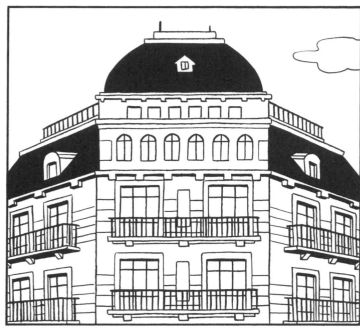

GOOD MORNING. I'D LIKE TO SPEAK WITH THE MAN OF THE HOUSE.

LIKE I SAID, I TOLD THE POLICE EVERYTHING I KNOW ABOUT MY SON.

OK, BUT...

GOOD DAY, SIR.

KNOCK KNOCK

BAR GRACIA.
KIOSKO GRAU.
BAR "ADELANTAD
BARBERIA RAM
MONTJUIC QUA
TABAQUERÍA
ESTANCO
BAR PRA

MONTJUIC QUARRY

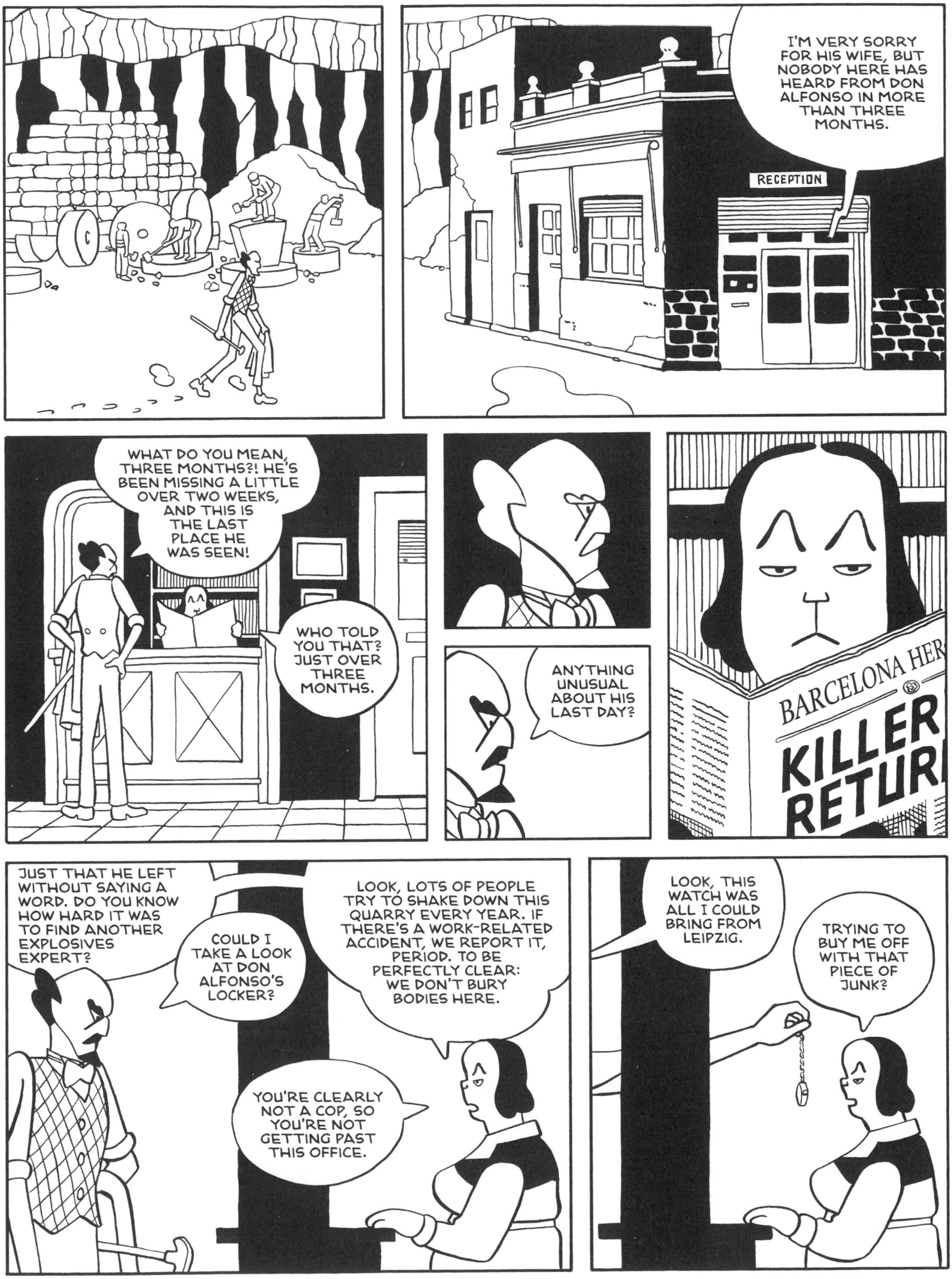
I'M VERY SORRY FOR HIS WIFE, BUT NOBODY HERE HAS HEARD FROM DON ALFONSO IN MORE THAN THREE MONTHS.
RECEPTION
WHAT DO YOU MEAN, THREE MONTHS?! HE'S BEEN MISSING A LITTLE OVER TWO WEEKS, AND THIS IS THE LAST PLACE HE WAS SEEN!
WHO TOLD YOU THAT? JUST OVER THREE MONTHS.
ANYTHING UNUSUAL ABOUT HIS LAST DAY?
BARCELONA HER
KILLER RETUR
JUST THAT HE LEFT WITHOUT SAYING A WORD. DO YOU KNOW HOW HARD IT WAS TO FIND ANOTHER EXPLOSIVES EXPERT?
COULD I TAKE A LOOK AT DON ALFONSO'S LOCKER?
LOOK, LOTS OF PEOPLE TRY TO SHAKE DOWN THIS QUARRY EVERY YEAR. IF THERE'S A WORK-RELATED ACCIDENT, WE REPORT IT, PERIOD. TO BE PERFECTLY CLEAR: WE DON'T BURY BODIES HERE.
YOU'RE CLEARLY NOT A COP, SO YOU'RE NOT GETTING PAST THIS OFFICE.
LOOK, THIS WATCH WAS ALL I COULD BRING FROM LEIPZIG.
TRYING TO BUY ME OFF WITH THAT PIECE OF JUNK?

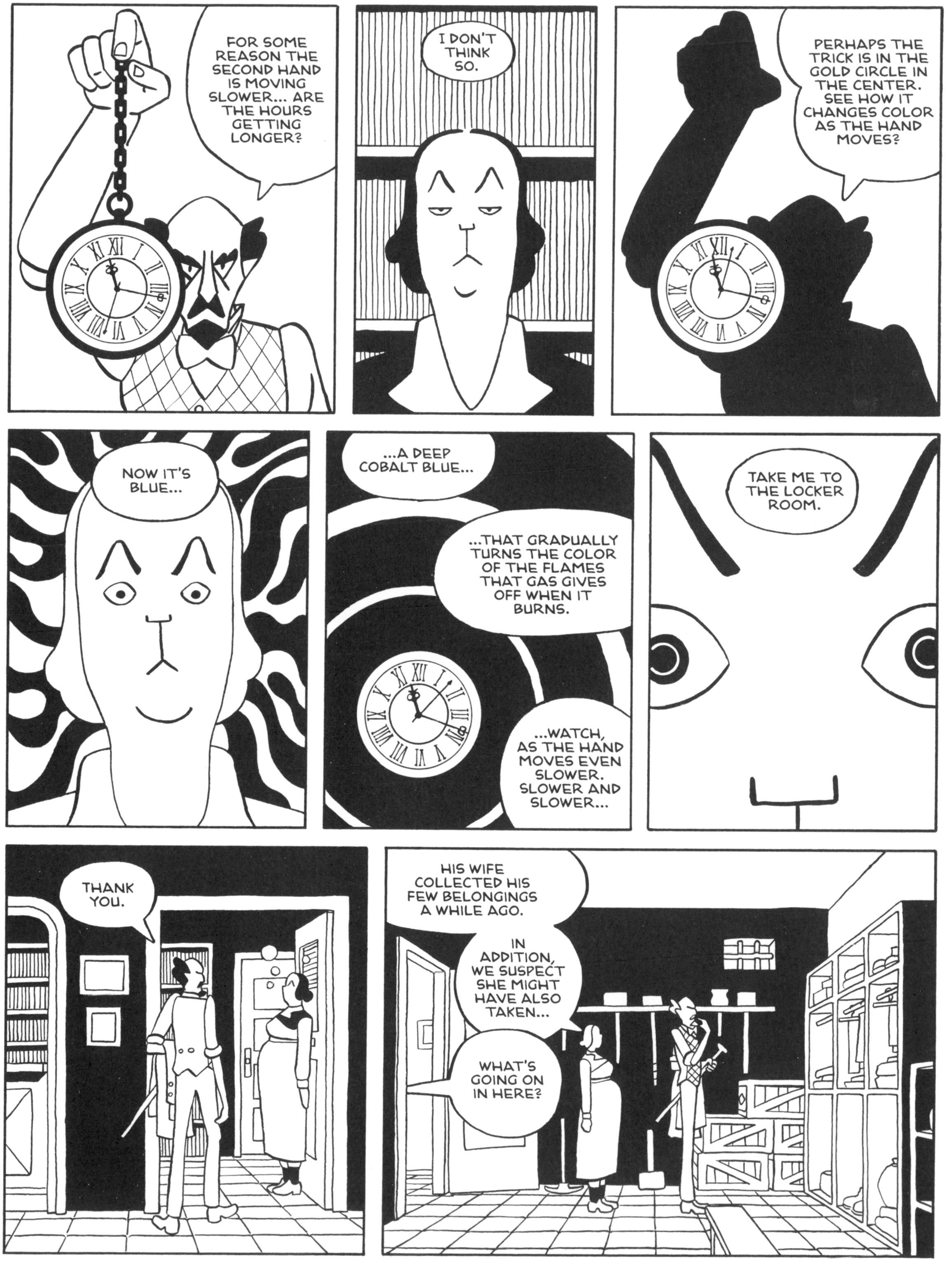
FOR SOME REASON THE SECOND HAND IS MOVING SLOWER... ARE THE HOURS GETTING LONGER?
I DON'T THINK SO.
PERHAPS THE TRICK IS IN THE GOLD CIRCLE IN THE CENTER. SEE HOW IT CHANGES COLOR AS THE HAND MOVES?
NOW IT'S BLUE...
...A DEEP COBALT BLUE...
...THAT GRADUALLY TURNS THE COLOR OF THE FLAMES THAT GAS GIVES OFF WHEN IT BURNS.
...WATCH, AS THE HAND MOVES EVEN SLOWER. SLOWER AND SLOWER...
TAKE ME TO THE LOCKER ROOM.
THANK YOU.
HIS WIFE COLLECTED HIS FEW BELONGINGS A WHILE AGO.
IN ADDITION, WE SUSPECT SHE MIGHT HAVE ALSO TAKEN...
WHAT'S GOING ON IN HERE?

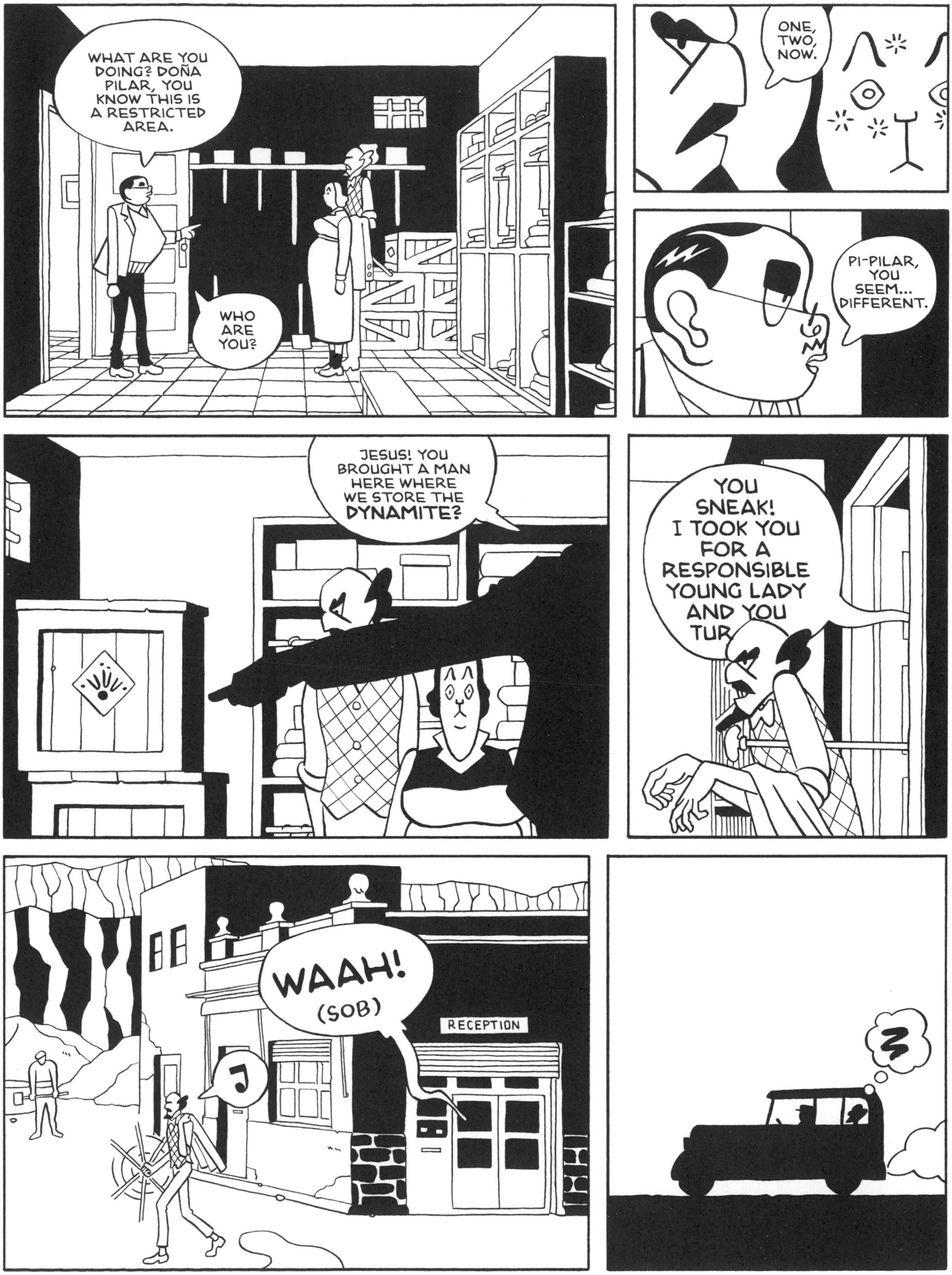
WHAT ARE YOU DOING? DOÑA PILAR, YOU KNOW THIS IS A RESTRICTED AREA.
WHO ARE YOU?
ONE, TWO, NOW.
PI-PILAR, YOU SEEM... DIFFERENT.
JESUS! YOU BROUGHT A MAN HERE WHERE WE STORE THE **DYNAMITE**?
YOU SNEAK! I TOOK YOU FOR A RESPONSIBLE YOUNG LADY AND YOU TUR
WAAH! (SOB)
RECEPTION

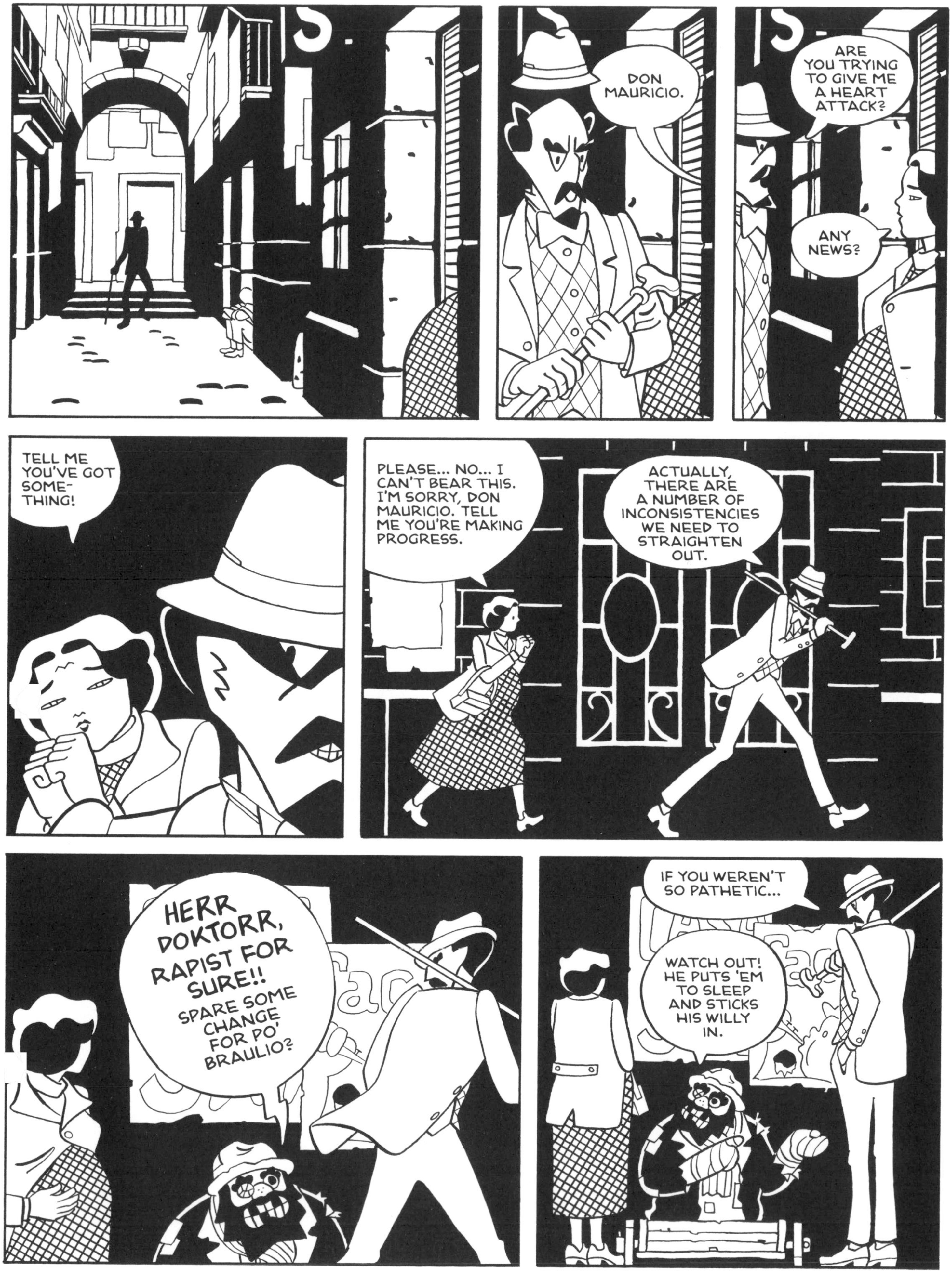
DON MAURICIO.
ARE YOU TRYING TO GIVE ME A HEART ATTACK?
ANY NEWS?
TELL ME YOU'VE GOT SOME-THING!
PLEASE... NO... I CAN'T BEAR THIS. I'M SORRY, DON MAURICIO. TELL ME YOU'RE MAKING PROGRESS.
ACTUALLY, THERE ARE A NUMBER OF INCONSISTENCIES WE NEED TO STRAIGHTEN OUT.
HERR DOKTORR, RAPIST FOR SURE!! SPARE SOME CHANGE FOR PO' BRAULIO?
IF YOU WEREN'T SO PATHETIC...
WATCH OUT! HE PUTS 'EM TO SLEEP AND STICKS HIS WILLY IN.

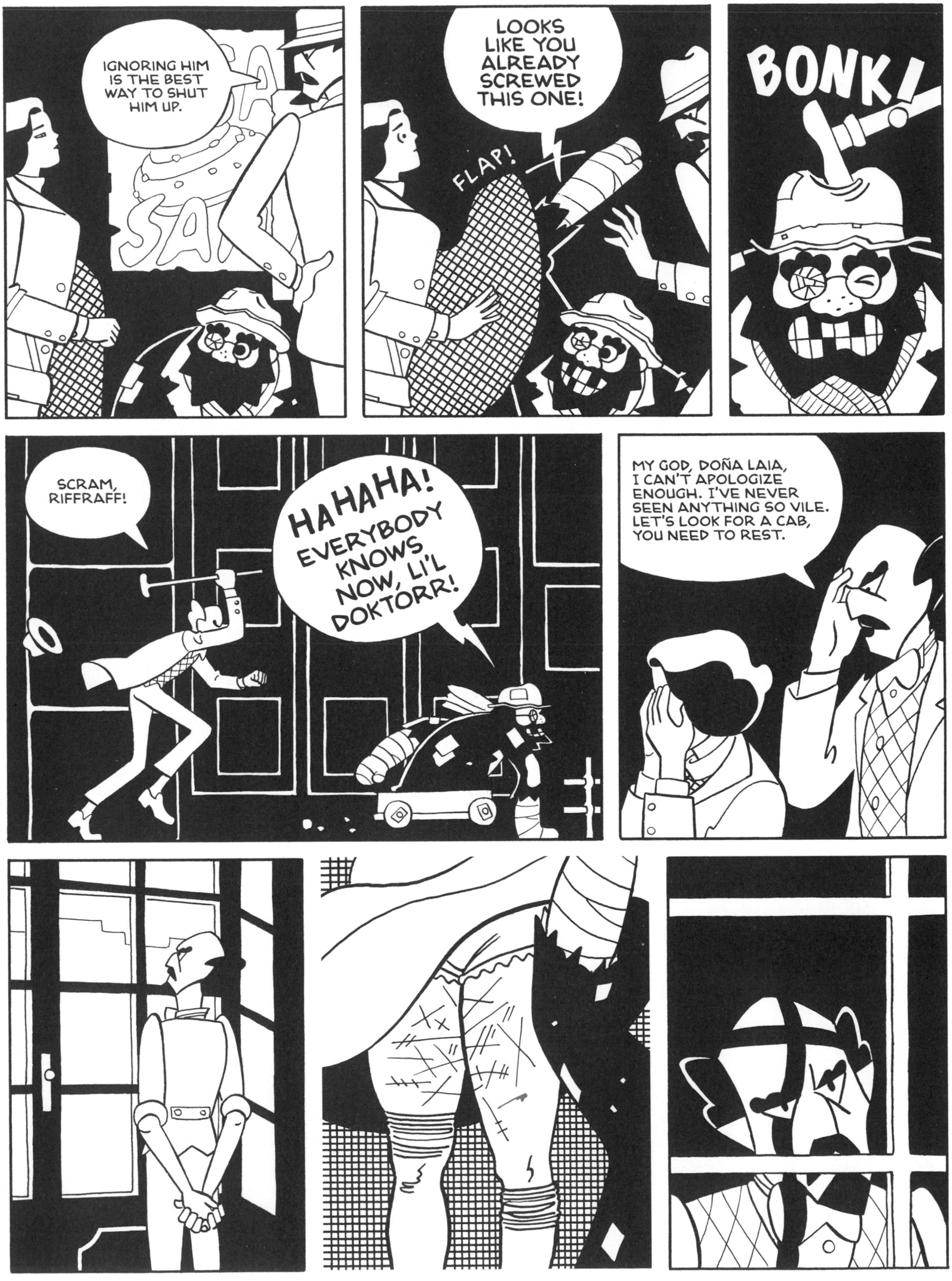
IGNORING HIM IS THE BEST WAY TO SHUT HIM UP.
LOOKS LIKE YOU ALREADY SCREWED THIS ONE!
FLAP!
BONK!
SCRAM, RIFFRAFF!
HAHAHA! EVERYBODY KNOWS NOW, LI'L DOKTORR!
MY GOD, DOÑA LAIA, I CAN'T APOLOGIZE ENOUGH. I'VE NEVER SEEN ANYTHING SO VILE. LET'S LOOK FOR A CAB, YOU NEED TO REST.

5

Calorie Bomb

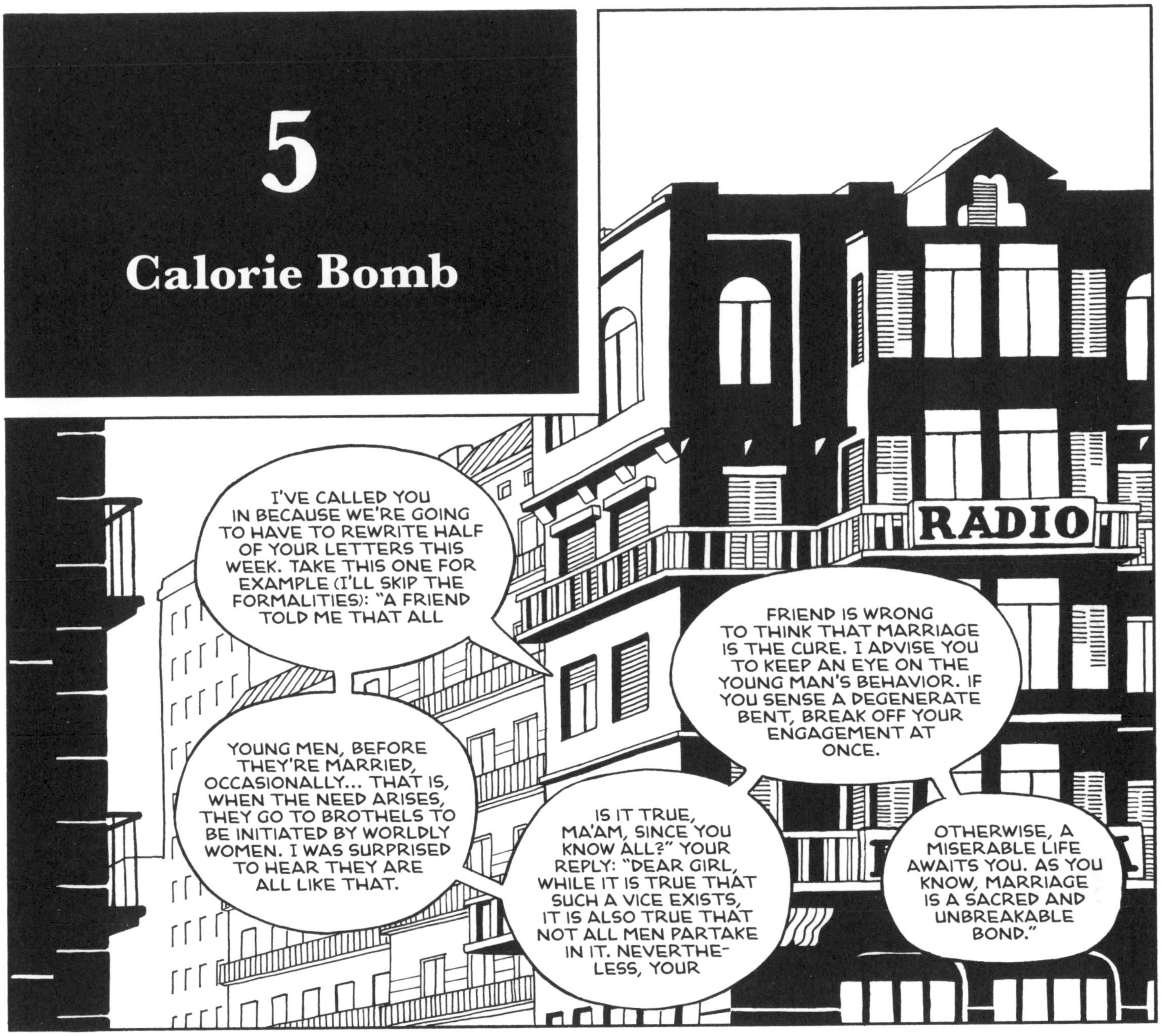
I'VE CALLED YOU IN BECAUSE WE'RE GOING TO HAVE TO REWRITE HALF OF YOUR LETTERS THIS WEEK. TAKE THIS ONE FOR EXAMPLE (I'LL SKIP THE FORMALITIES): "A FRIEND TOLD ME THAT ALL
YOUNG MEN, BEFORE THEY'RE MARRIED, OCCASIONALLY... THAT IS, WHEN THE NEED ARISES, THEY GO TO BROTHELS TO BE INITIATED BY WORLDLY WOMEN. I WAS SURPRISED TO HEAR THEY ARE ALL LIKE THAT.
IS IT TRUE, MA'AM, SINCE YOU KNOW ALL?" YOUR REPLY: "DEAR GIRL, WHILE IT IS TRUE THAT SUCH A VICE EXISTS, IT IS ALSO TRUE THAT NOT ALL MEN PARTAKE IN IT. NEVERTHE-LESS, YOUR
FRIEND IS WRONG TO THINK THAT MARRIAGE IS THE CURE. I ADVISE YOU TO KEEP AN EYE ON THE YOUNG MAN'S BEHAVIOR. IF YOU SENSE A DEGENERATE BENT, BREAK OFF YOUR ENGAGEMENT AT ONCE.
OTHERWISE, A MISERABLE LIFE AWAITS YOU. AS YOU KNOW, MARRIAGE IS A SACRED AND UNBREAKABLE BOND."
RADIO

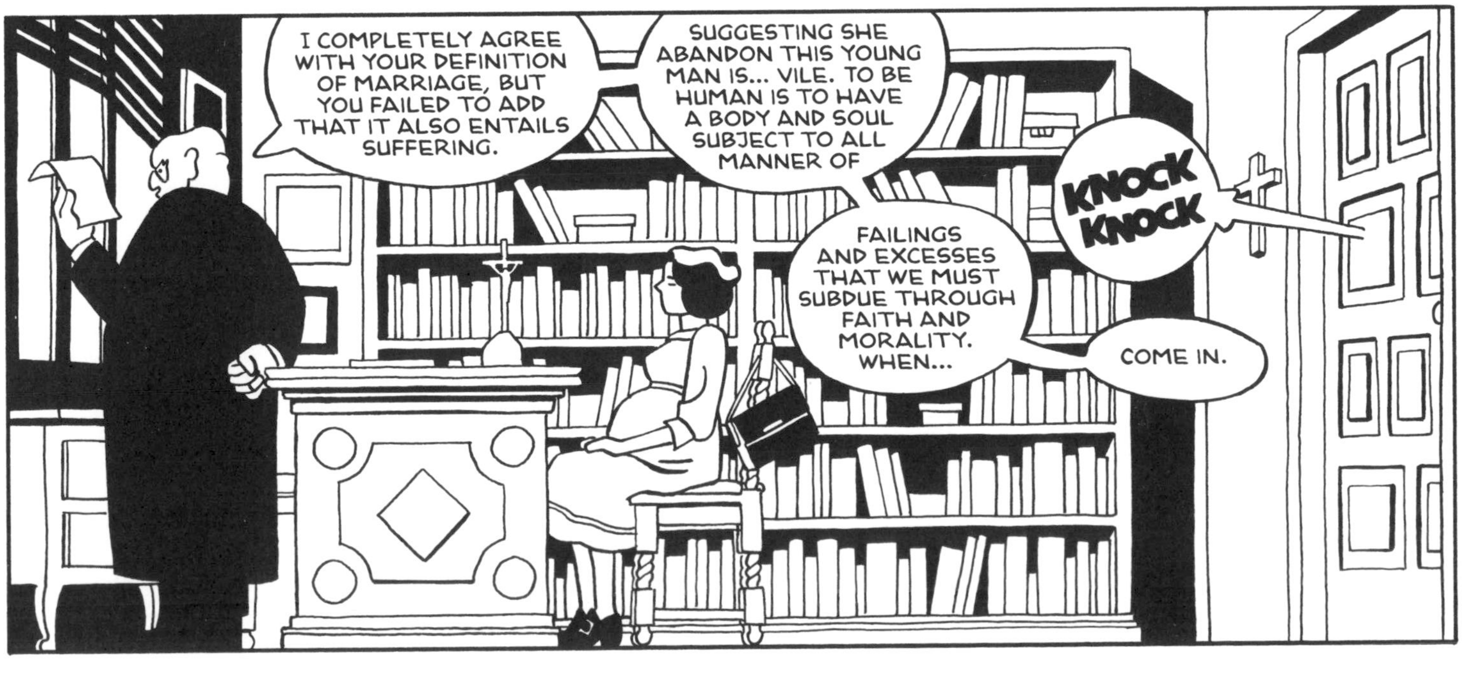
I COMPLETELY AGREE WITH YOUR DEFINITION OF MARRIAGE, BUT YOU FAILED TO ADD THAT IT ALSO ENTAILS SUFFERING.
SUGGESTING SHE ABANDON THIS YOUNG MAN IS... VILE. TO BE HUMAN IS TO HAVE A BODY AND SOUL SUBJECT TO ALL MANNER OF
FAILINGS AND EXCESSES THAT WE MUST SUBDUE THROUGH FAITH AND MORALITY. WHEN...
KNOCK KNOCK
COME IN.

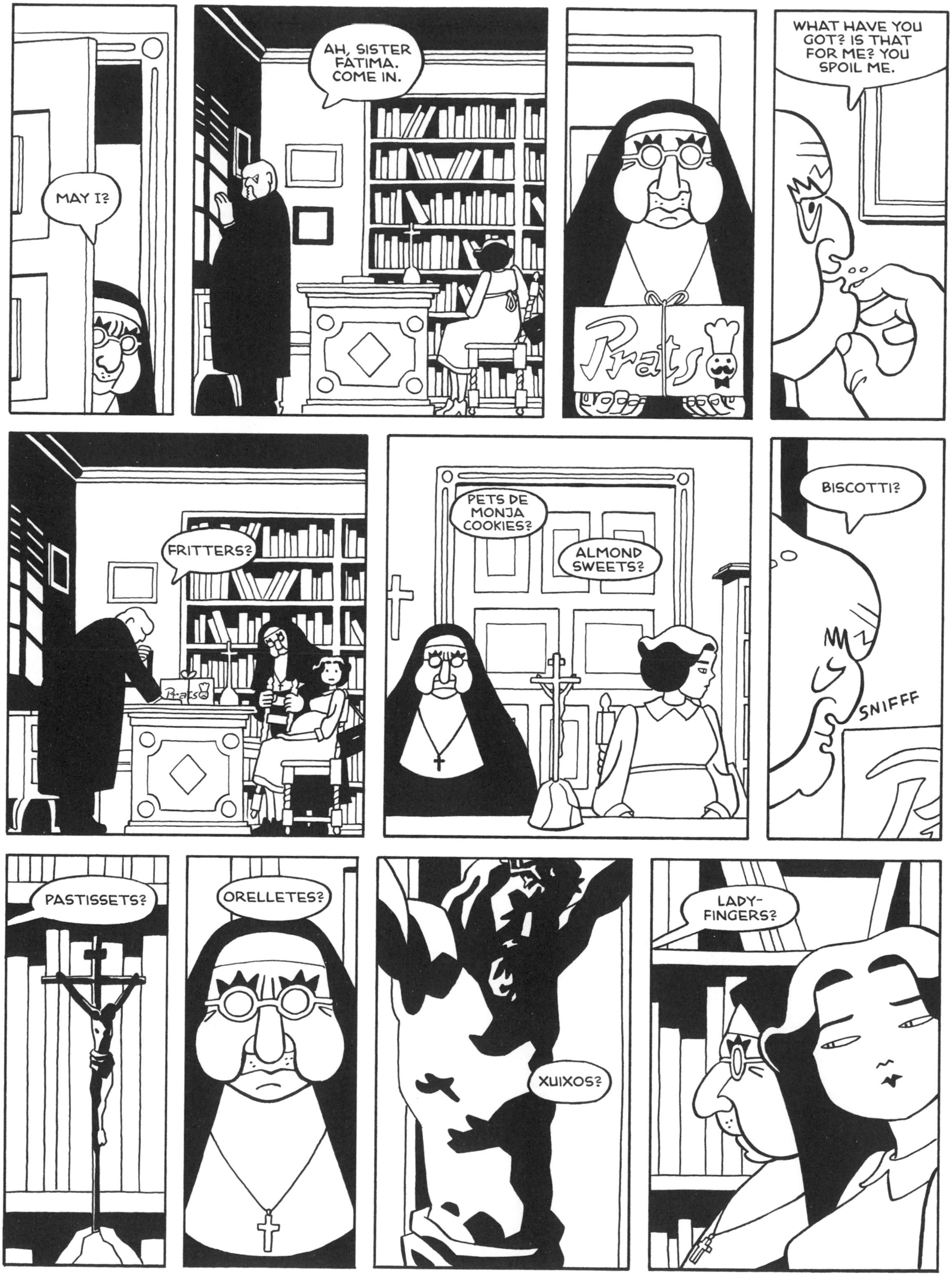
MAY I?
AH, SISTER FATIMA. COME IN.
Prats
WHAT HAVE YOU GOT? IS THAT FOR ME? YOU SPOIL ME.
FRITTERS?
Prats
PETS DE MONJA COOKIES?
ALMOND SWEETS?
BISCOTTI?
SNIFFF
PASTISSETS?
ORELLETES?
XUIXOS?
LADY-FINGERS?

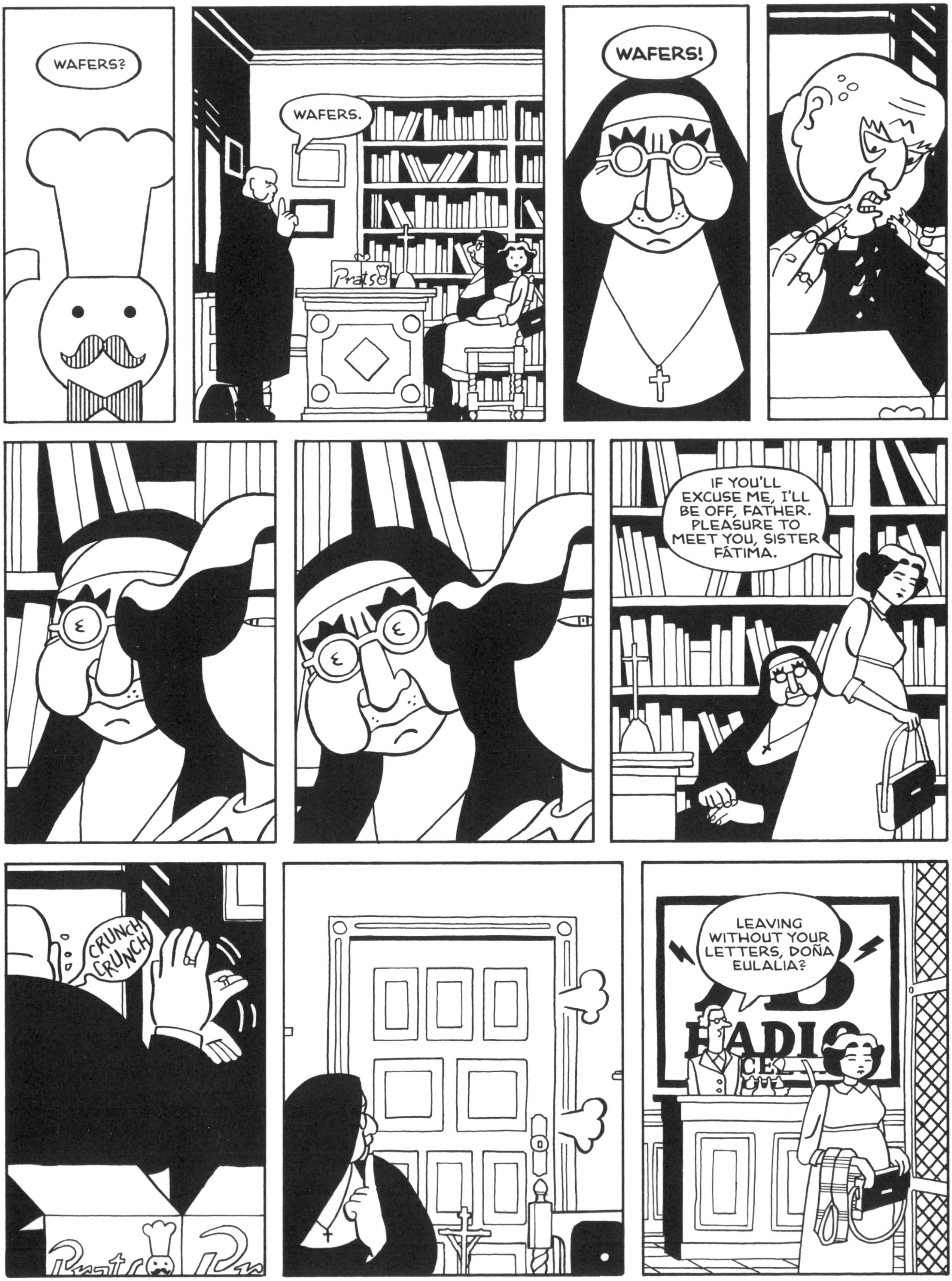
WAFERS?
WAFERS.
Prats
WAFERS!
IF YOU'LL EXCUSE ME, I'LL BE OFF, FATHER. PLEASURE TO MEET YOU, SISTER FÁTIMA.
CRUNCH CRUNCH
LEAVING WITHOUT YOUR LETTERS, DOÑA EULALIA?
RADIO

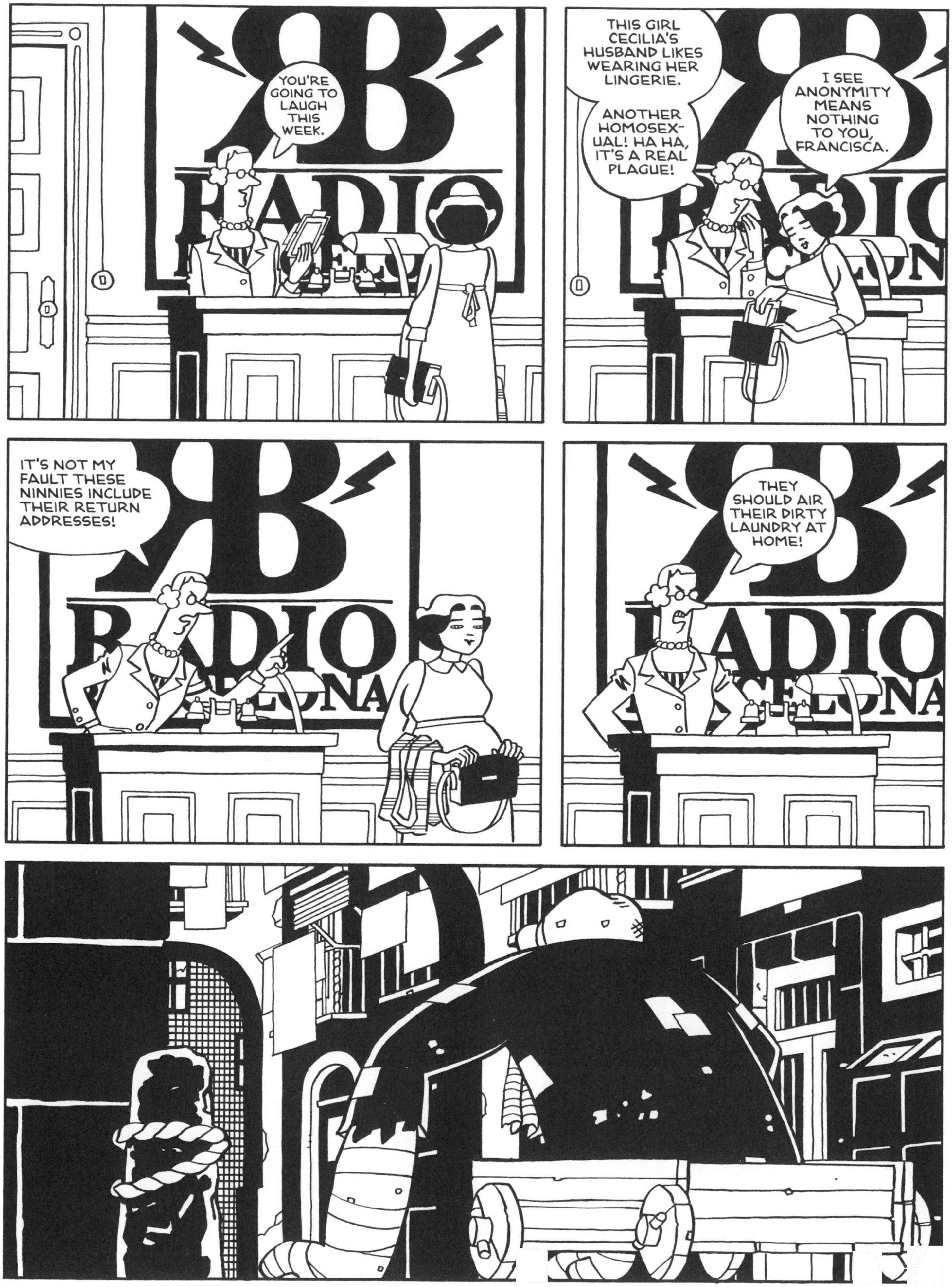

YOU'RE GOING TO LAUGH THIS WEEK.
THIS GIRL CECILIA'S HUSBAND LIKES WEARING HER LINGERIE.
ANOTHER HOMOSEX-UAL! HA HA, IT'S A REAL PLAGUE!
I SEE ANONYMITY MEANS NOTHING TO YOU, FRANCISCA.
IT'S NOT MY FAULT THESE NINNIES INCLUDE THEIR RETURN ADDRESSES!
THEY SHOULD AIR THEIR DIRTY LAUNDRY AT HOME!

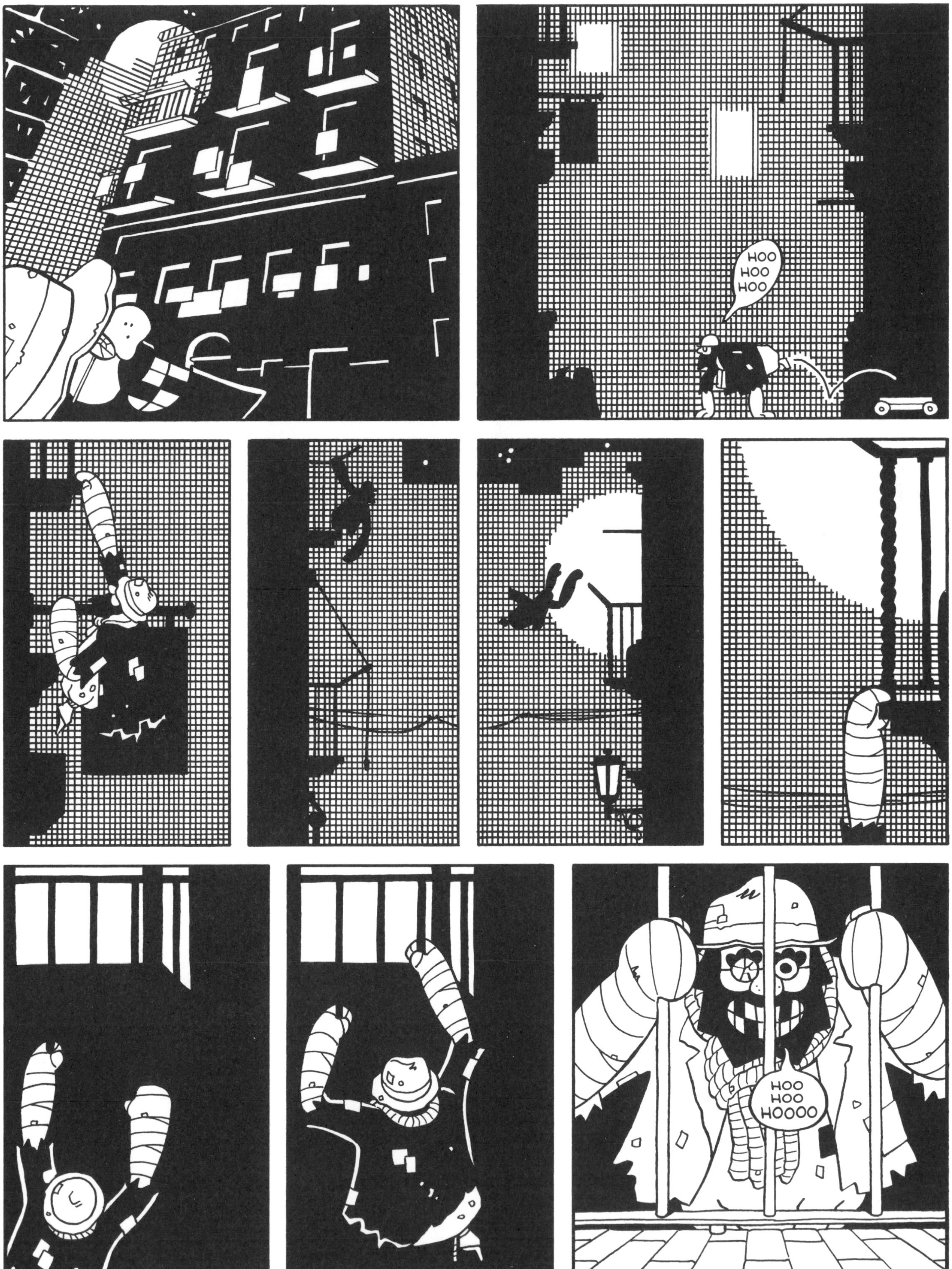
HOO
HOO
HOO
HOO
HOO
HOOOO

6

The Hunt

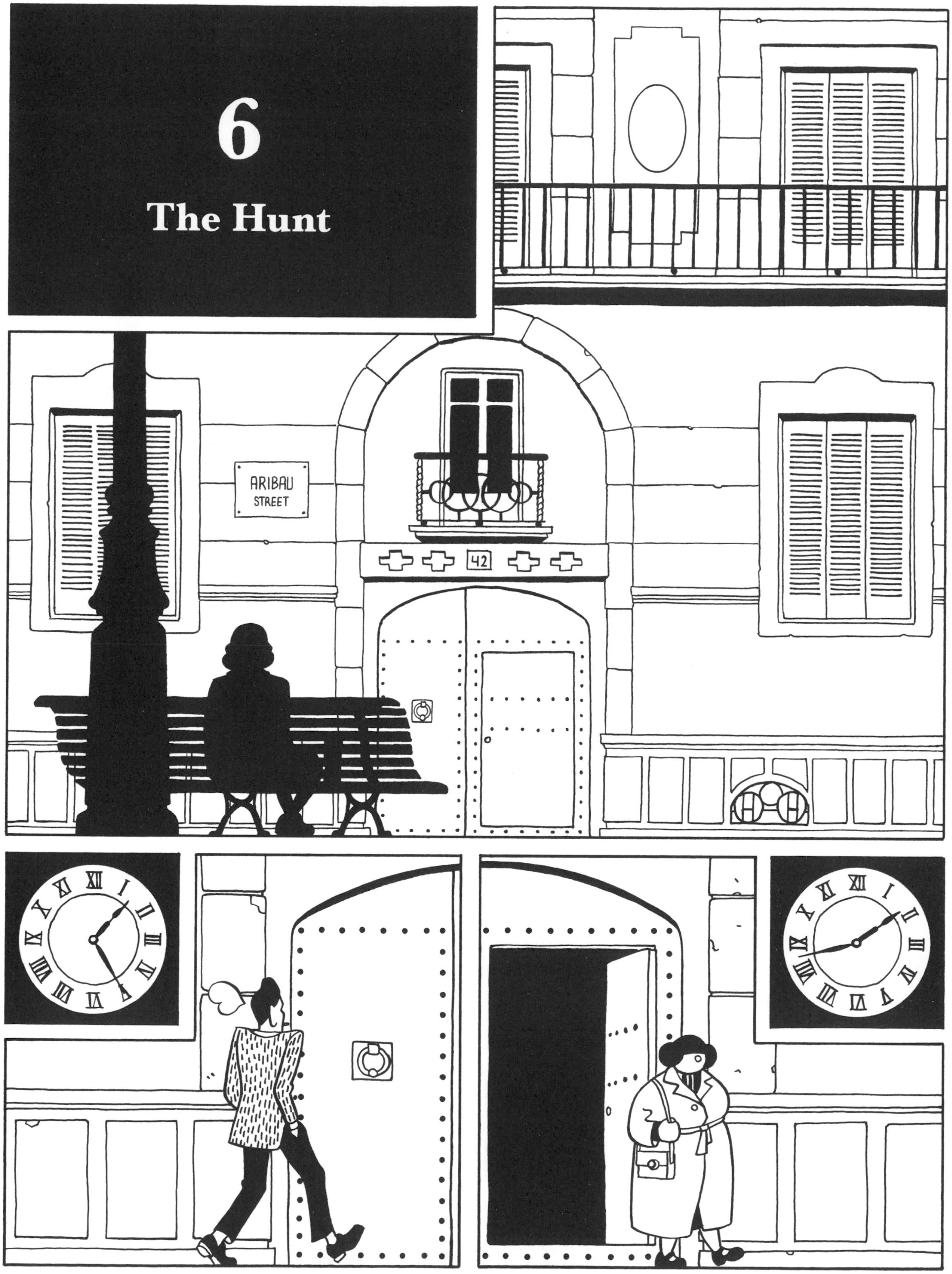

ARIBAU
STREET
42

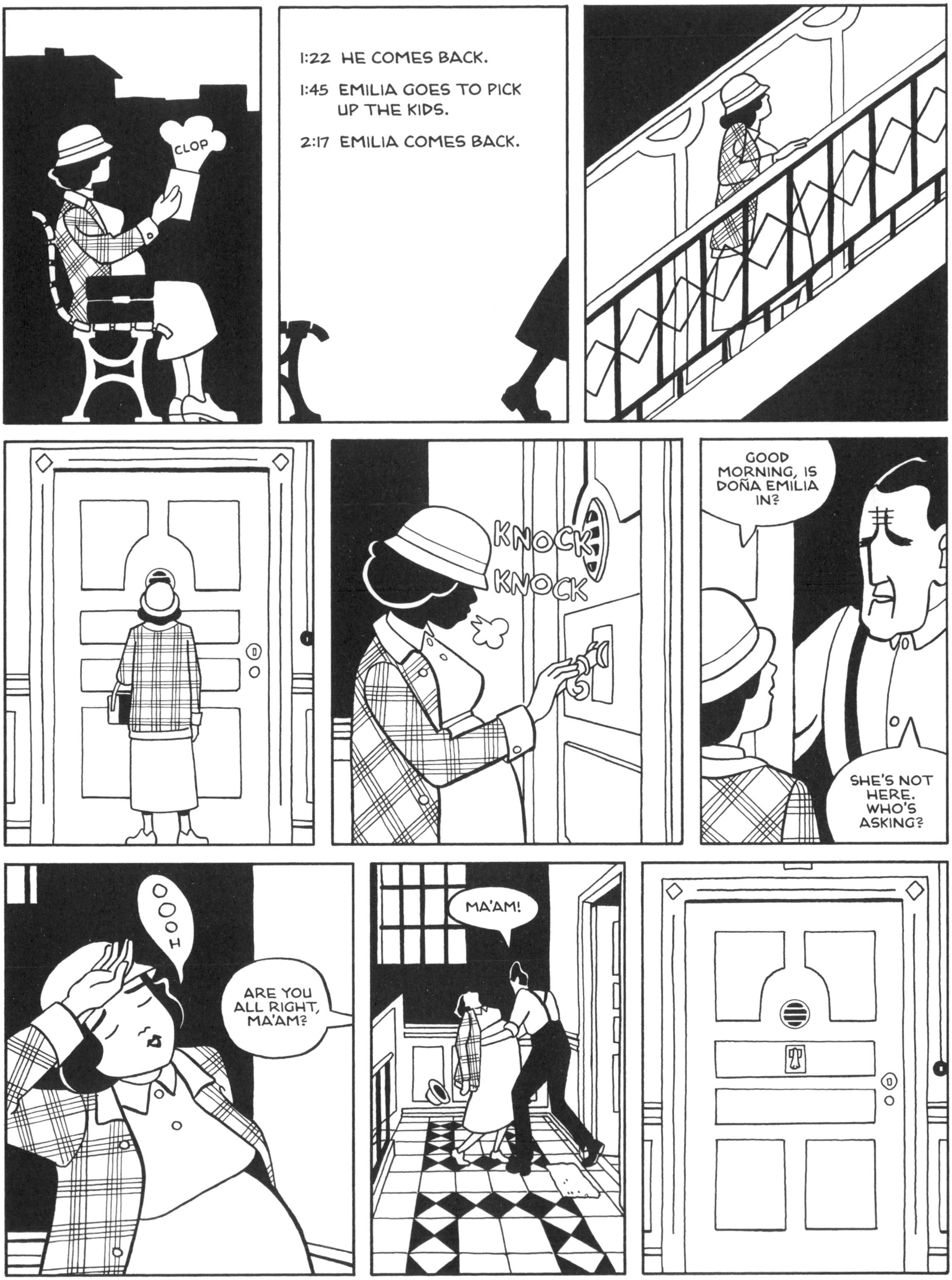
CLOP
1:22 HE COMES BACK.
1:45 EMILIA GOES TO PICK UP THE KIDS.
2:17 EMILIA COMES BACK.
KNOCK KNOCK
GOOD MORNING, IS DOÑA EMILIA IN?
SHE'S NOT HERE. WHO'S ASKING?
OOOH
ARE YOU ALL RIGHT, MA'AM?
MA'AM!

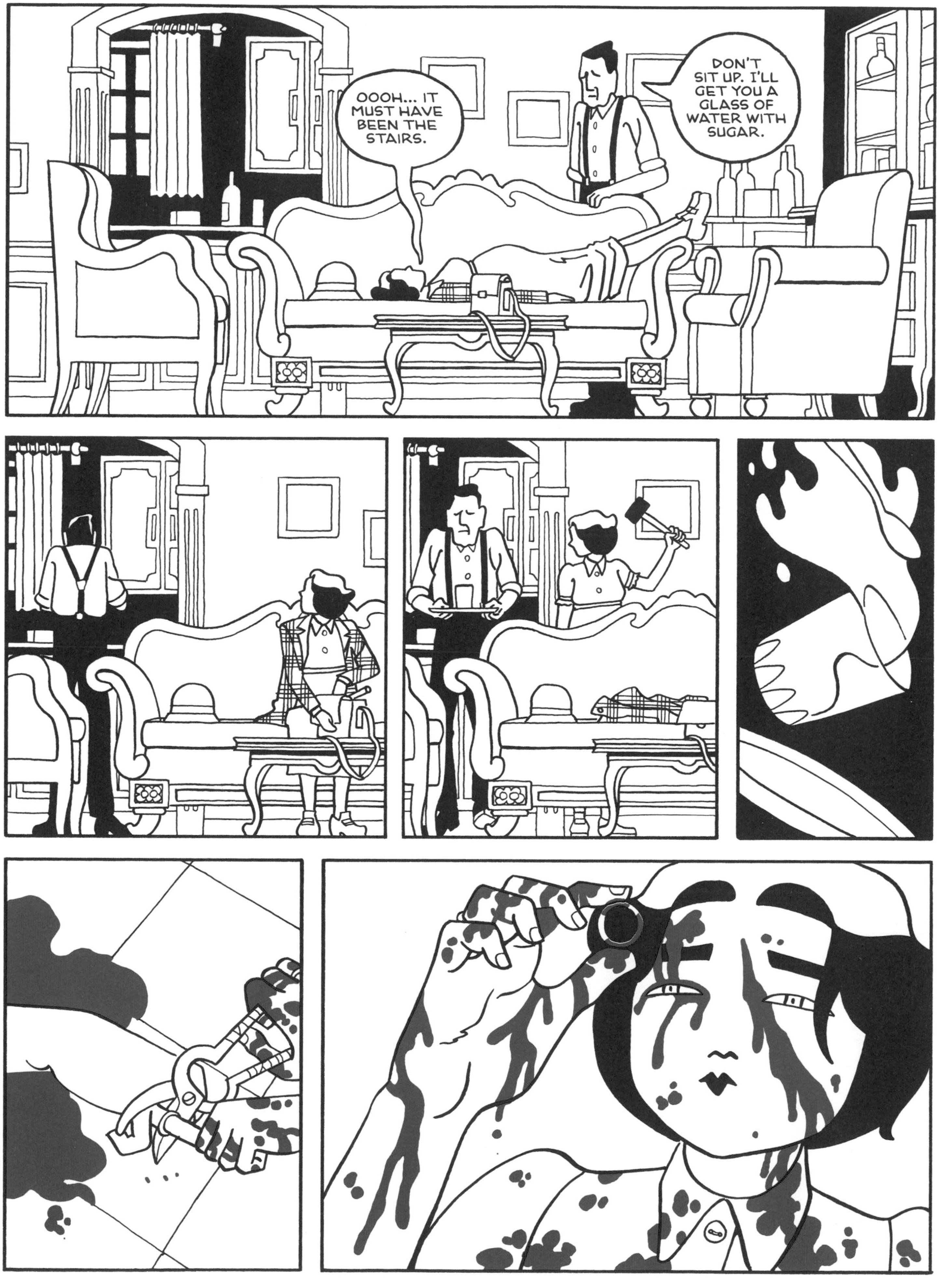
OOOH... IT MUST HAVE BEEN THE STAIRS.
DON'T SIT UP. I'LL GET YOU A GLASS OF WATER WITH SUGAR.

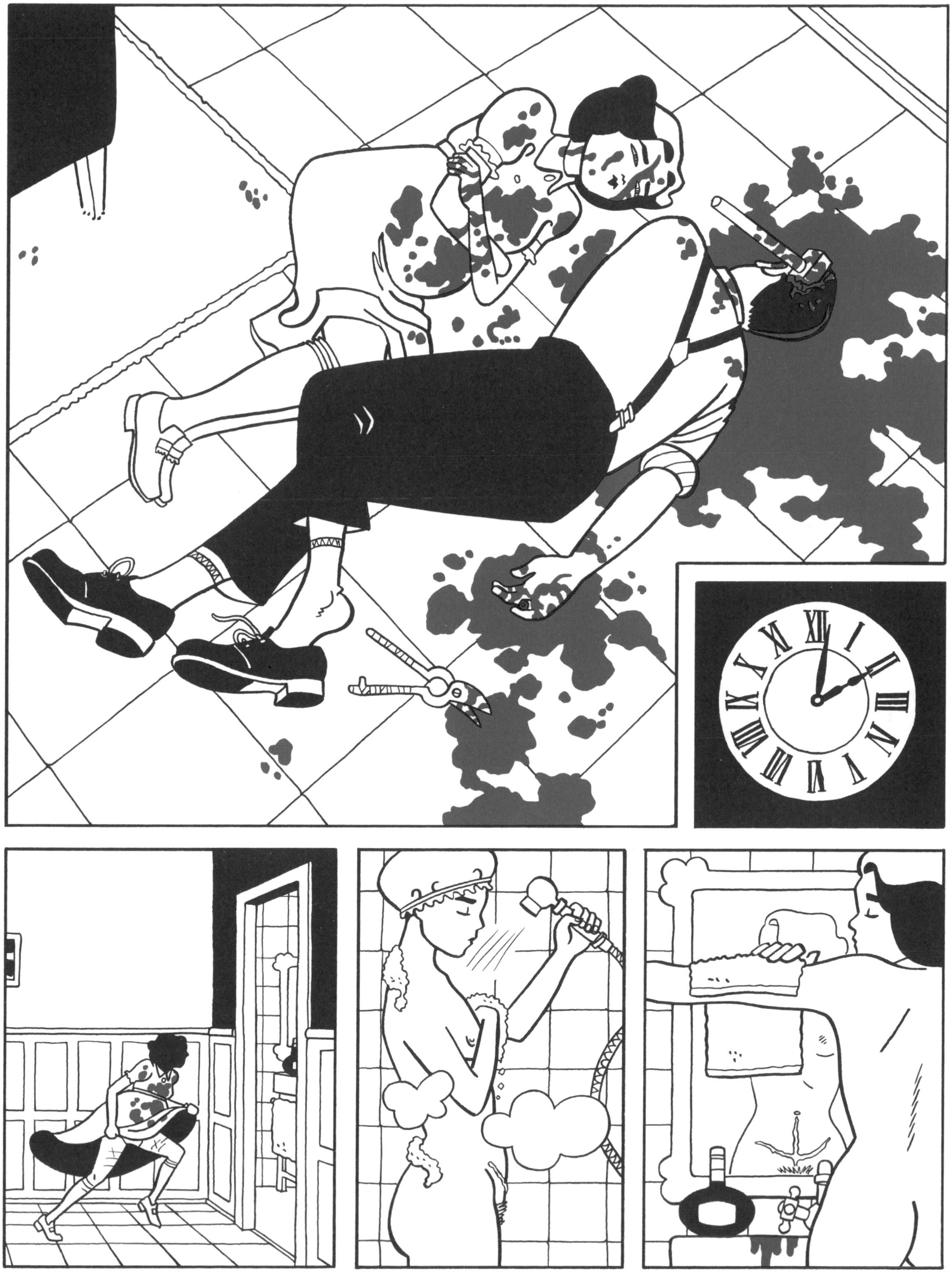

OBEDIENT
GIRL

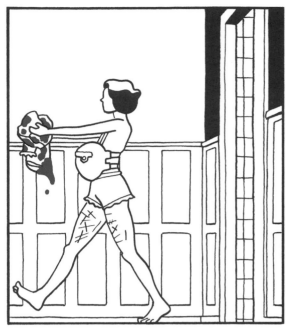

7

Thursday

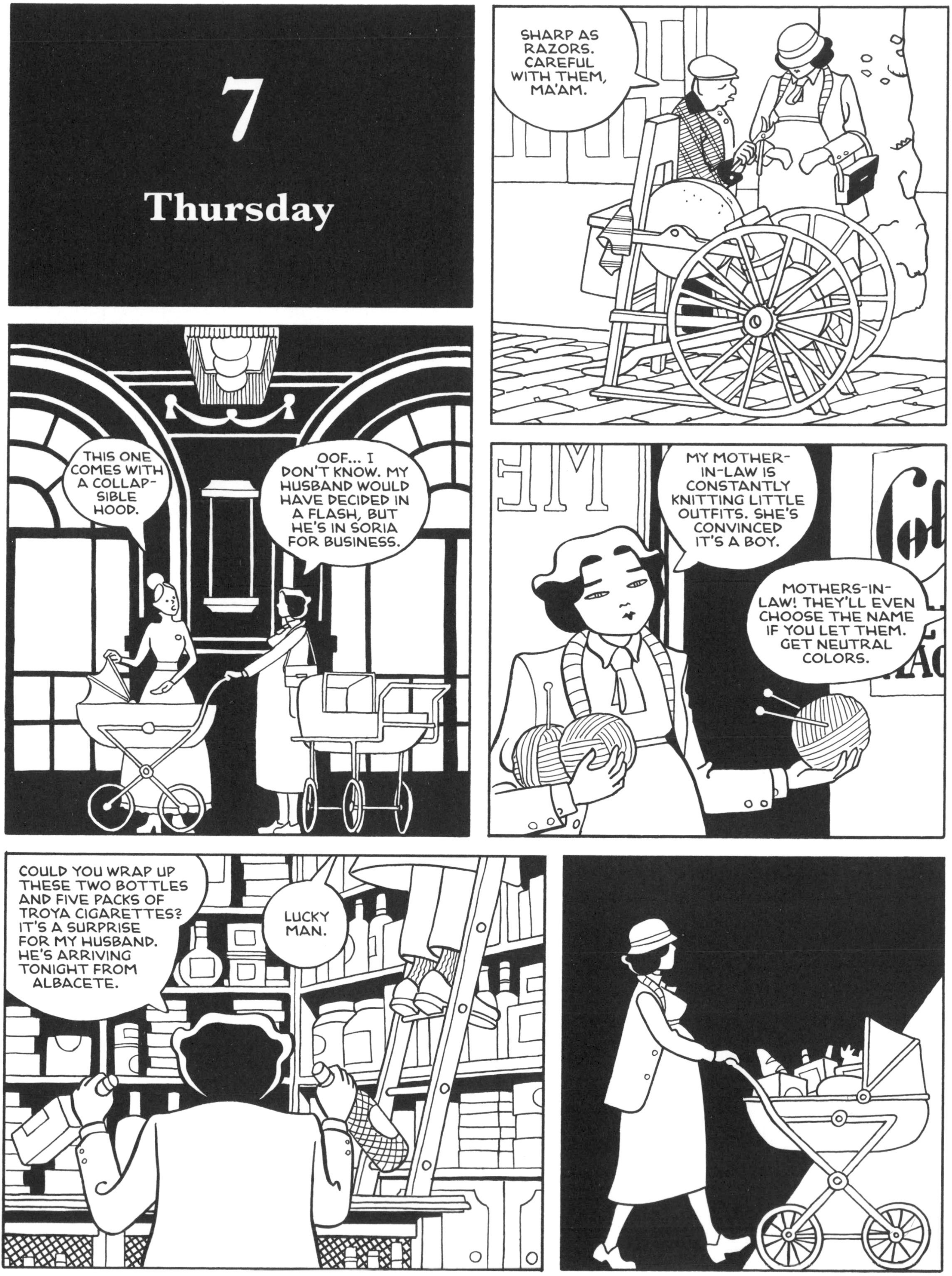

SHARP AS RAZORS. CAREFUL WITH THEM, MA'AM.
THIS ONE COMES WITH A COLLAPSIBLE HOOD.
OOF... I DON'T KNOW. MY HUSBAND WOULD HAVE DECIDED IN A FLASH, BUT HE'S IN SORIA FOR BUSINESS.
MY MOTHER-IN-LAW IS CONSTANTLY KNITTING LITTLE OUTFITS. SHE'S CONVINCED IT'S A BOY.
MOTHERS-IN-LAW! THEY'LL EVEN CHOOSE THE NAME IF YOU LET THEM. GET NEUTRAL COLORS.
COULD YOU WRAP UP THESE TWO BOTTLES AND FIVE PACKS OF TROYA CIGARETTES? IT'S A SURPRISE FOR MY HUSBAND. HE'S ARRIVING TONIGHT FROM ALBACETE.
LUCKY MAN.

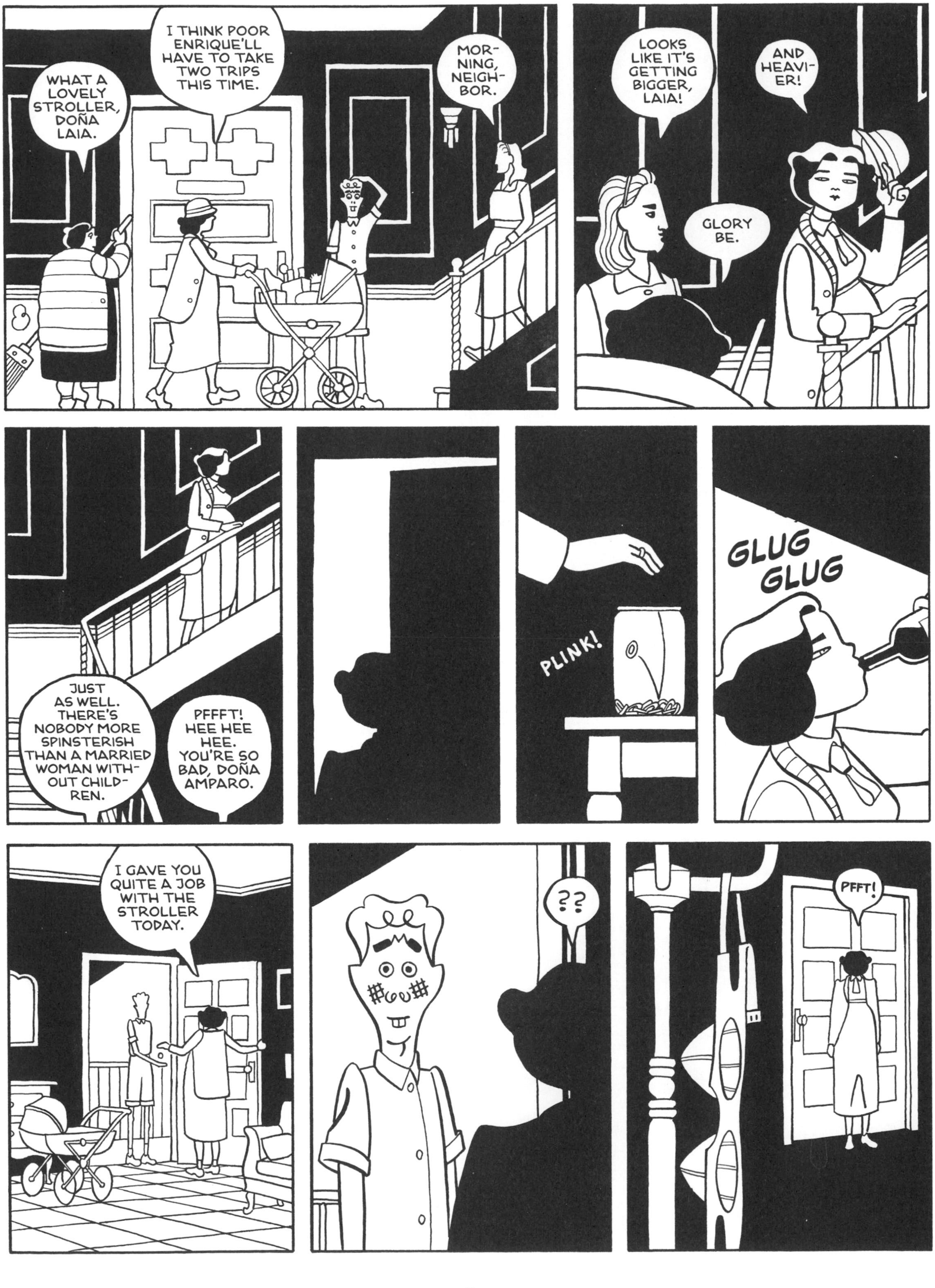
WHAT A LOVELY STROLLER, DOÑA LAIA.
I THINK POOR ENRIQUE'LL HAVE TO TAKE TWO TRIPS THIS TIME.
MOR-NING, NEIGH-BOR.
LOOKS LIKE IT'S GETTING BIGGER, LAIA!
AND HEAVI-ER!
GLORY BE.
JUST AS WELL. THERE'S NOBODY MORE SPINSTERISH THAN A MARRIED WOMAN WITH-OUT CHILD-REN.
PFFFT! HEE HEE HEE. YOU'RE SO BAD, DOÑA AMPARO.
PLINK!
GLUG GLUG
I GAVE YOU QUITE A JOB WITH THE STROLLER TODAY.
??
PFFT!

CLAP
APCLAP
APCLAP
KNOCK
OCK KN
KNOCK
KNOCK
KNOCK
KNOCK
KNOCK

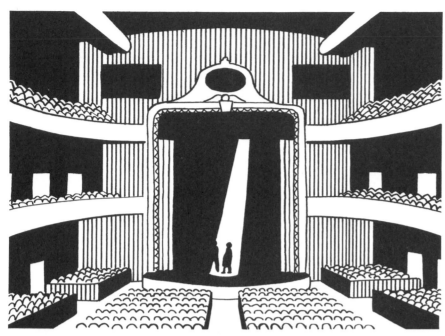

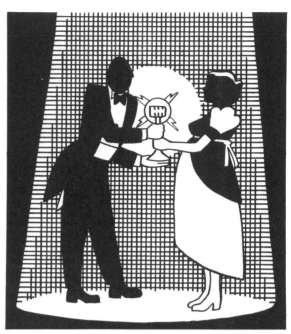

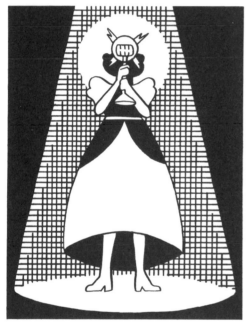

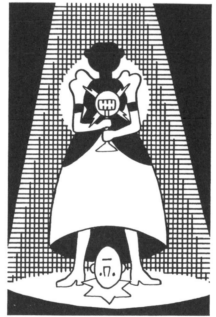

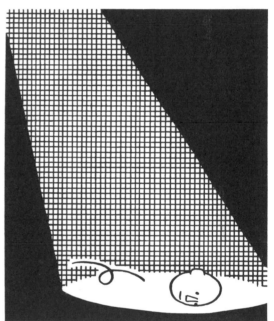

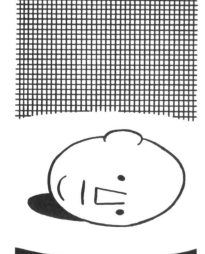

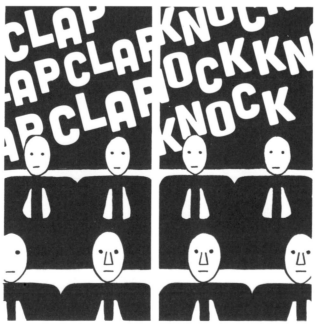

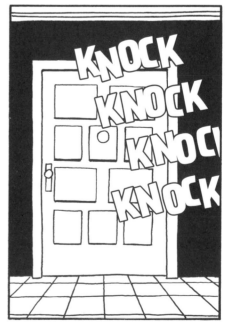

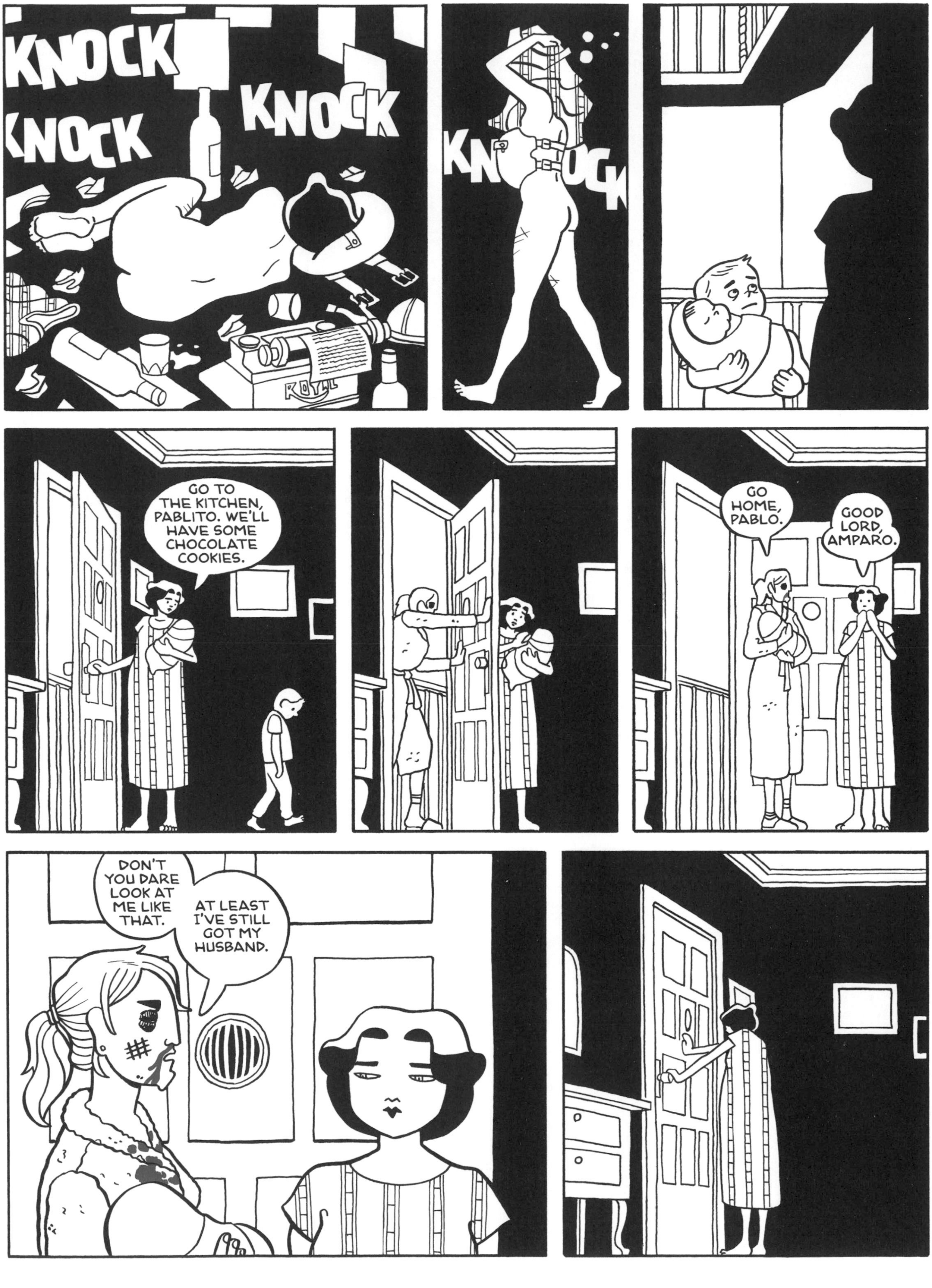
KNOCK
KNOCK
KNOCK
KNOCK
GO TO THE KITCHEN, PABLITO. WE'LL HAVE SOME CHOCOLATE COOKIES.
GO HOME, PABLO.
GOOD LORD, AMPARO.
DON'T YOU DARE LOOK AT ME LIKE THAT.
AT LEAST I'VE STILL GOT MY HUSBAND.

8
The Bloodhound Without a Bone

YOU'LL FEEL BETTER TOMORROW, YOU'LL SEE. CAREFUL ON THE STAIRS.

DOÑA LAIA, COME IN, PLEASE.

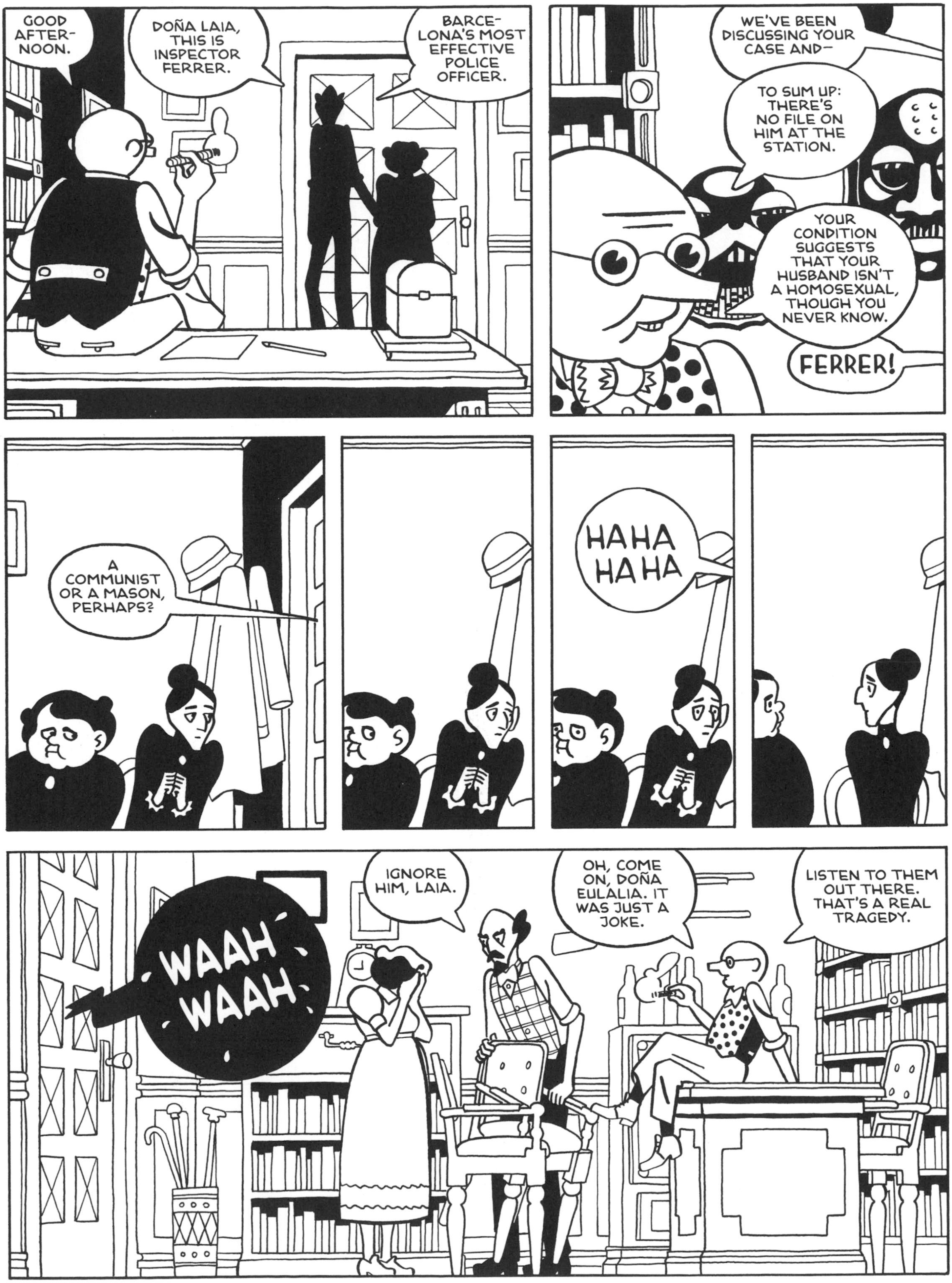
GOOD AFTERNOON.
DOÑA LAIA, THIS IS INSPECTOR FERRER.
BARCELONA'S MOST EFFECTIVE POLICE OFFICER.
WE'VE BEEN DISCUSSING YOUR CASE AND—
TO SUM UP: THERE'S NO FILE ON HIM AT THE STATION.
YOUR CONDITION SUGGESTS THAT YOUR HUSBAND ISN'T A HOMOSEXUAL, THOUGH YOU NEVER KNOW.
FERRER!
A COMMUNIST OR A MASON, PERHAPS?
HAHA HAHA
WAAH WAAH
IGNORE HIM, LAIA.
OH, COME ON, DOÑA EULALIA. IT WAS JUST A JOKE.
LISTEN TO THEM OUT THERE. THAT'S A REAL TRAGEDY.

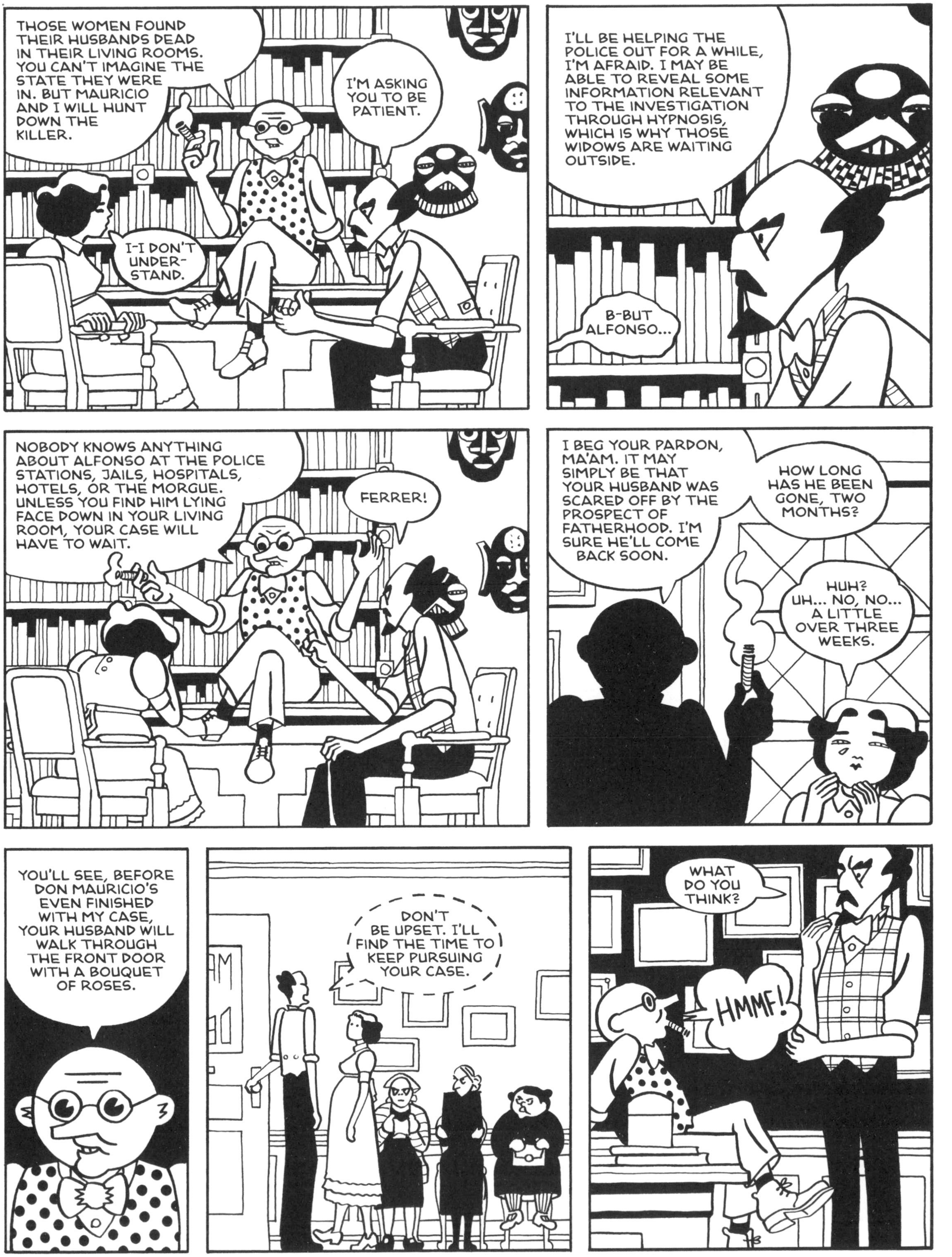
THOSE WOMEN FOUND THEIR HUSBANDS DEAD IN THEIR LIVING ROOMS. YOU CAN'T IMAGINE THE STATE THEY WERE IN. BUT MAURICIO AND I WILL HUNT DOWN THE KILLER.
I'M ASKING YOU TO BE PATIENT.
I-I DON'T UNDER-STAND.
I'LL BE HELPING THE POLICE OUT FOR A WHILE, I'M AFRAID. I MAY BE ABLE TO REVEAL SOME INFORMATION RELEVANT TO THE INVESTIGATION THROUGH HYPNOSIS, WHICH IS WHY THOSE WIDOWS ARE WAITING OUTSIDE.
B-BUT ALFONSO...
NOBODY KNOWS ANYTHING ABOUT ALFONSO AT THE POLICE STATIONS, JAILS, HOSPITALS, HOTELS, OR THE MORGUE. UNLESS YOU FIND HIM LYING FACE DOWN IN YOUR LIVING ROOM, YOUR CASE WILL HAVE TO WAIT.
FERRER!
I BEG YOUR PARDON, MA'AM. IT MAY SIMPLY BE THAT YOUR HUSBAND WAS SCARED OFF BY THE PROSPECT OF FATHERHOOD. I'M SURE HE'LL COME BACK SOON.
HOW LONG HAS HE BEEN GONE, TWO MONTHS?
HUH? UH... NO, NO... A LITTLE OVER THREE WEEKS.
YOU'LL SEE, BEFORE DON MAURICIO'S EVEN FINISHED WITH MY CASE, YOUR HUSBAND WILL WALK THROUGH THE FRONT DOOR WITH A BOUQUET OF ROSES.
DON'T BE UPSET. I'LL FIND THE TIME TO KEEP PURSUING YOUR CASE.
WHAT DO YOU THINK?
HMMF!

9

Splash!

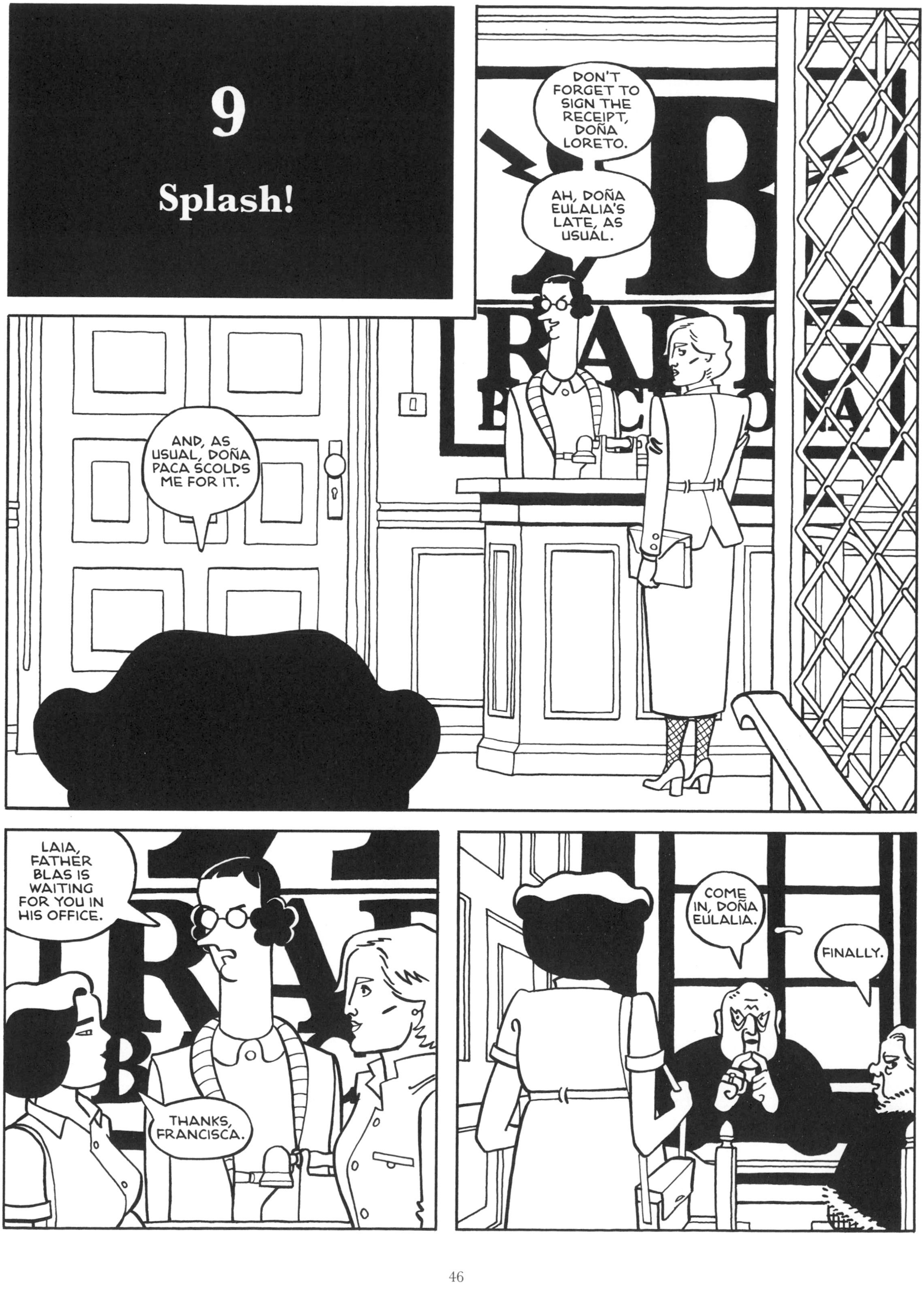
DON'T FORGET TO SIGN THE RECEIPT, DOÑA LORETO.
AH, DOÑA EULALIA'S LATE, AS USUAL.
AND, AS USUAL, DOÑA PACA SCOLDS ME FOR IT.
LAIA, FATHER BLAS IS WAITING FOR YOU IN HIS OFFICE.
THANKS, FRANCISCA.
COME IN, DOÑA EULALIA.
FINALLY.

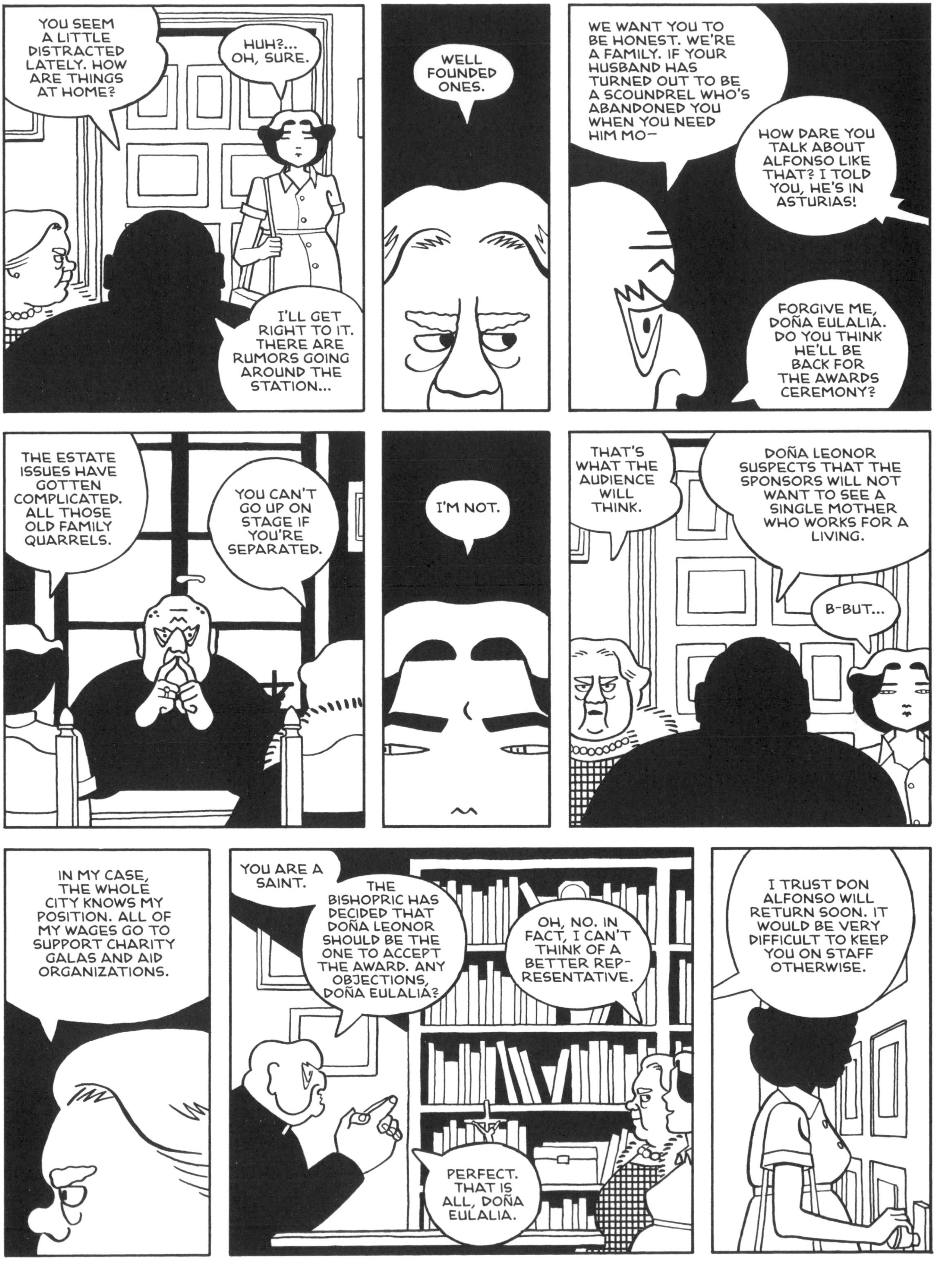
YOU SEEM A LITTLE DISTRACTED LATELY. HOW ARE THINGS AT HOME?
HUH?... OH, SURE.
I'LL GET RIGHT TO IT. THERE ARE RUMORS GOING AROUND THE STATION...
WELL FOUNDED ONES.
WE WANT YOU TO BE HONEST. WE'RE A FAMILY. IF YOUR HUSBAND HAS TURNED OUT TO BE A SCOUNDREL WHO'S ABANDONED YOU WHEN YOU NEED HIM MO—
HOW DARE YOU TALK ABOUT ALFONSO LIKE THAT? I TOLD YOU, HE'S IN ASTURIAS!
FORGIVE ME, DOÑA EULALIA. DO YOU THINK HE'LL BE BACK FOR THE AWARDS CEREMONY?
THE ESTATE ISSUES HAVE GOTTEN COMPLICATED. ALL THOSE OLD FAMILY QUARRELS.
YOU CAN'T GO UP ON STAGE IF YOU'RE SEPARATED.
I'M NOT.
THAT'S WHAT THE AUDIENCE WILL THINK.
DOÑA LEONOR SUSPECTS THAT THE SPONSORS WILL NOT WANT TO SEE A SINGLE MOTHER WHO WORKS FOR A LIVING.
B-BUT...
IN MY CASE, THE WHOLE CITY KNOWS MY POSITION. ALL OF MY WAGES GO TO SUPPORT CHARITY GALAS AND AID ORGANIZATIONS.
YOU ARE A SAINT.
THE BISHOPRIC HAS DECIDED THAT DOÑA LEONOR SHOULD BE THE ONE TO ACCEPT THE AWARD. ANY OBJECTIONS, DOÑA EULALIA?
OH, NO. IN FACT, I CAN'T THINK OF A BETTER REP-RESENTATIVE.
PERFECT. THAT IS ALL, DOÑA EULALIA.
I TRUST DON ALFONSO WILL RETURN SOON. IT WOULD BE VERY DIFFICULT TO KEEP YOU ON STAFF OTHERWISE.

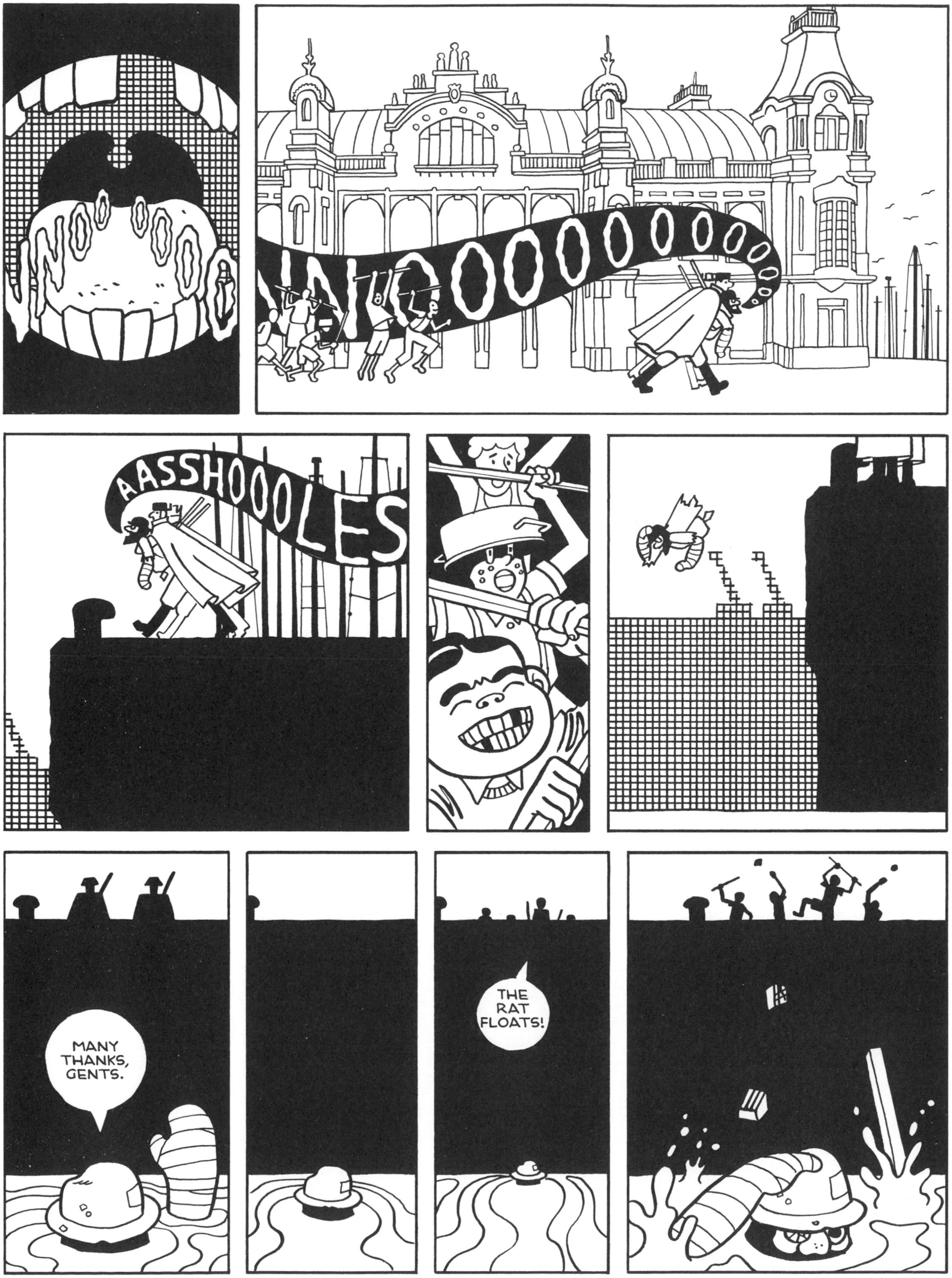
NOOOOO
NOOOOOOOOOOOO
AASSHOOOLES
MANY THANKS, GENTS.
THE RAT FLOATS!

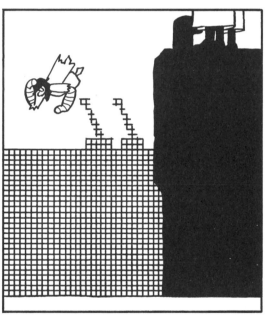

10

Pathos Season

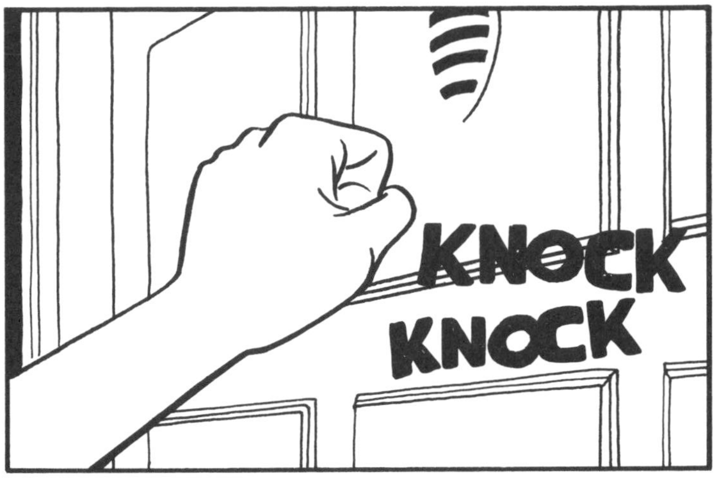
KNOCK
KNOCK

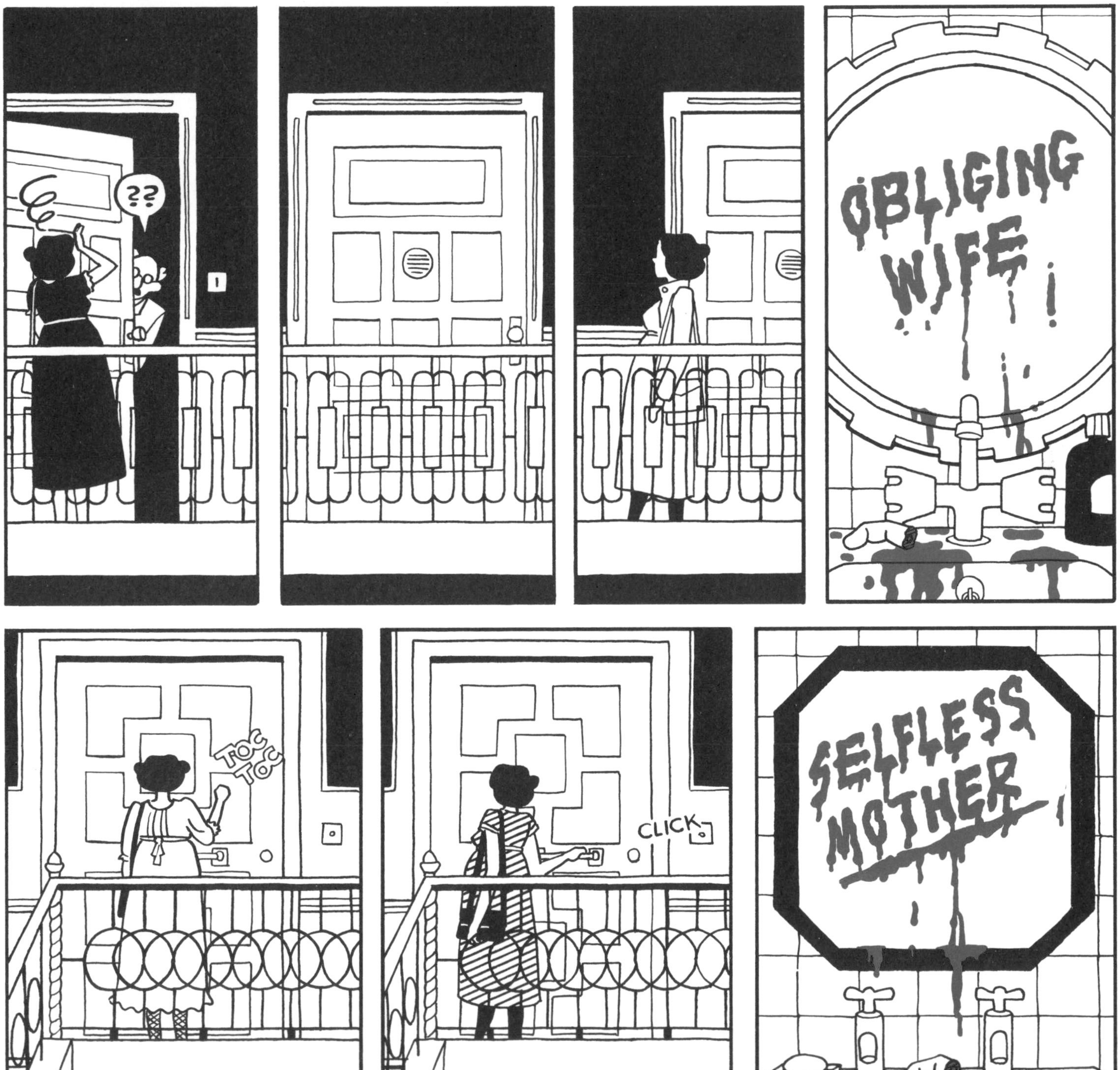
??
OBLIGING
WIFE
!
TOC
TOC
CLICK
SELFLESS
MOTHER

11

The Detective and the Pendulum

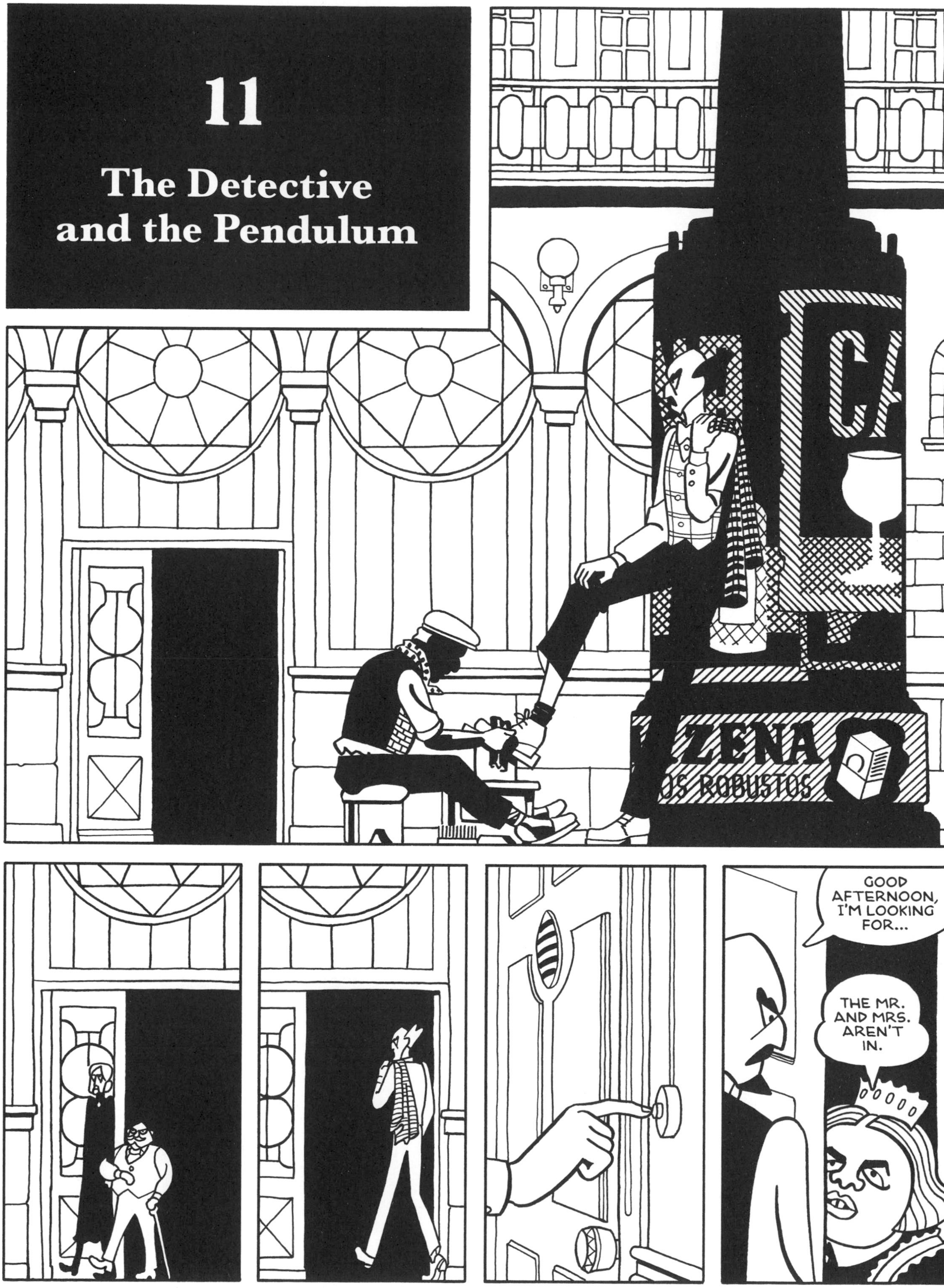
CA
ZENA
OS ROBUSTOS
GOOD AFTERNOON, I'M LOOKING FOR...
THE MR. AND MRS. AREN'T IN.

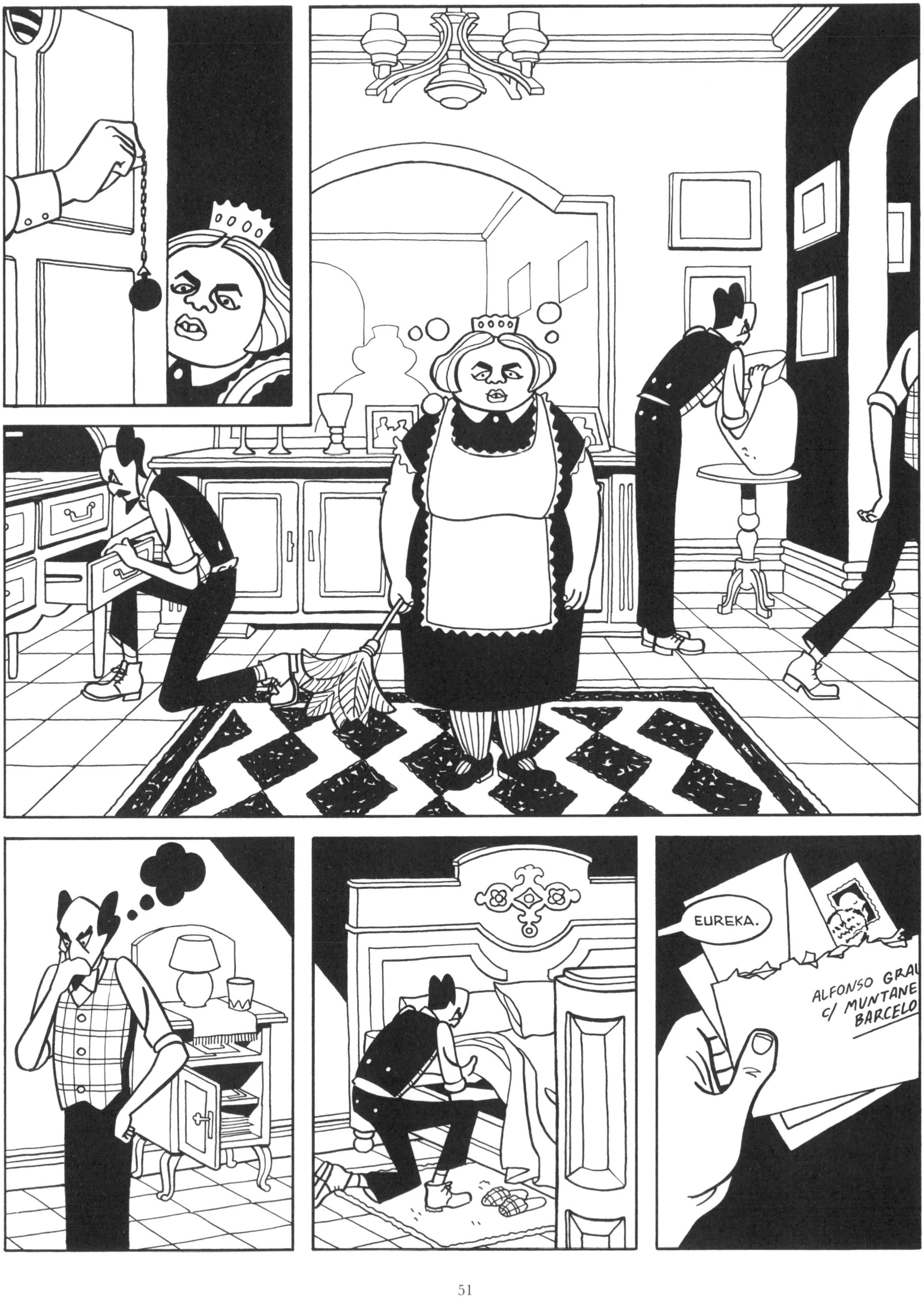
EUREKA.
ALFONSO GRAU
C/ MUNTANE
BARCELO

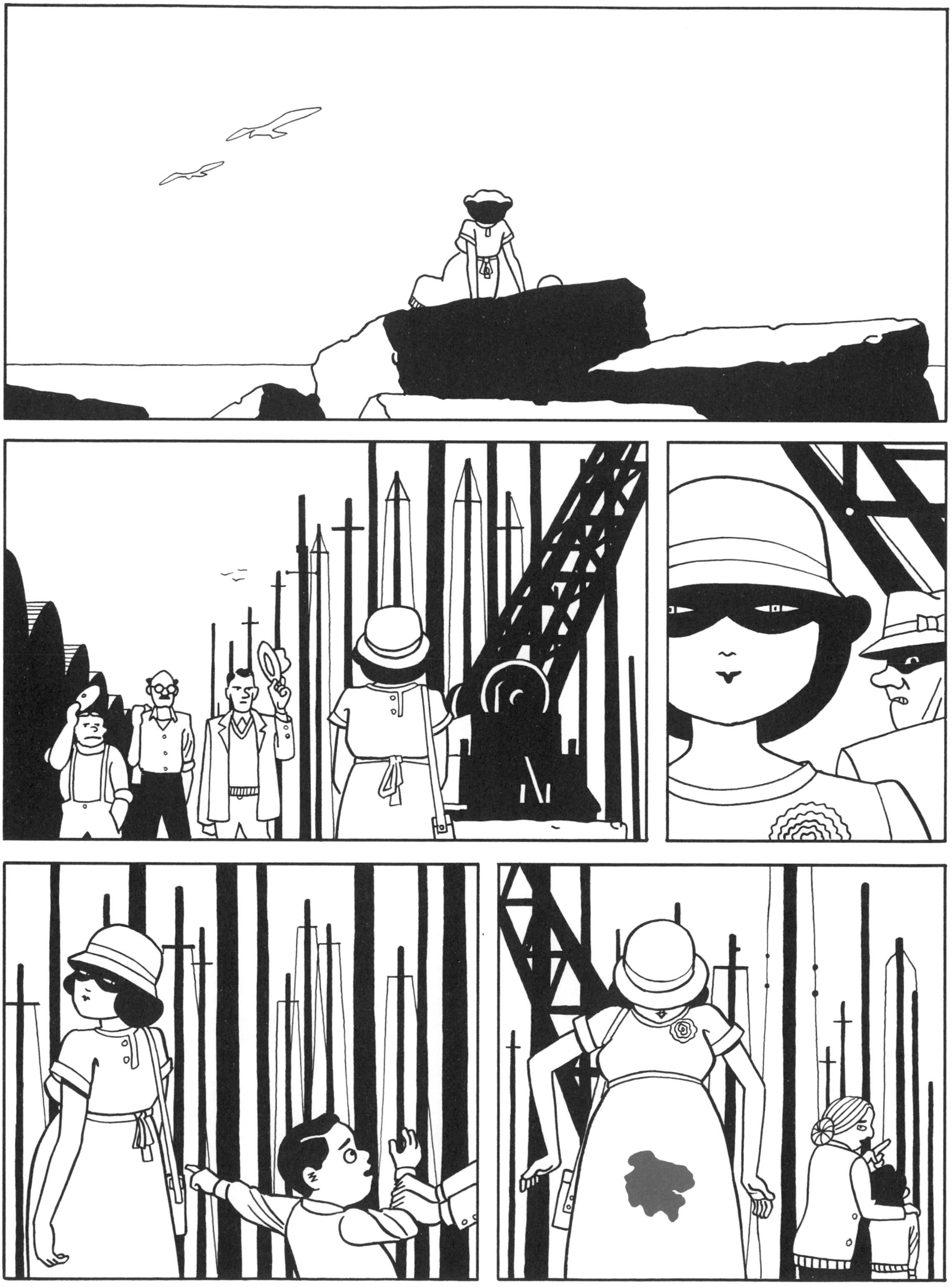

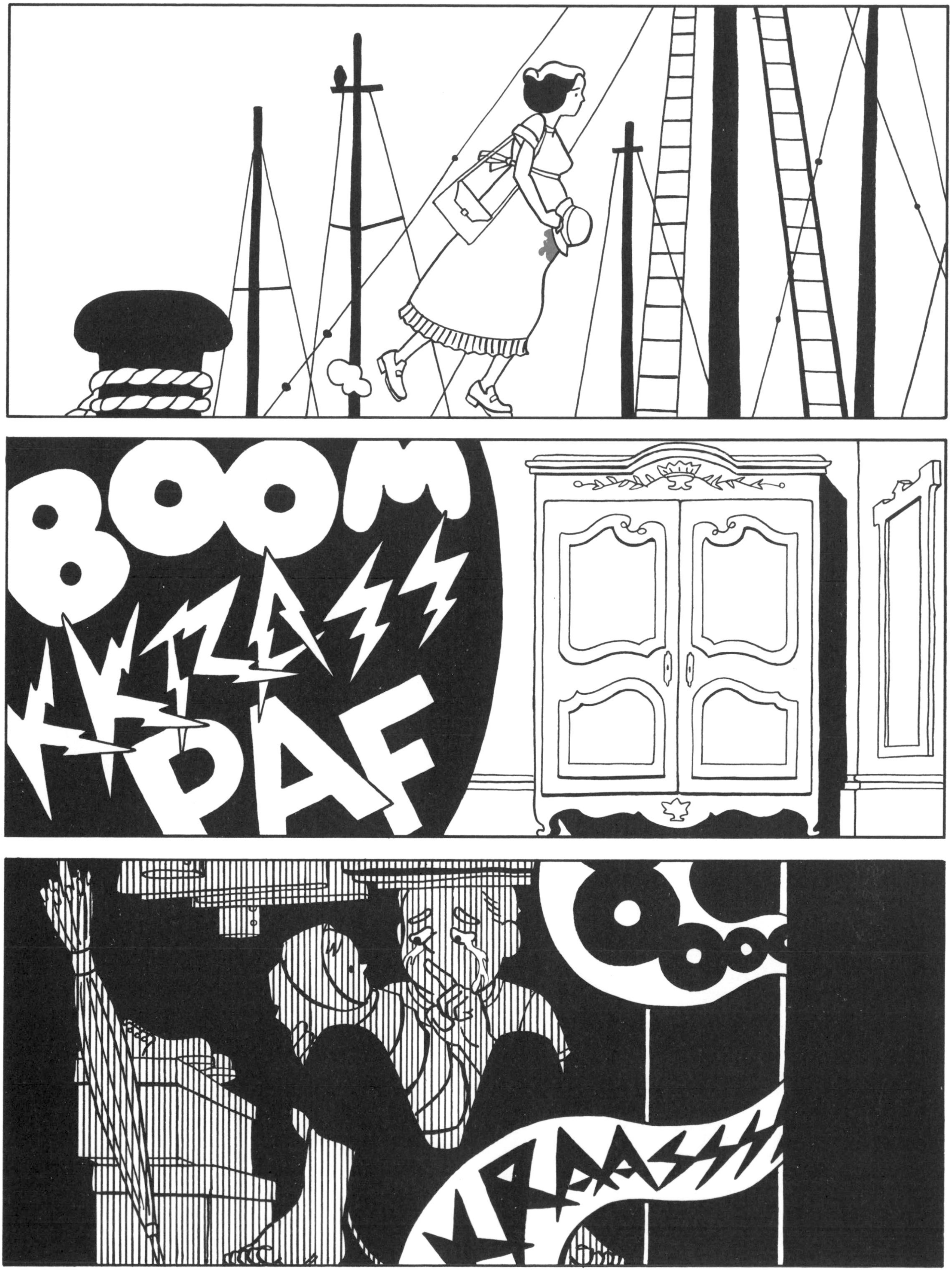
BOOM
PAF

12

You Will Earn Your Bread By the Sweat of Someone Else's Brow

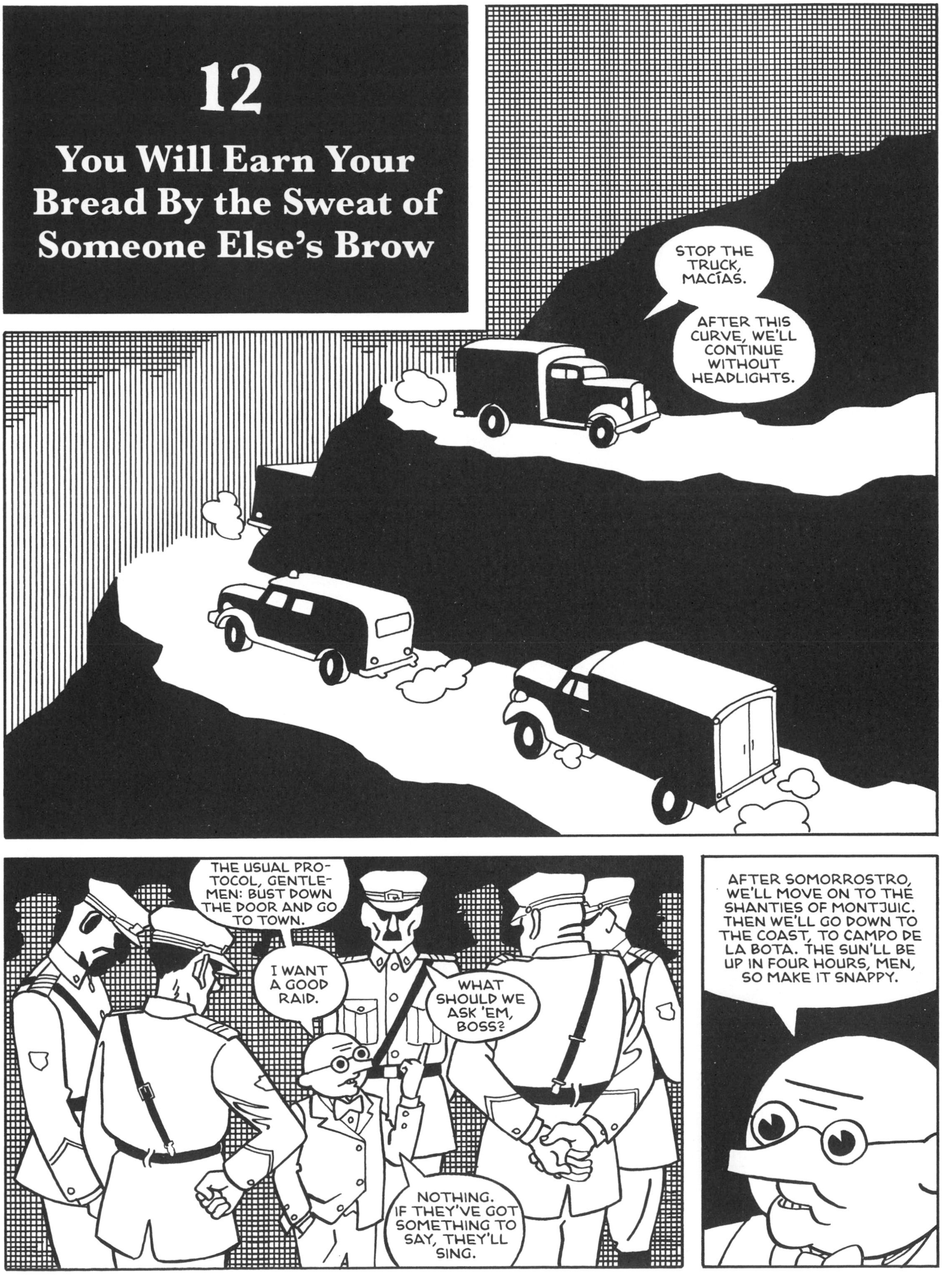
STOP THE TRUCK, MACÍAS.
AFTER THIS CURVE, WE'LL CONTINUE WITHOUT HEADLIGHTS.
THE USUAL PROTOCOL, GENTLEMEN: BUST DOWN THE DOOR AND GO TO TOWN.
I WANT A GOOD RAID.
WHAT SHOULD WE ASK 'EM, BOSS?
NOTHING. IF THEY'VE GOT SOMETHING TO SAY, THEY'LL SING.
AFTER SOMORROSTRO, WE'LL MOVE ON TO THE SHANTIES OF MONTJUIC. THEN WE'LL GO DOWN TO THE COAST, TO CAMPO DE LA BOTA. THE SUN'LL BE UP IN FOUR HOURS, MEN, SO MAKE IT SNAPPY.

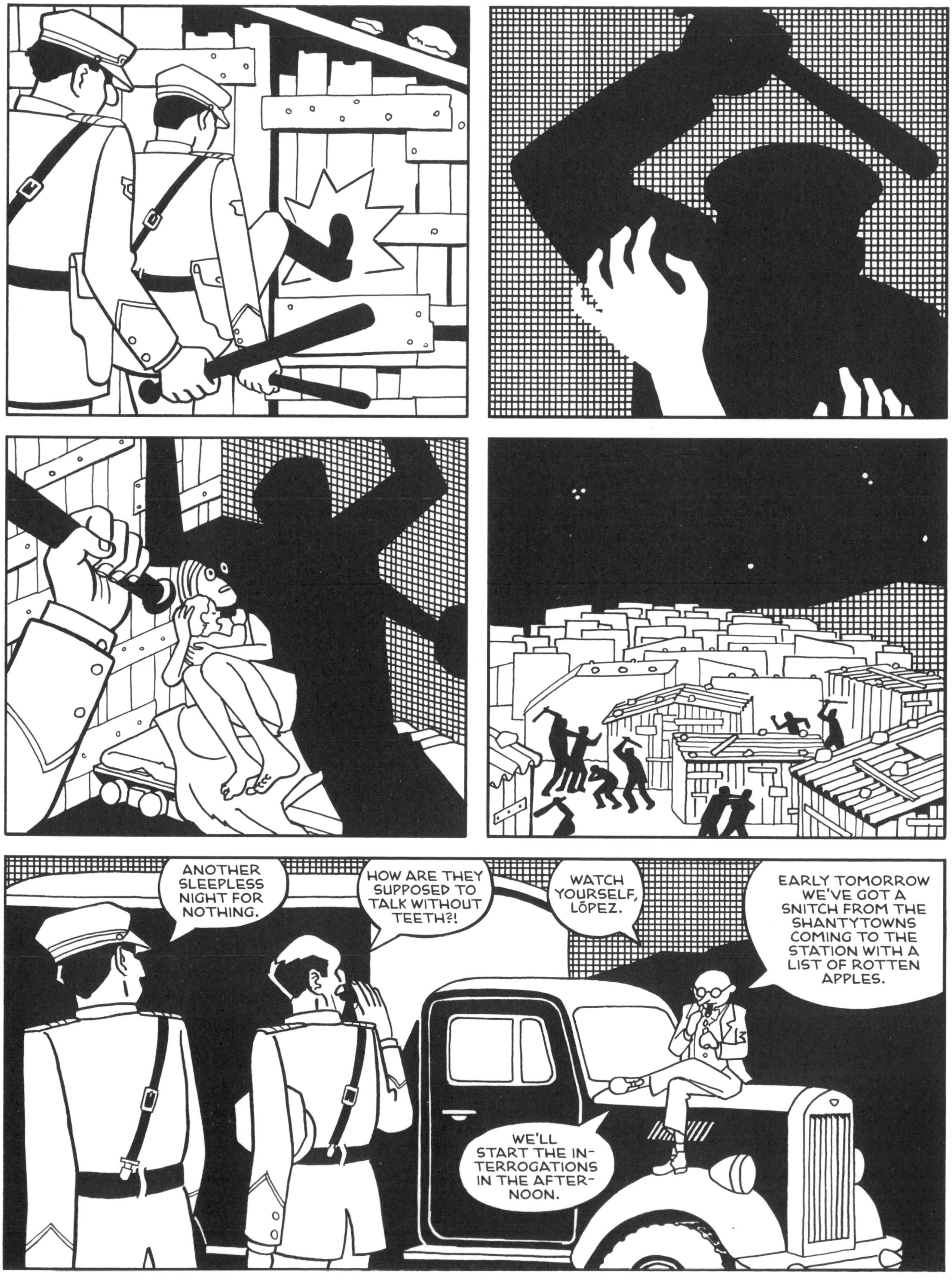
ANOTHER SLEEPLESS NIGHT FOR NOTHING.
HOW ARE THEY SUPPOSED TO TALK WITHOUT TEETH?!
WATCH YOURSELF, LÓPEZ.
EARLY TOMORROW WE'VE GOT A SNITCH FROM THE SHANTYTOWNS COMING TO THE STATION WITH A LIST OF ROTTEN APPLES.
WE'LL START THE INTERROGATIONS IN THE AFTERNOON.

13

Sisters

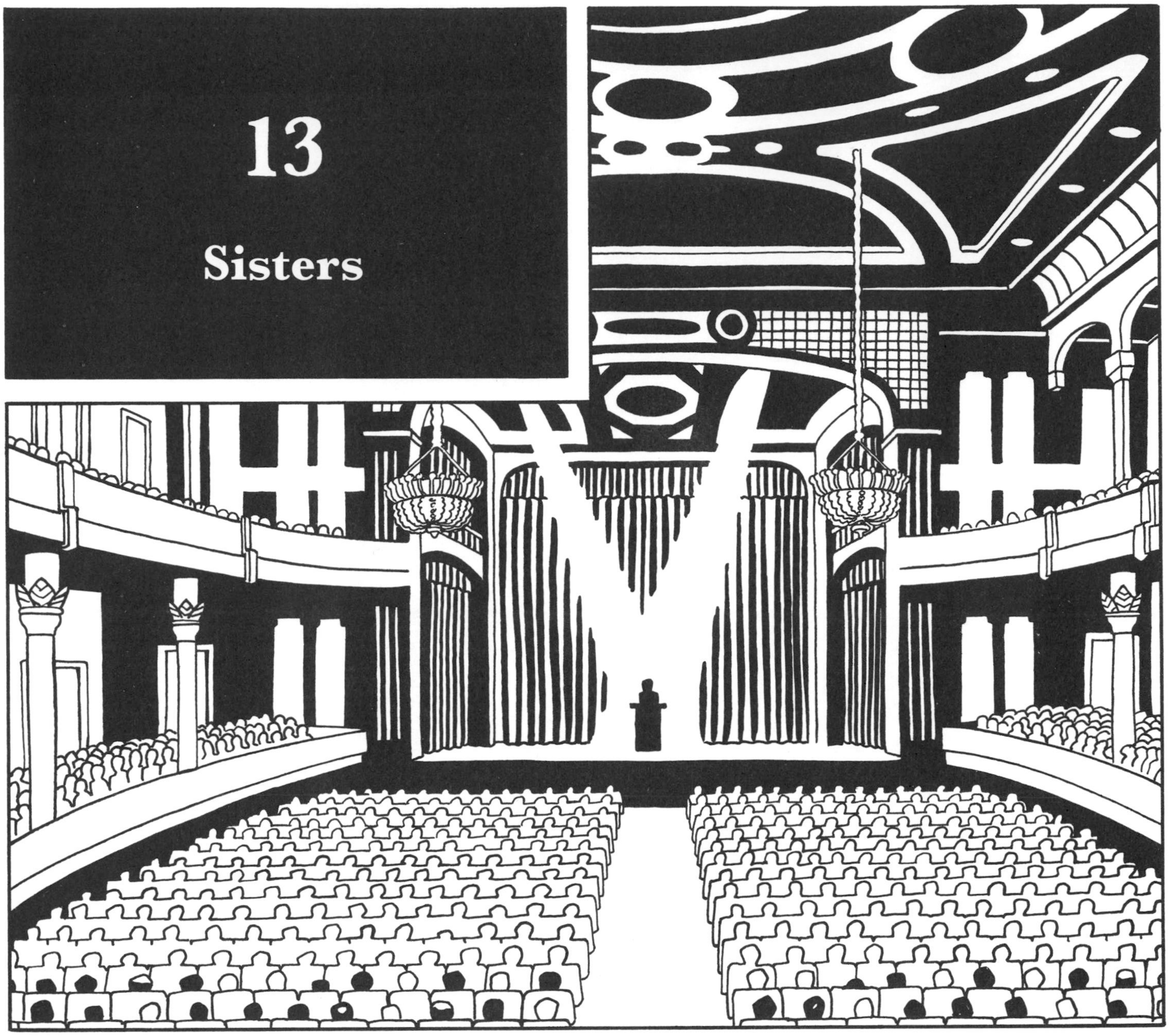

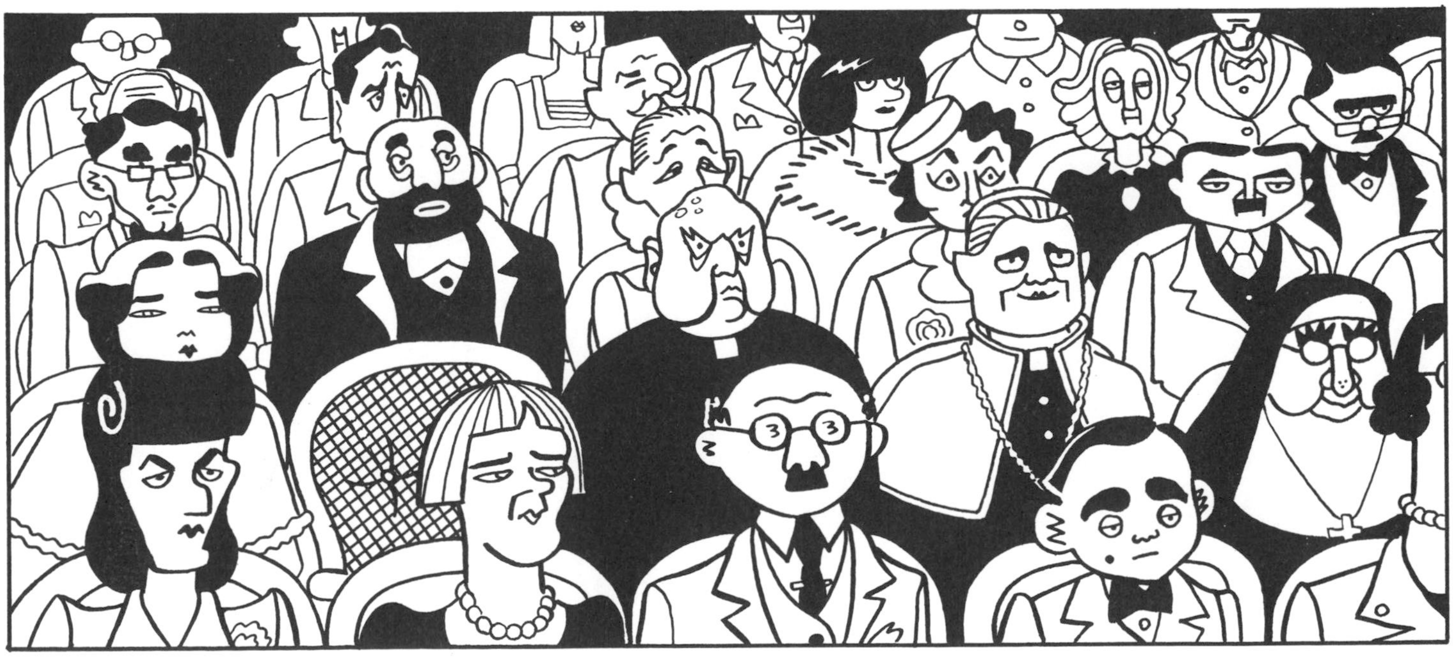

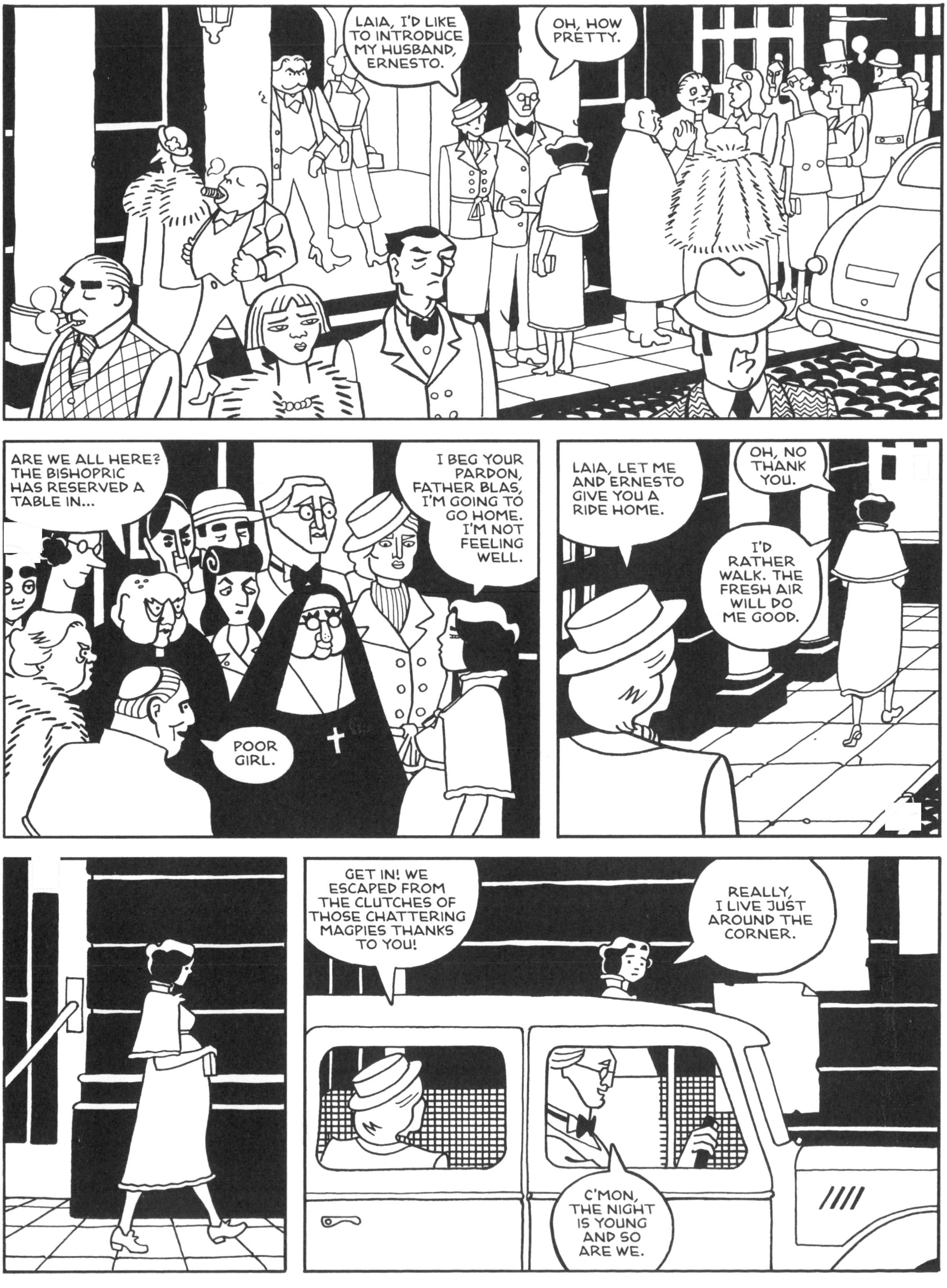
LAIA, I'D LIKE TO INTRODUCE MY HUSBAND, ERNESTO.
OH, HOW PRETTY.
ARE WE ALL HERE? THE BISHOPRIC HAS RESERVED A TABLE IN...
I BEG YOUR PARDON, FATHER BLAS, I'M GOING TO GO HOME. I'M NOT FEELING WELL.
POOR GIRL.
LAIA, LET ME AND ERNESTO GIVE YOU A RIDE HOME.
OH, NO THANK YOU.
I'D RATHER WALK. THE FRESH AIR WILL DO ME GOOD.
GET IN! WE ESCAPED FROM THE CLUTCHES OF THOSE CHATTERING MAGPIES THANKS TO YOU!
REALLY, I LIVE JUST AROUND THE CORNER.
C'MON, THE NIGHT IS YOUNG AND SO ARE WE.

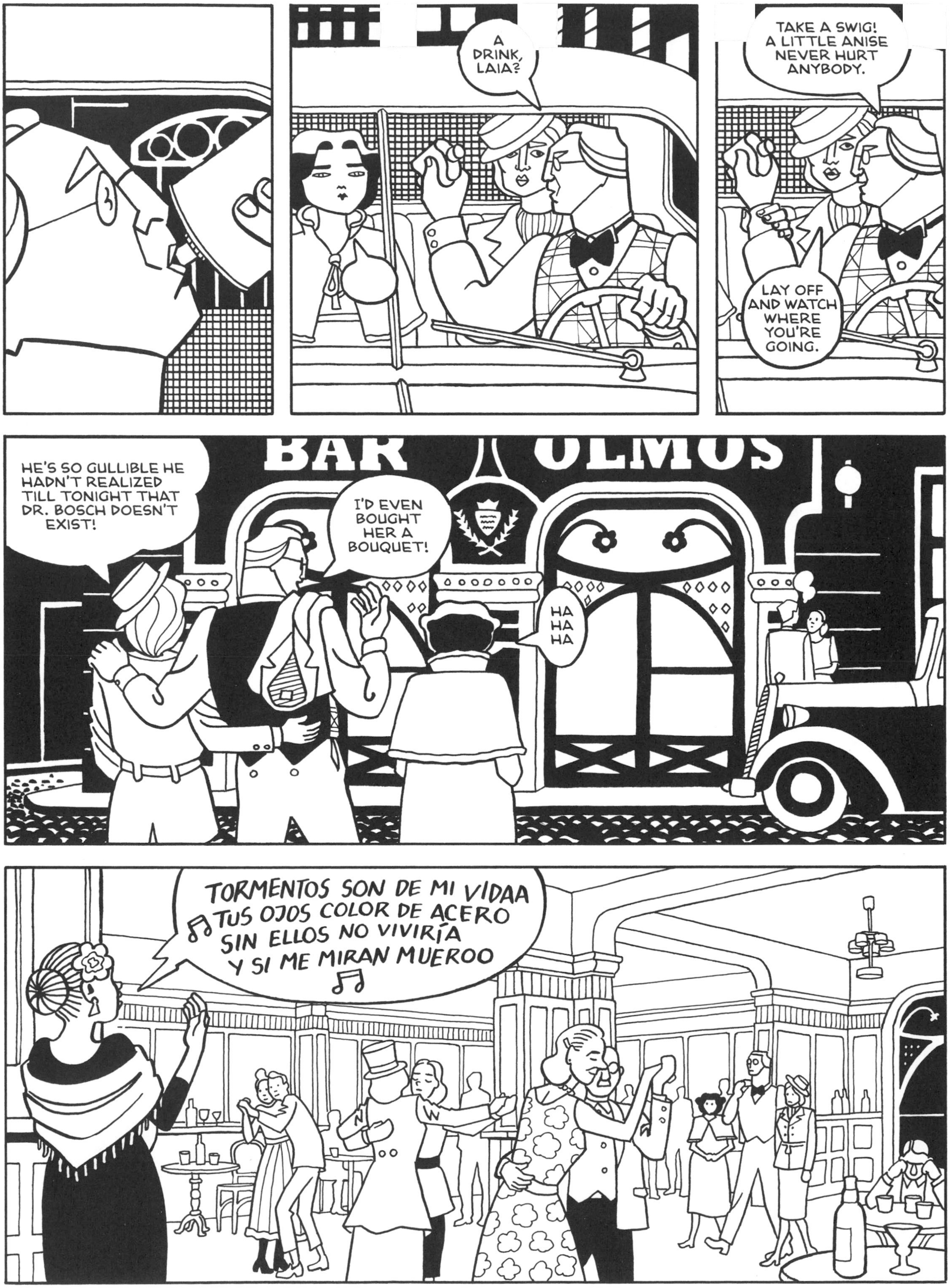
A DRINK, LAIA?
TAKE A SWIG! A LITTLE ANISE NEVER HURT ANYBODY.
LAY OFF AND WATCH WHERE YOU'RE GOING.
BAR OLMOS
HE'S SO GULLIBLE HE HADN'T REALIZED TILL TONIGHT THAT DR. BOSCH DOESN'T EXIST!
I'D EVEN BOUGHT HER A BOUQUET!
HA HA HA
TORMENTOS SON DE MI VIDAA
TUS OJOS COLOR DE ACERO
SIN ELLOS NO VIVIRÍA
Y SI ME MIRAN MUEROO

RI
HAVE YOU CHOSEN A NAME YET?
SOFÍA. LIKE ALFONSO'S MOTHER.
AND IF IT'S A BOY?
IT WON'T BE.
WELL, LAIA'S A LOVELY NAME.
RI
LAIA SOUNDS NICE, BUT EULALIA IS AWFUL.
EXCEPT WHEN COMPARED TO LORETO.
HA HA, HOW SWEET.
SAYS "THE IMPORTANCE OF BEING ERNESTO."

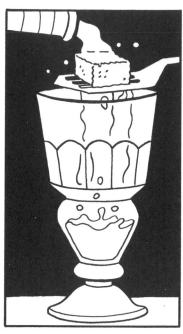

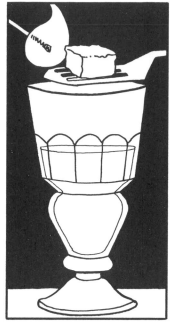

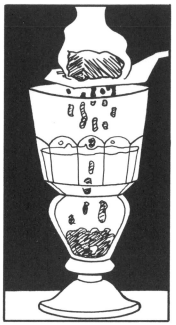

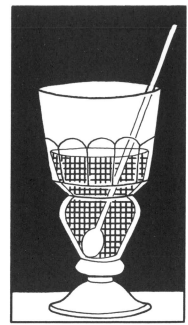

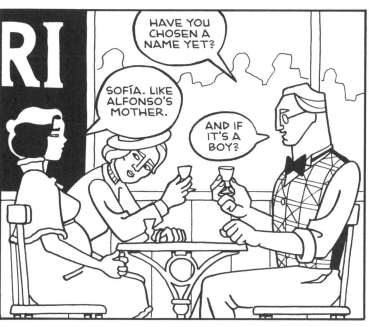

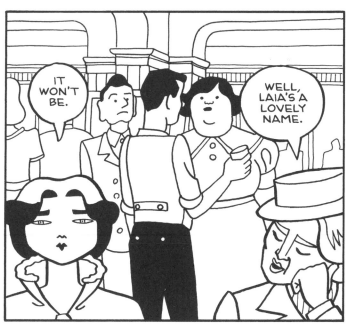

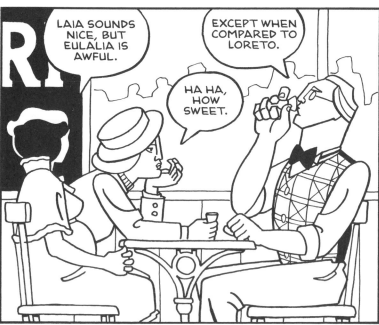

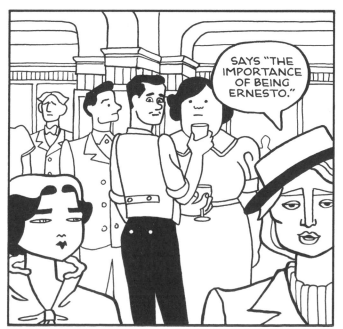

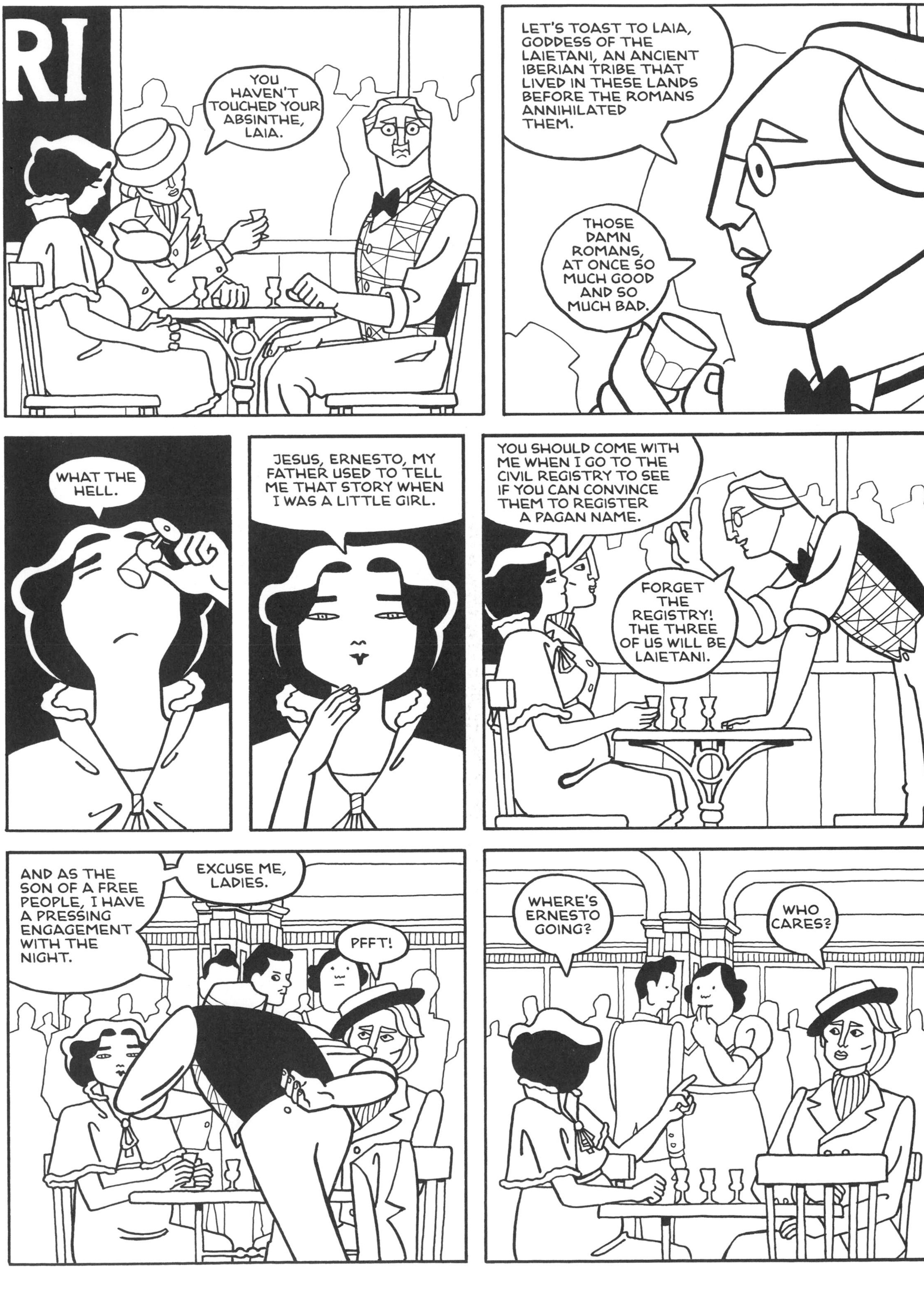
RI
YOU HAVEN'T TOUCHED YOUR ABSINTHE, LAIA.
LET'S TOAST TO LAIA, GODDESS OF THE LAIETANI, AN ANCIENT IBERIAN TRIBE THAT LIVED IN THESE LANDS BEFORE THE ROMANS ANNIHILATED THEM.
THOSE DAMN ROMANS, AT ONCE SO MUCH GOOD AND SO MUCH BAD.
WHAT THE HELL.
JESUS, ERNESTO, MY FATHER USED TO TELL ME THAT STORY WHEN I WAS A LITTLE GIRL.
YOU SHOULD COME WITH ME WHEN I GO TO THE CIVIL REGISTRY TO SEE IF YOU CAN CONVINCE THEM TO REGISTER A PAGAN NAME.
FORGET THE REGISTRY! THE THREE OF US WILL BE LAIETANI.
AND AS THE SON OF A FREE PEOPLE, I HAVE A PRESSING ENGAGEMENT WITH THE NIGHT.
EXCUSE ME, LADIES.
PFFT!
WHERE'S ERNESTO GOING?
WHO CARES?

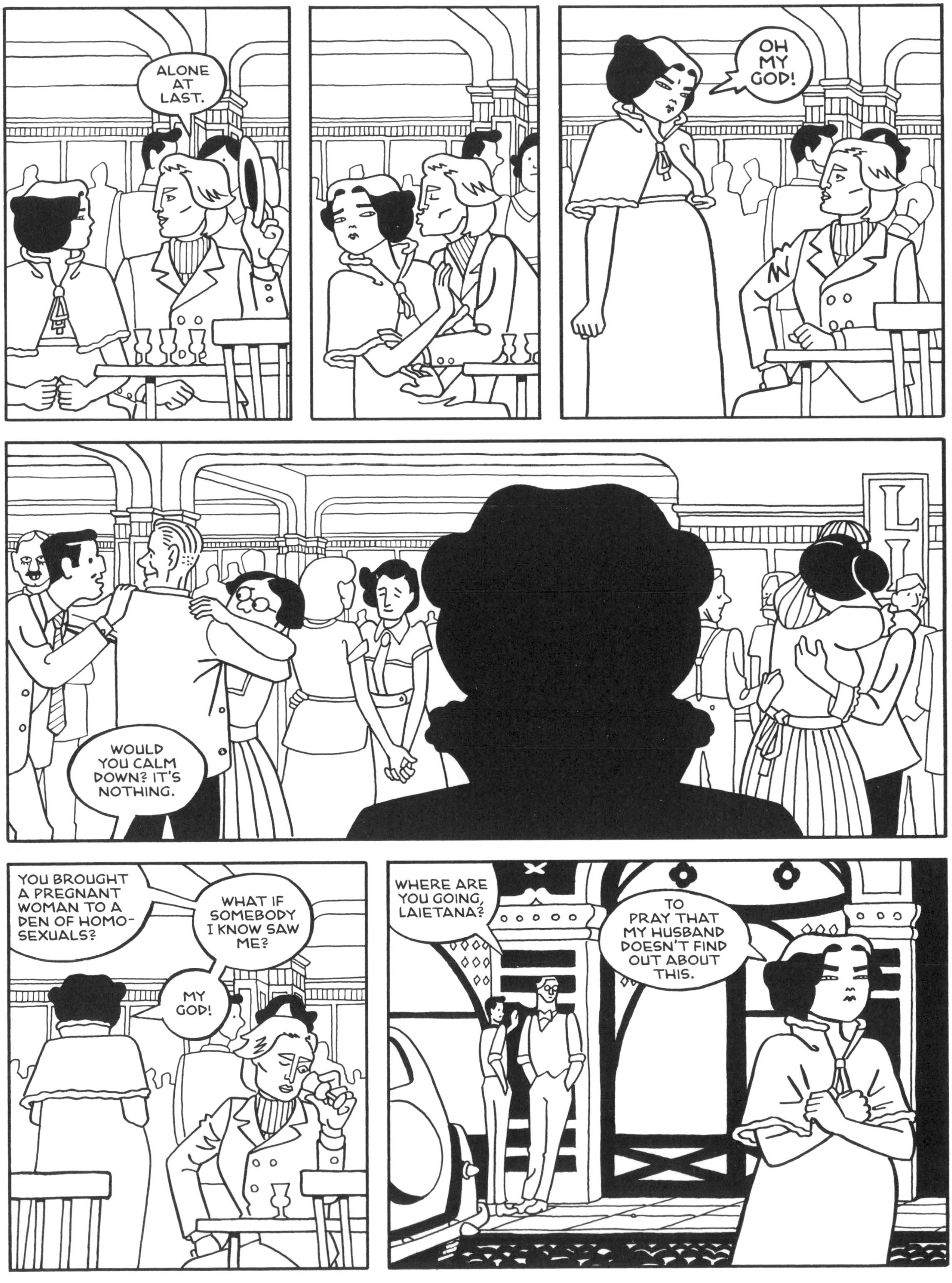
ALONE AT LAST.
OH MY GOD!
WOULD YOU CALM DOWN? IT'S NOTHING.
YOU BROUGHT A PREGNANT WOMAN TO A DEN OF HOMO-SEXUALS?
WHAT IF SOMEBODY I KNOW SAW ME?
MY GOD!
WHERE ARE YOU GOING, LAIETANA?
TO PRAY THAT MY HUSBAND DOESN'T FIND OUT ABOUT THIS.

14
The Hunt (II)

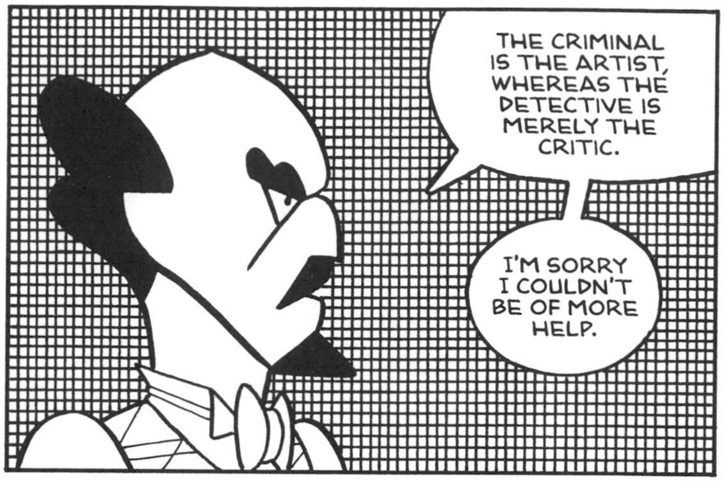
THE CRIMINAL IS THE ARTIST, WHEREAS THE DETECTIVE IS MERELY THE CRITIC.
I'M SORRY I COULDN'T BE OF MORE HELP.

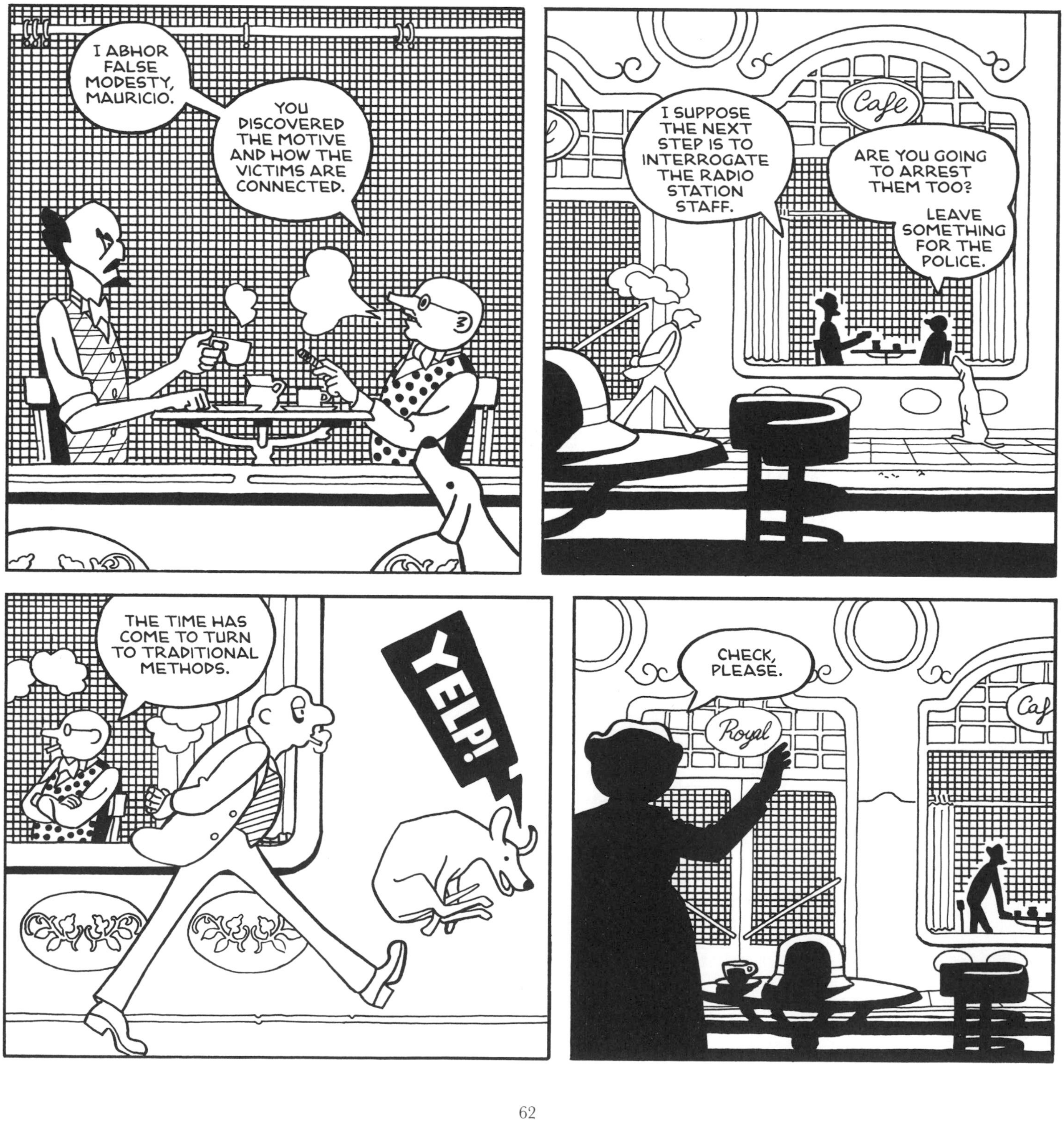
I ABHOR FALSE MODESTY, MAURICIO.
YOU DISCOVERED THE MOTIVE AND HOW THE VICTIMS ARE CONNECTED.
Café
I SUPPOSE THE NEXT STEP IS TO INTERROGATE THE RADIO STATION STAFF.
ARE YOU GOING TO ARREST THEM TOO?
LEAVE SOMETHING FOR THE POLICE.
THE TIME HAS COME TO TURN TO TRADITIONAL METHODS.
YELP!
CHECK, PLEASE.
Royal

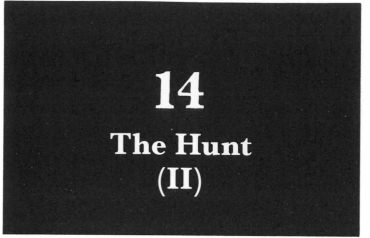

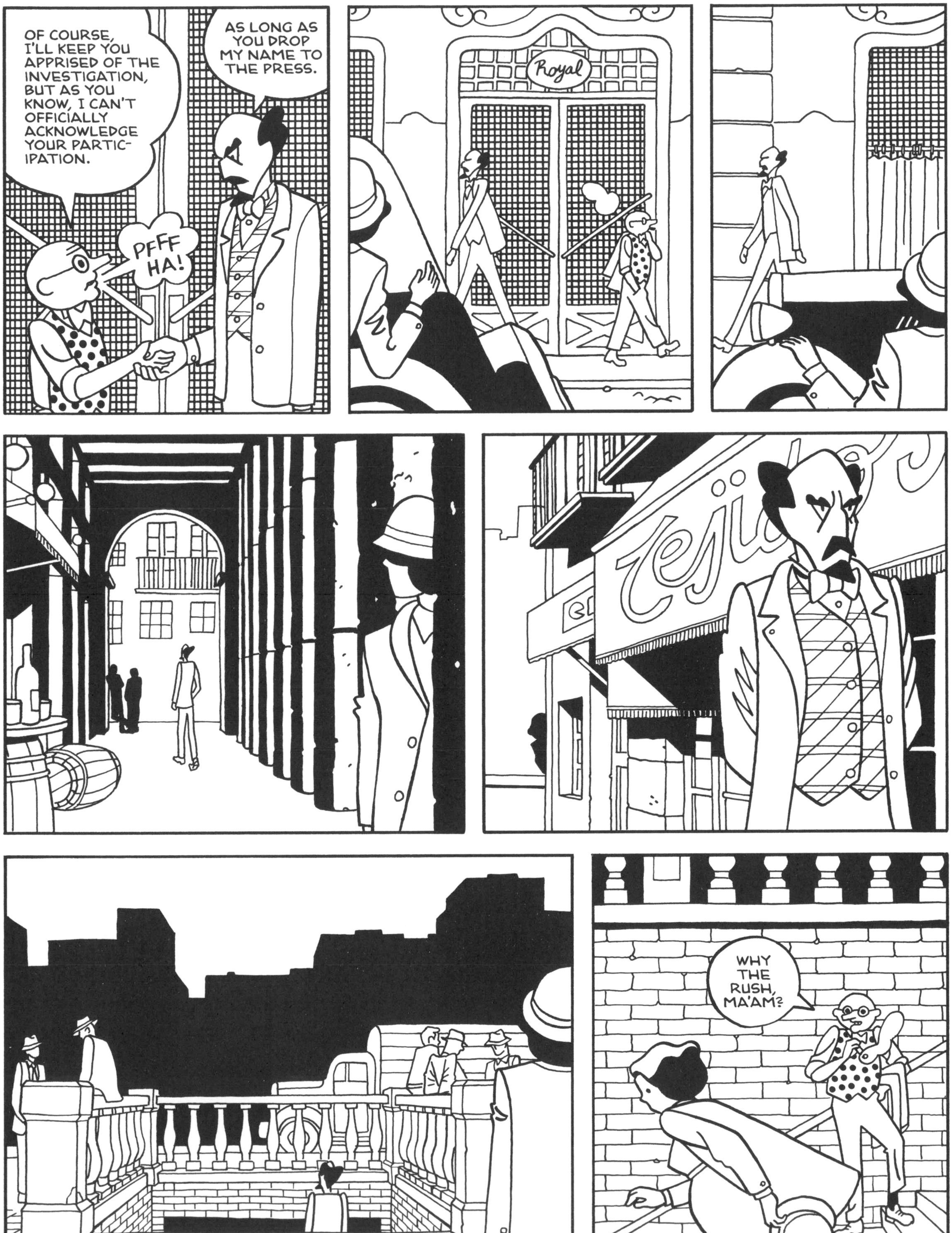
OF COURSE, I'LL KEEP YOU APPRISED OF THE INVESTIGATION, BUT AS YOU KNOW, I CAN'T OFFICIALLY ACKNOWLEDGE YOUR PARTICIPATION.
AS LONG AS YOU DROP MY NAME TO THE PRESS.
PFFF HA!
Royal
WHY THE RUSH, MA'AM?

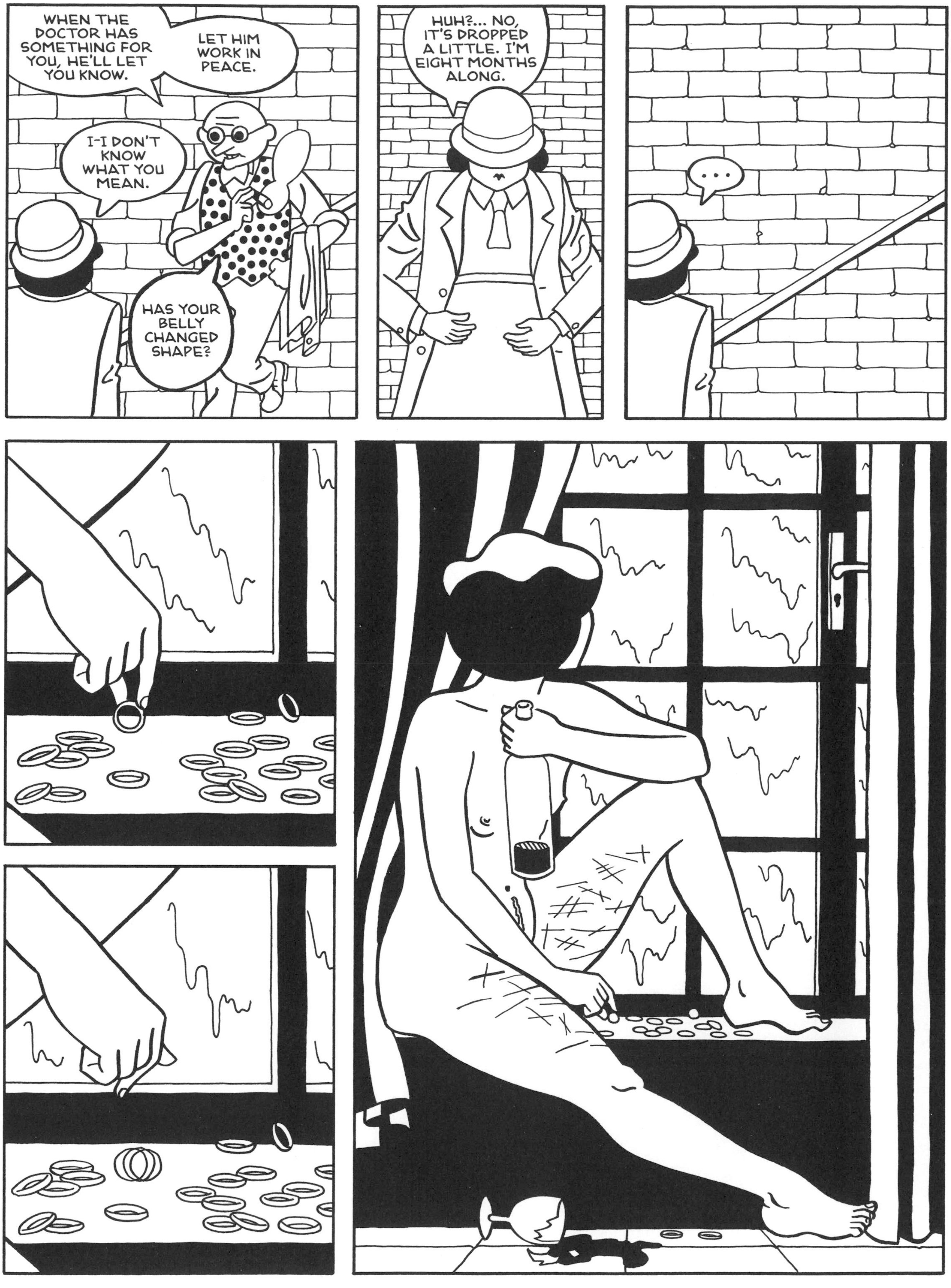
WHEN THE DOCTOR HAS SOMETHING FOR YOU, HE'LL LET YOU KNOW.
LET HIM WORK IN PEACE.
I-I DON'T KNOW WHAT YOU MEAN.
HAS YOUR BELLY CHANGED SHAPE?
HUH?... NO, IT'S DROPPED A LITTLE. I'M EIGHT MONTHS ALONG.
...

15

The Errand Boy

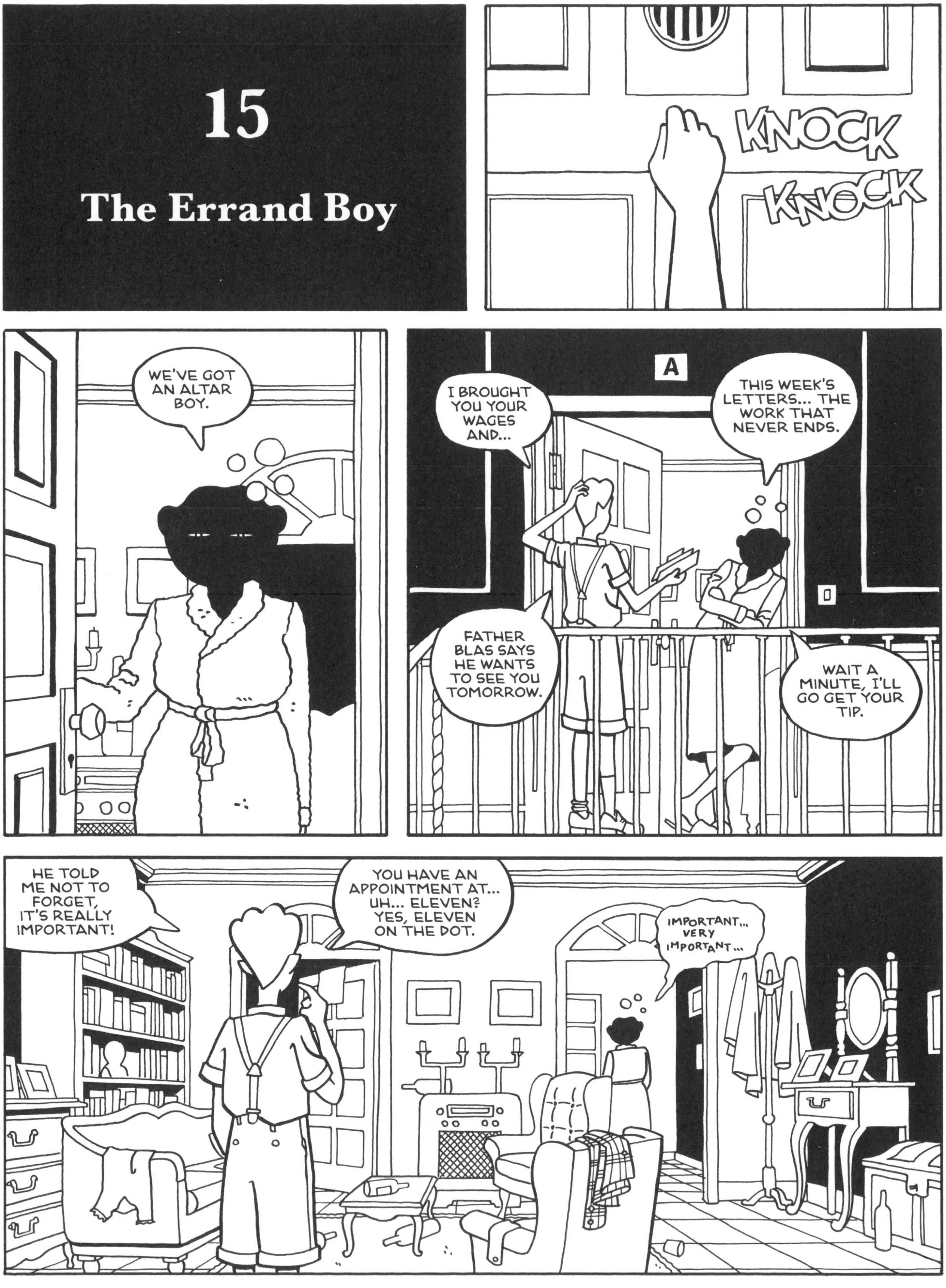

KNOCK
KNOCK
WE'VE GOT AN ALTAR BOY.
A
I BROUGHT YOU YOUR WAGES AND...
THIS WEEK'S LETTERS... THE WORK THAT NEVER ENDS.
FATHER BLAS SAYS HE WANTS TO SEE YOU TOMORROW.
WAIT A MINUTE, I'LL GO GET YOUR TIP.
HE TOLD ME NOT TO FORGET, IT'S REALLY IMPORTANT!
YOU HAVE AN APPOINTMENT AT... UH... ELEVEN? YES, ELEVEN ON THE DOT.
IMPORTANT... VERY IMPORTANT...

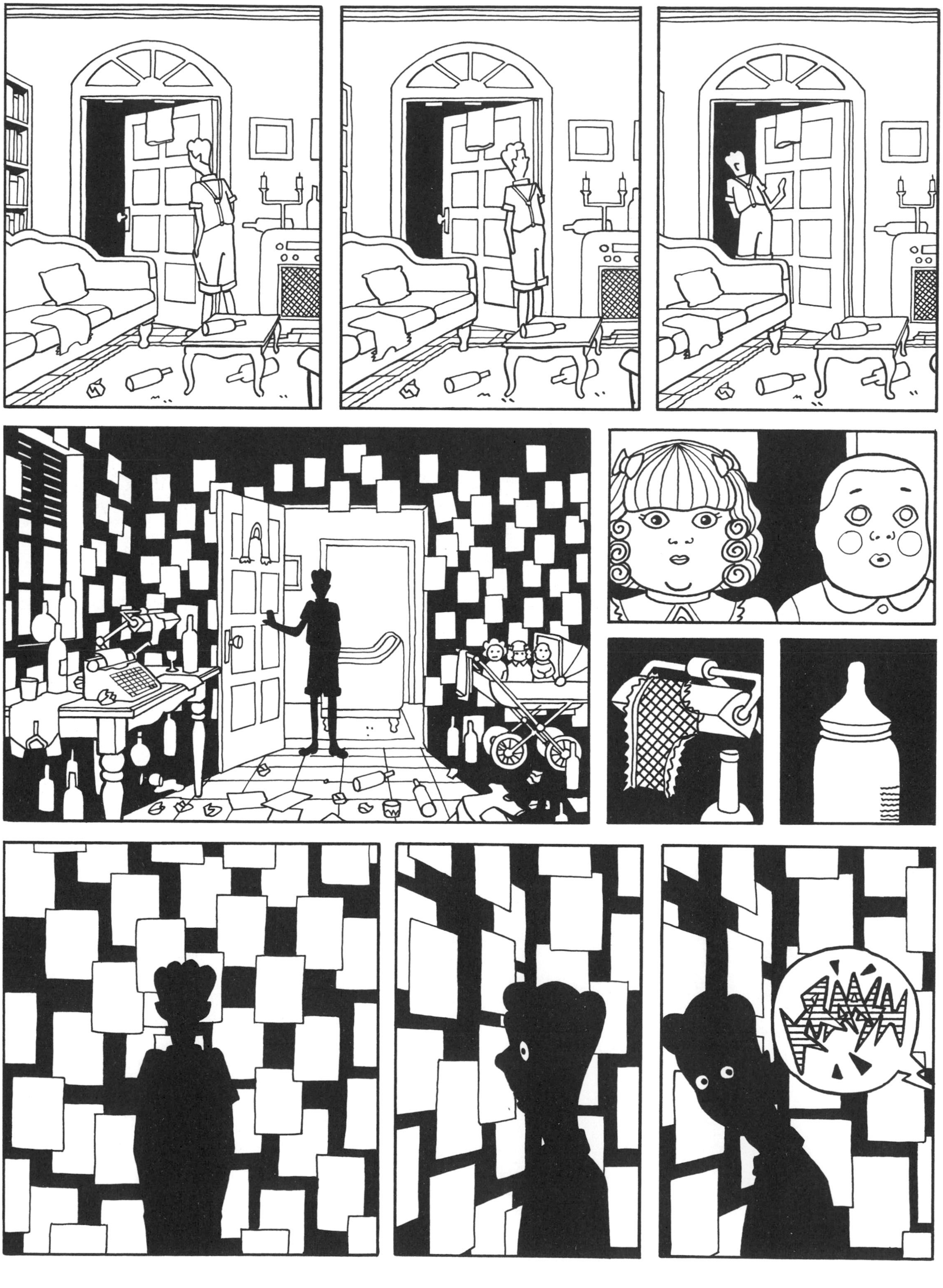

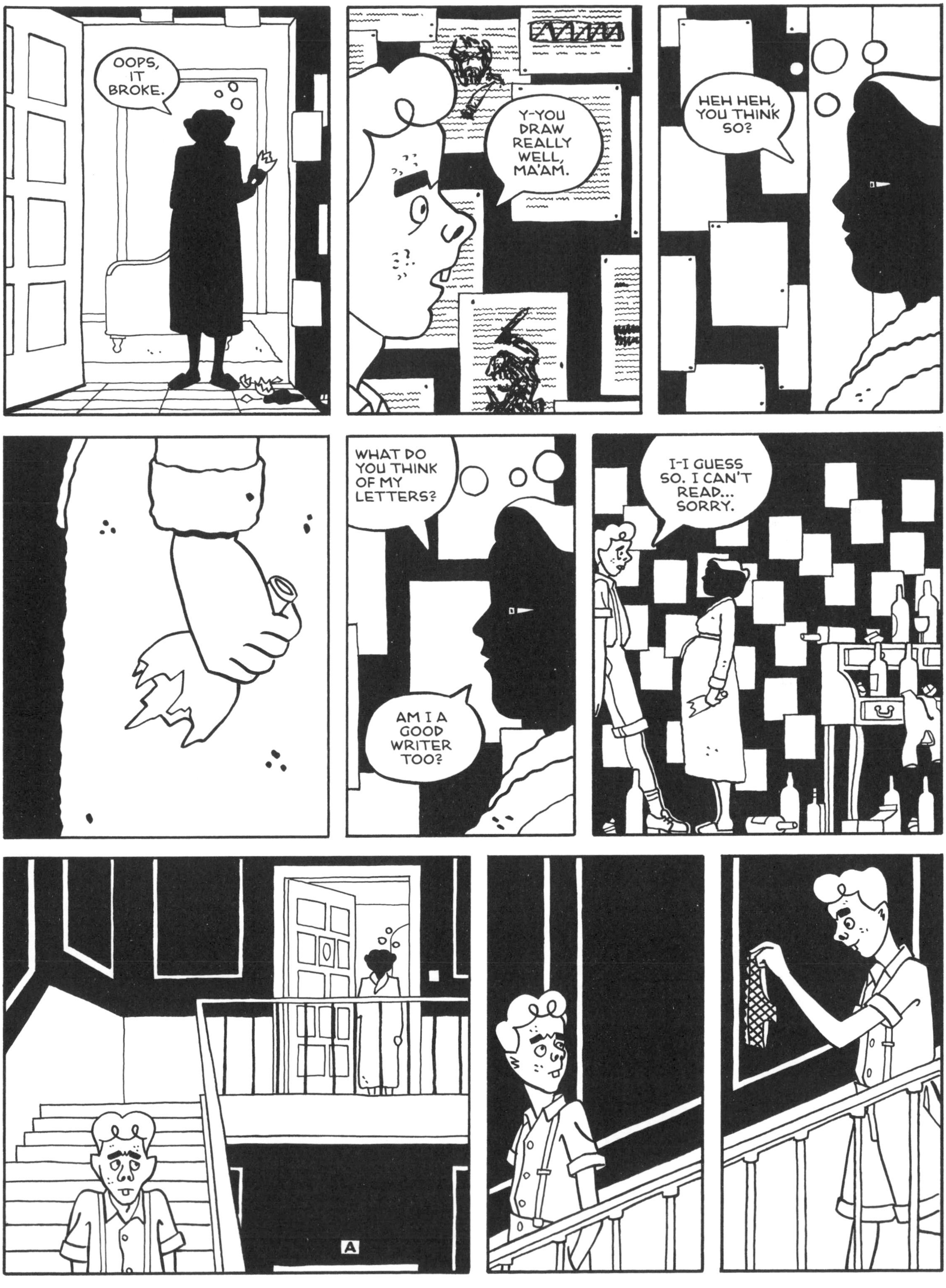
OOPS, IT BROKE.
Y-YOU DRAW REALLY WELL, MA'AM.
HEH HEH, YOU THINK SO?
WHAT DO YOU THINK OF MY LETTERS?
AM I A GOOD WRITER TOO?
I-I GUESS SO. I CAN'T READ... SORRY.
A

16

The Waiter

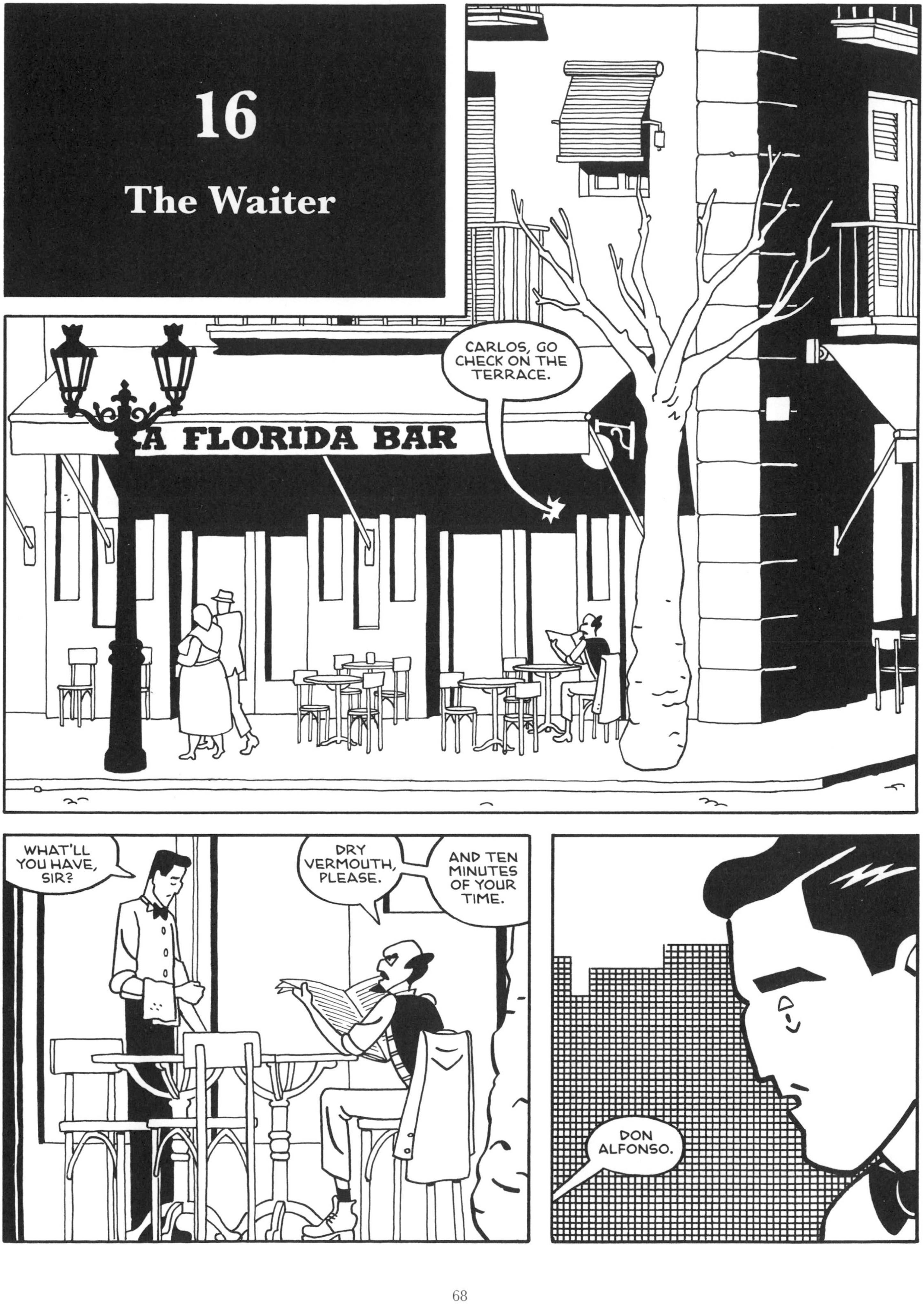

LA FLORIDA BAR
CARLOS, GO CHECK ON THE TERRACE.
WHAT'LL YOU HAVE, SIR?
DRY VERMOUTH, PLEASE.
AND TEN MINUTES OF YOUR TIME.
DON ALFONSO.

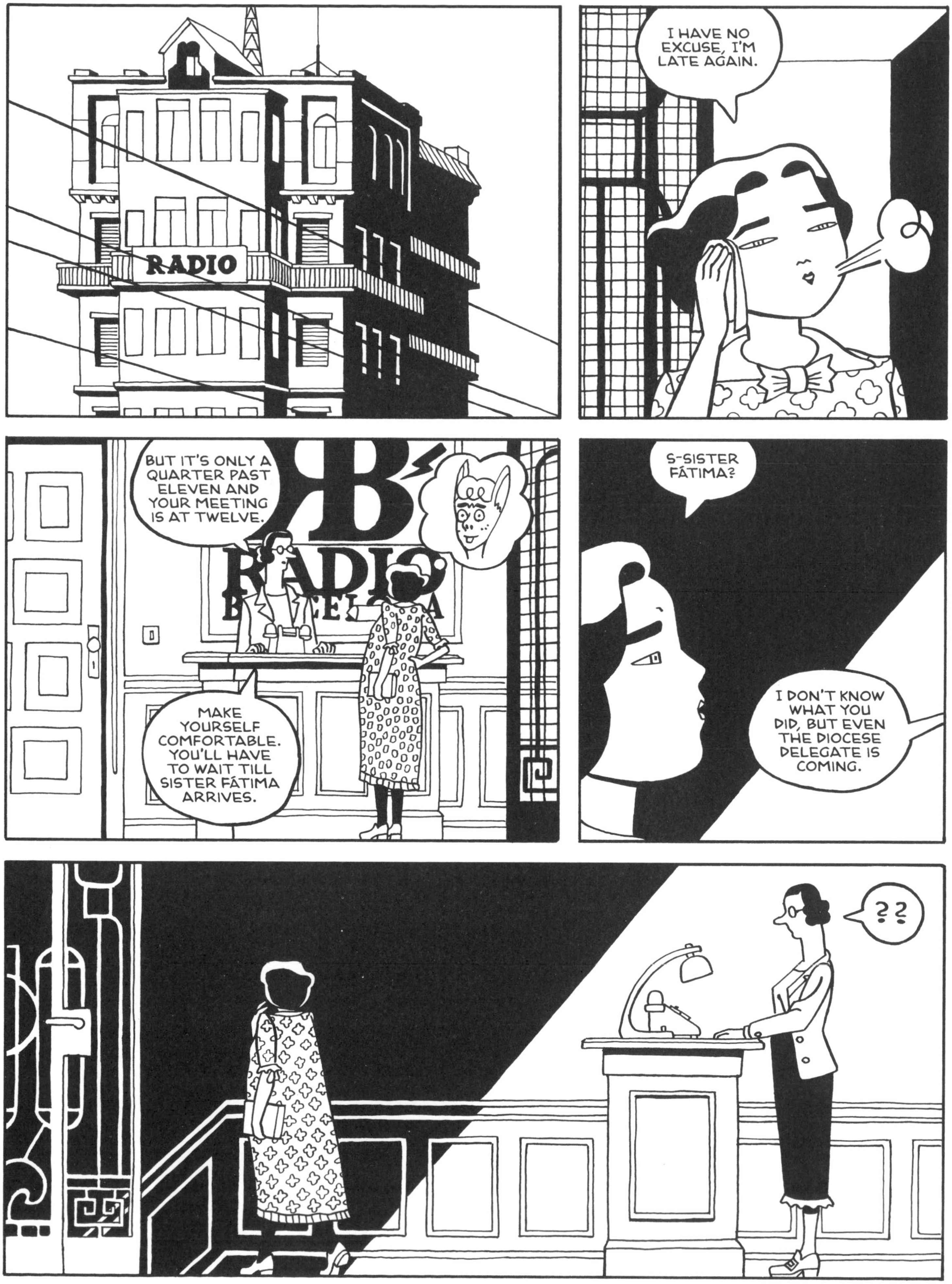
RADIO
I HAVE NO EXCUSE, I'M LATE AGAIN.
BUT IT'S ONLY A QUARTER PAST ELEVEN AND YOUR MEETING IS AT TWELVE.
MAKE YOURSELF COMFORTABLE. YOU'LL HAVE TO WAIT TILL SISTER FÁTIMA ARRIVES.
S-SISTER FÁTIMA?
I DON'T KNOW WHAT YOU DID, BUT EVEN THE DIOCESE DELEGATE IS COMING.
??

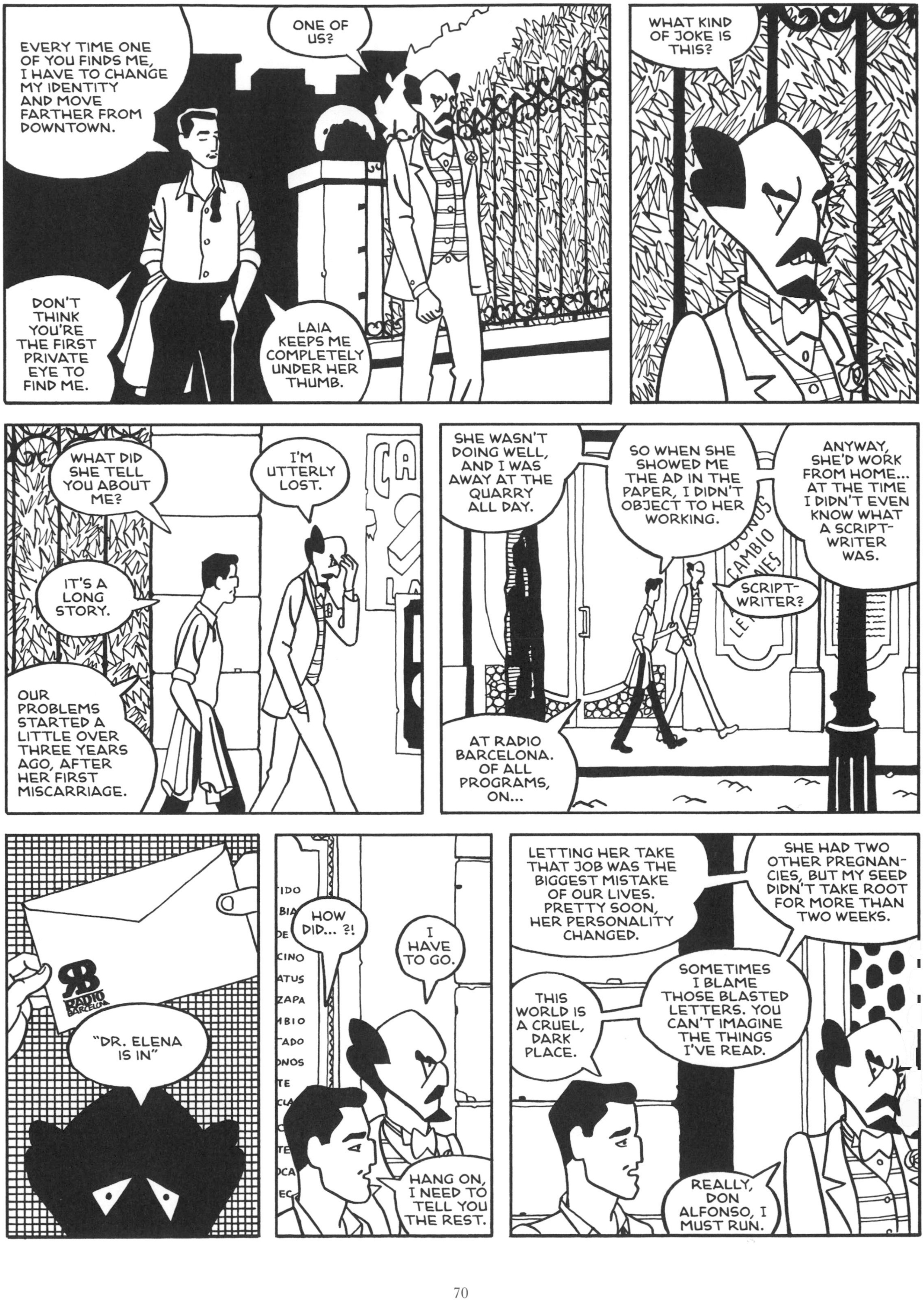
EVERY TIME ONE OF YOU FINDS ME, I HAVE TO CHANGE MY IDENTITY AND MOVE FARTHER FROM DOWNTOWN.
ONE OF US?
DON'T THINK YOU'RE THE FIRST PRIVATE EYE TO FIND ME.
LAIA KEEPS ME COMPLETELY UNDER HER THUMB.
WHAT KIND OF JOKE IS THIS?
WHAT DID SHE TELL YOU ABOUT ME?
I'M UTTERLY LOST.
IT'S A LONG STORY.
OUR PROBLEMS STARTED A LITTLE OVER THREE YEARS AGO, AFTER HER FIRST MISCARRIAGE.
SHE WASN'T DOING WELL, AND I WAS AWAY AT THE QUARRY ALL DAY.
SO WHEN SHE SHOWED ME THE AD IN THE PAPER, I DIDN'T OBJECT TO HER WORKING.
ANYWAY, SHE'D WORK FROM HOME... AT THE TIME I DIDN'T EVEN KNOW WHAT A SCRIPT-WRITER WAS.
SCRIPT-WRITER?
AT RADIO BARCELONA. OF ALL PROGRAMS, ON...
RADIO BARCELONA
"DR. ELENA IS IN"
HOW DID... ?!
I HAVE TO GO.
HANG ON, I NEED TO TELL YOU THE REST.
LETTING HER TAKE THAT JOB WAS THE BIGGEST MISTAKE OF OUR LIVES. PRETTY SOON, HER PERSONALITY CHANGED.
SHE HAD TWO OTHER PREGNANCIES, BUT MY SEED DIDN'T TAKE ROOT FOR MORE THAN TWO WEEKS.
THIS WORLD IS A CRUEL, DARK PLACE.
SOMETIMES I BLAME THOSE BLASTED LETTERS. YOU CAN'T IMAGINE THE THINGS I'VE READ.
REALLY, DON ALFONSO, I MUST RUN.

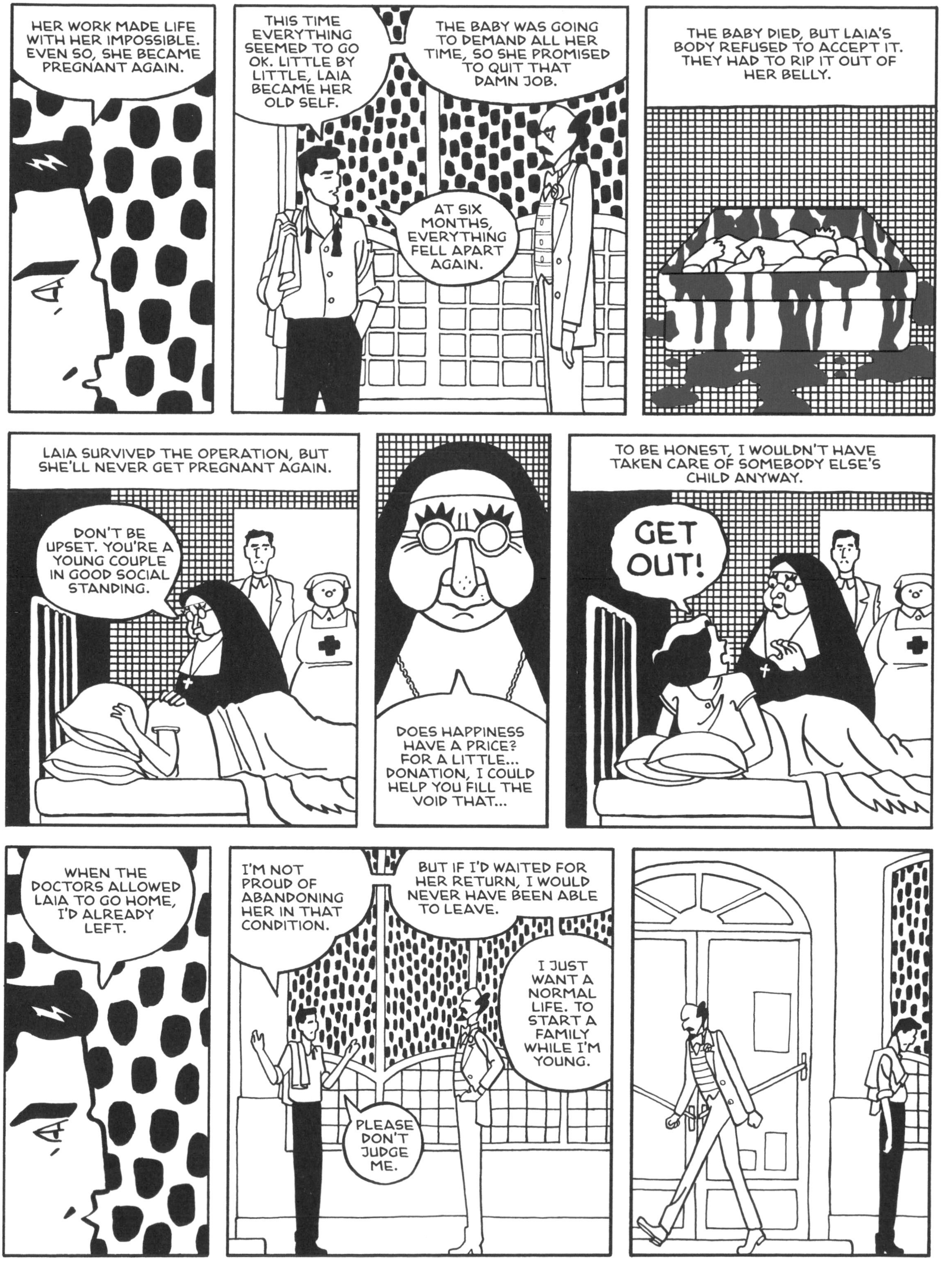
HER WORK MADE LIFE WITH HER IMPOSSIBLE. EVEN SO, SHE BECAME PREGNANT AGAIN.
THIS TIME EVERYTHING SEEMED TO GO OK. LITTLE BY LITTLE, LAIA BECAME HER OLD SELF.
THE BABY WAS GOING TO DEMAND ALL HER TIME, SO SHE PROMISED TO QUIT THAT DAMN JOB.
AT SIX MONTHS, EVERYTHING FELL APART AGAIN.
THE BABY DIED, BUT LAIA'S BODY REFUSED TO ACCEPT IT. THEY HAD TO RIP IT OUT OF HER BELLY.
LAIA SURVIVED THE OPERATION, BUT SHE'LL NEVER GET PREGNANT AGAIN.
DON'T BE UPSET. YOU'RE A YOUNG COUPLE IN GOOD SOCIAL STANDING.
DOES HAPPINESS HAVE A PRICE? FOR A LITTLE... DONATION, I COULD HELP YOU FILL THE VOID THAT...
TO BE HONEST, I WOULDN'T HAVE TAKEN CARE OF SOMEBODY ELSE'S CHILD ANYWAY.
GET OUT!
WHEN THE DOCTORS ALLOWED LAIA TO GO HOME, I'D ALREADY LEFT.
I'M NOT PROUD OF ABANDONING HER IN THAT CONDITION.
BUT IF I'D WAITED FOR HER RETURN, I WOULD NEVER HAVE BEEN ABLE TO LEAVE.
I JUST WANT A NORMAL LIFE. TO START A FAMILY WHILE I'M YOUNG.
PLEASE DON'T JUDGE ME.

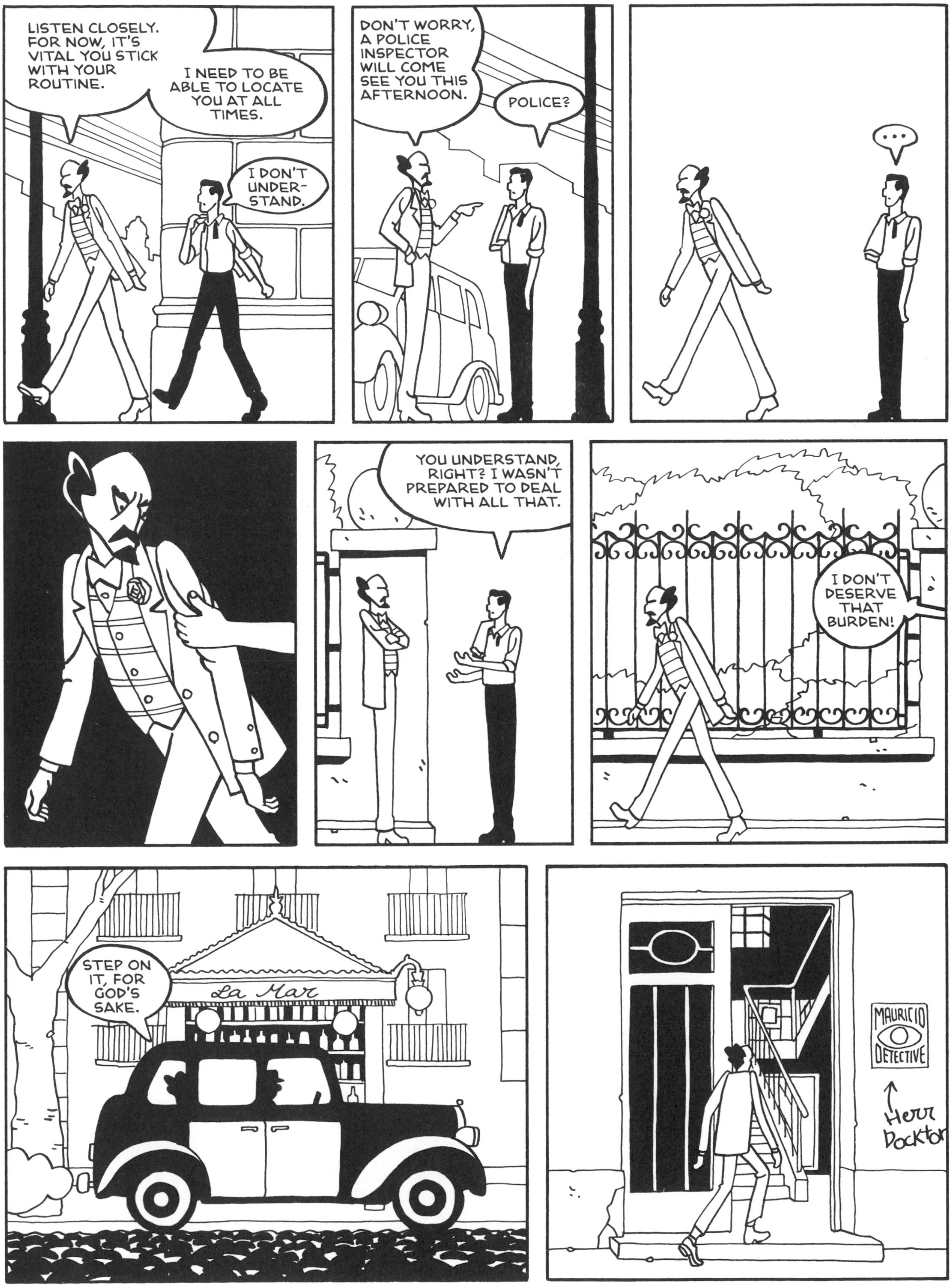
LISTEN CLOSELY. FOR NOW, IT'S VITAL YOU STICK WITH YOUR ROUTINE.
I NEED TO BE ABLE TO LOCATE YOU AT ALL TIMES.
I DON'T UNDER-STAND.
DON'T WORRY, A POLICE INSPECTOR WILL COME SEE YOU THIS AFTERNOON.
POLICE?
...
YOU UNDERSTAND, RIGHT? I WASN'T PREPARED TO DEAL WITH ALL THAT.
I DON'T DESERVE THAT BURDEN!
STEP ON IT, FOR GOD'S SAKE.
La Mar
MAURICIO DETECTIVE
Herr Docktor

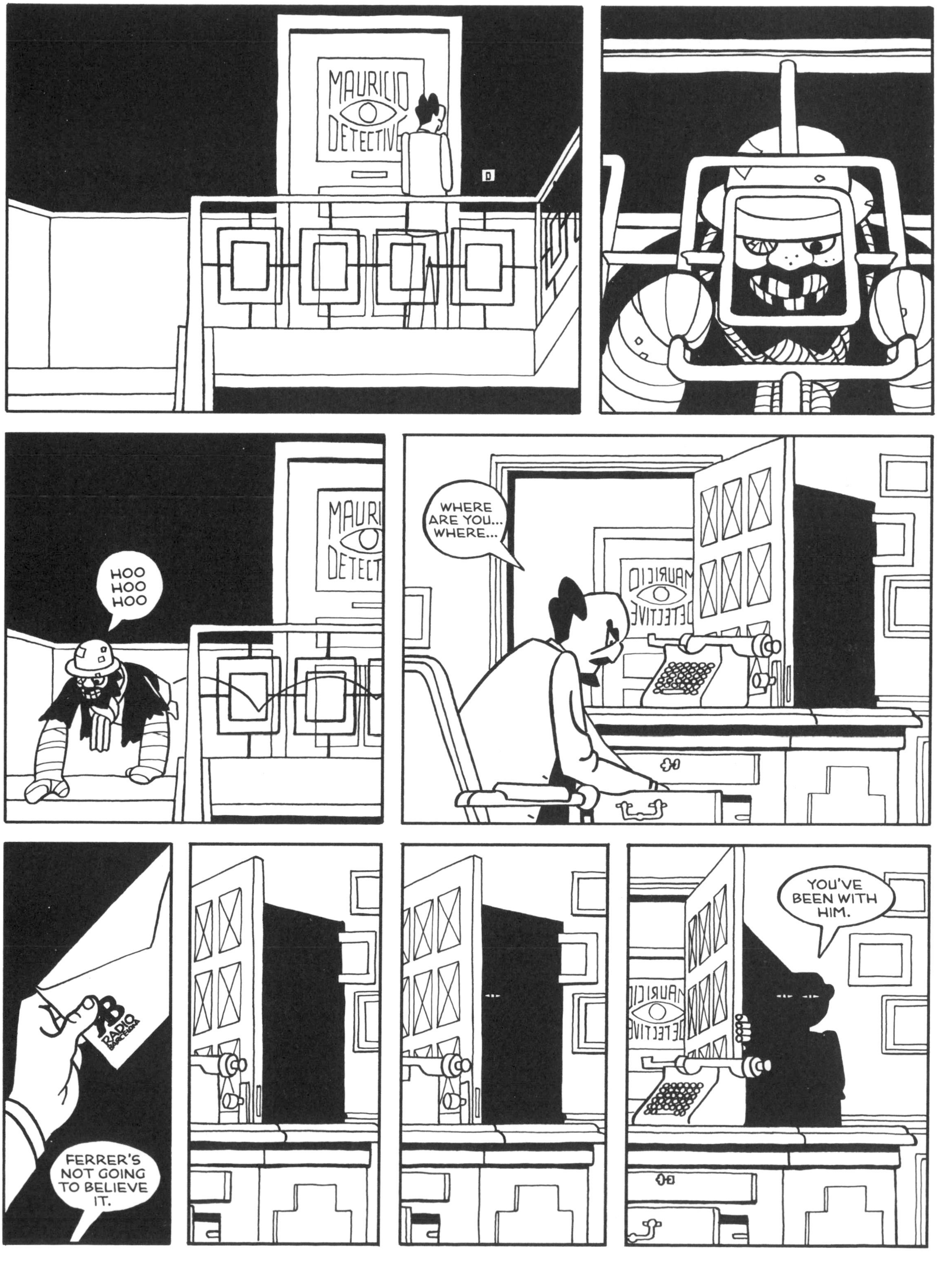
MAURICIO DETECTIVE
HOO HOO HOO
WHERE ARE YOU... WHERE...
RADIO BARCELONA
FERRER'S NOT GOING TO BELIEVE IT.
YOU'VE BEEN WITH HIM.

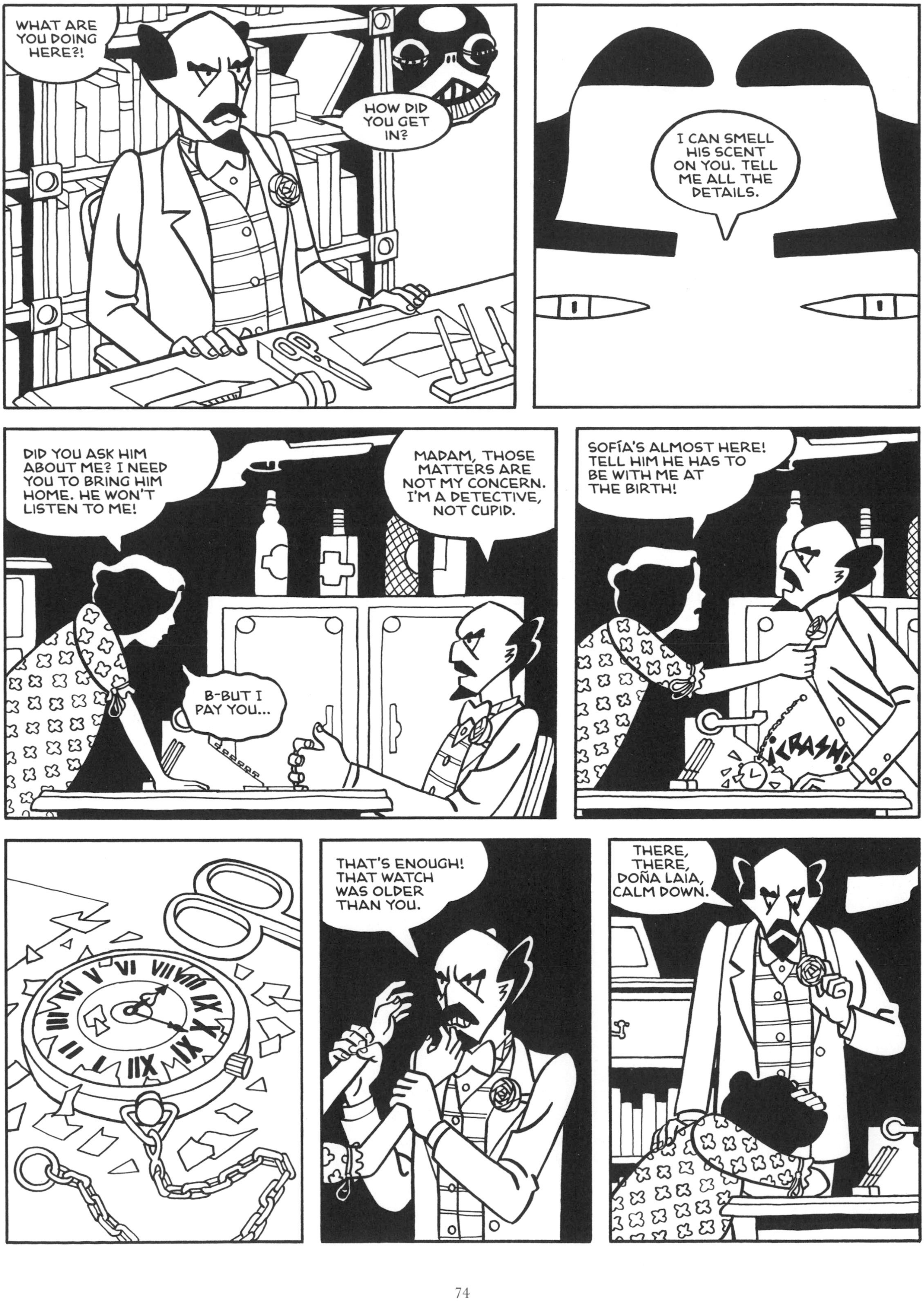
WHAT ARE YOU DOING HERE?!
HOW DID YOU GET IN?
I CAN SMELL HIS SCENT ON YOU. TELL ME ALL THE DETAILS.
DID YOU ASK HIM ABOUT ME? I NEED YOU TO BRING HIM HOME. HE WON'T LISTEN TO ME!
MADAM, THOSE MATTERS ARE NOT MY CONCERN. I'M A DETECTIVE, NOT CUPID.
B-BUT I PAY YOU...
SOFÍA'S ALMOST HERE! TELL HIM HE HAS TO BE WITH ME AT THE BIRTH!
¡CRASH!
THAT'S ENOUGH! THAT WATCH WAS OLDER THAN YOU.
THERE, THERE, DOÑA LAIA, CALM DOWN.

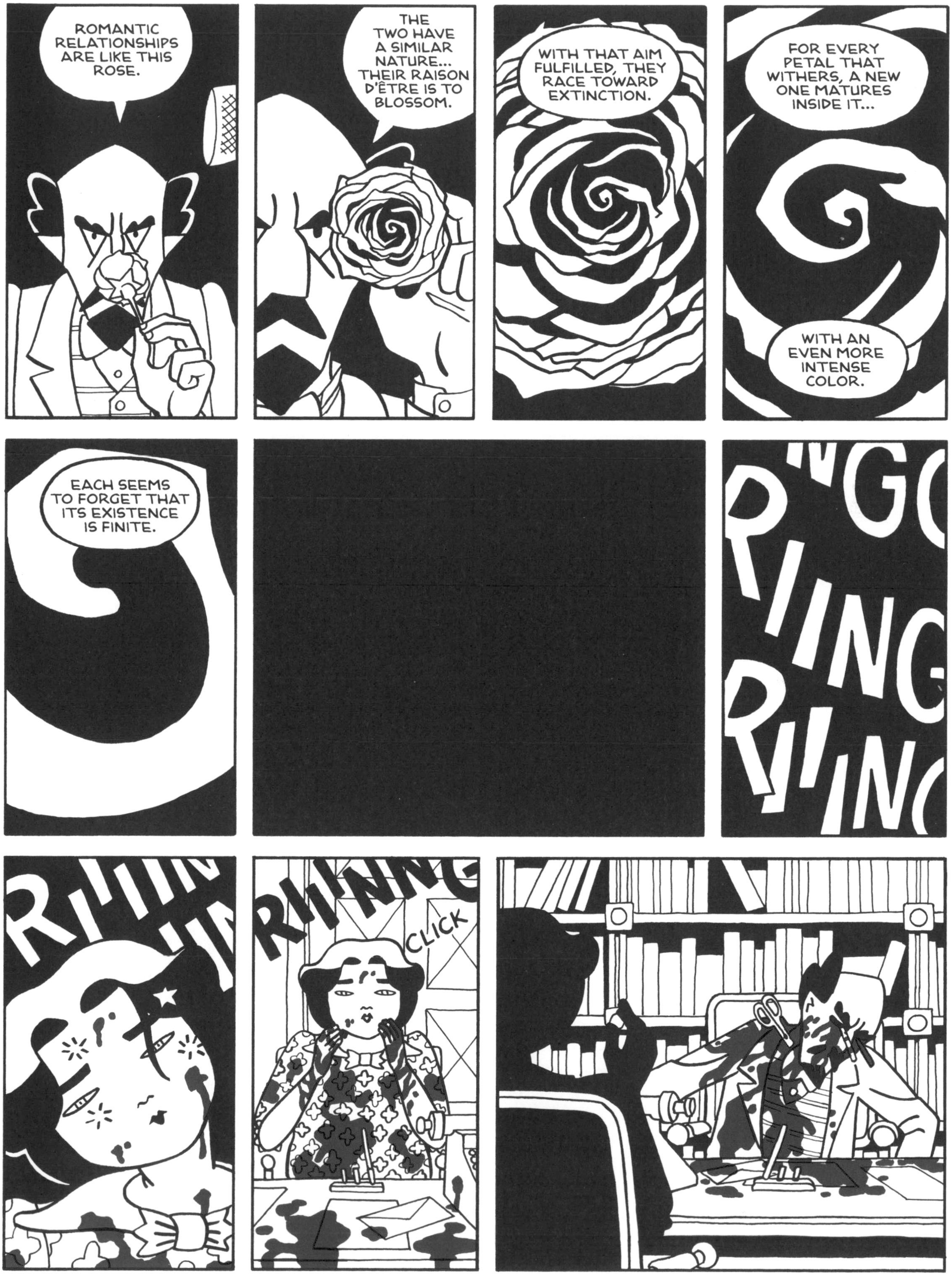
ROMANTIC RELATIONSHIPS ARE LIKE THIS ROSE.
THE TWO HAVE A SIMILAR NATURE... THEIR RAISON D'ÊTRE IS TO BLOSSOM.
WITH THAT AIM FULFILLED, THEY RACE TOWARD EXTINCTION.
FOR EVERY PETAL THAT WITHERS, A NEW ONE MATURES INSIDE IT...
WITH AN EVEN MORE INTENSE COLOR.
EACH SEEMS TO FORGET THAT ITS EXISTENCE IS FINITE.
CLICK

TAC TAC TAC TAC TAC TAC TAC TAC TAC TAC TAC TAC TAC TAC TAC

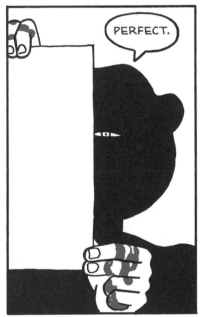

PERFECT.

MAURICIO DETECTIVE

PSST, BABY.

AIN'T YOU FORGETTIN' SOMETHING?

I'LL GIVE YOU SOMETHING BETTER THAN A FEW PESETAS.

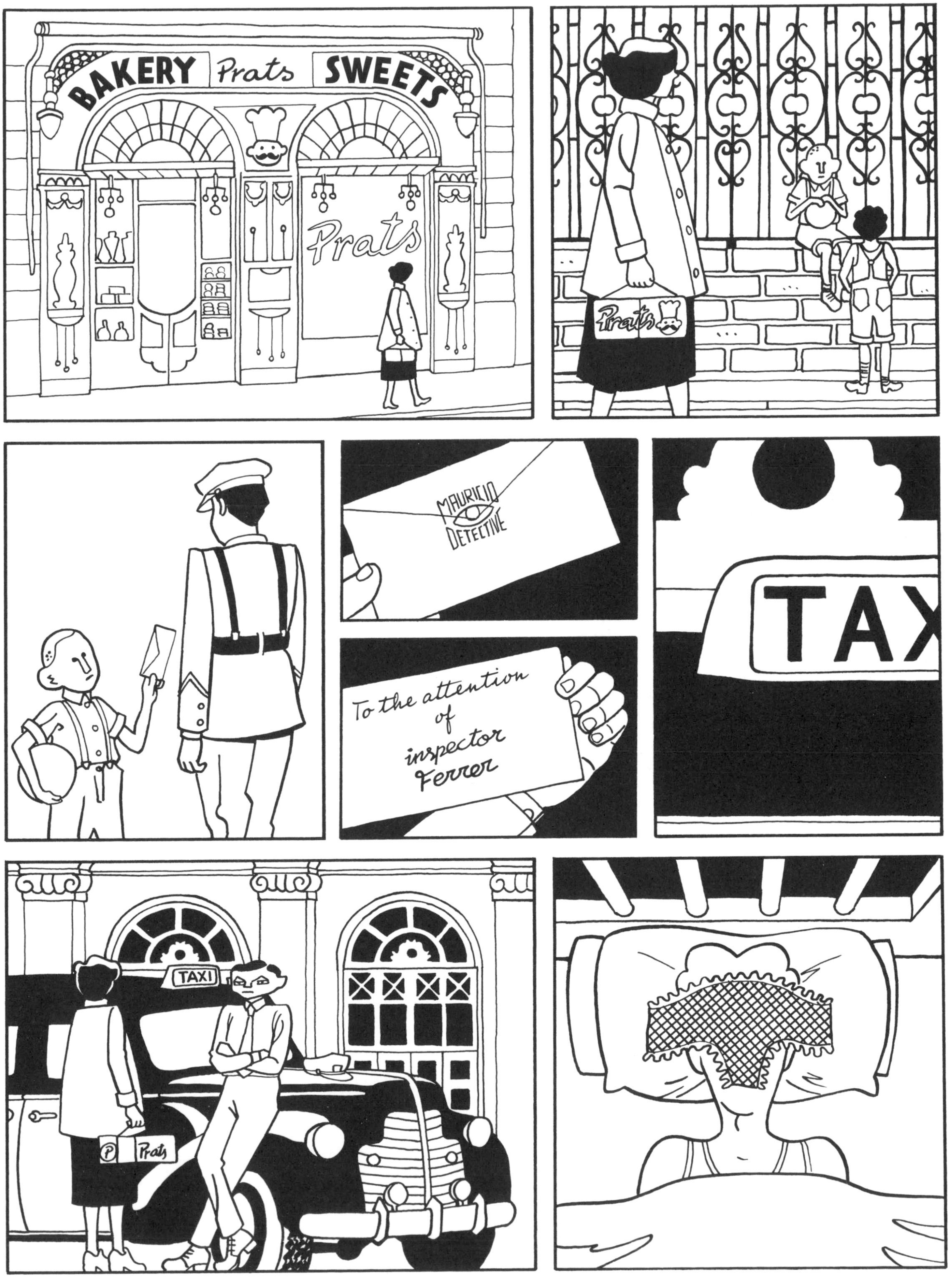
BAKERY
Prats
SWEETS
Prats
Prats
MAURICIO
DETECTIVE
To the attention of inspector Ferrer
TAX
TAXI
Prats

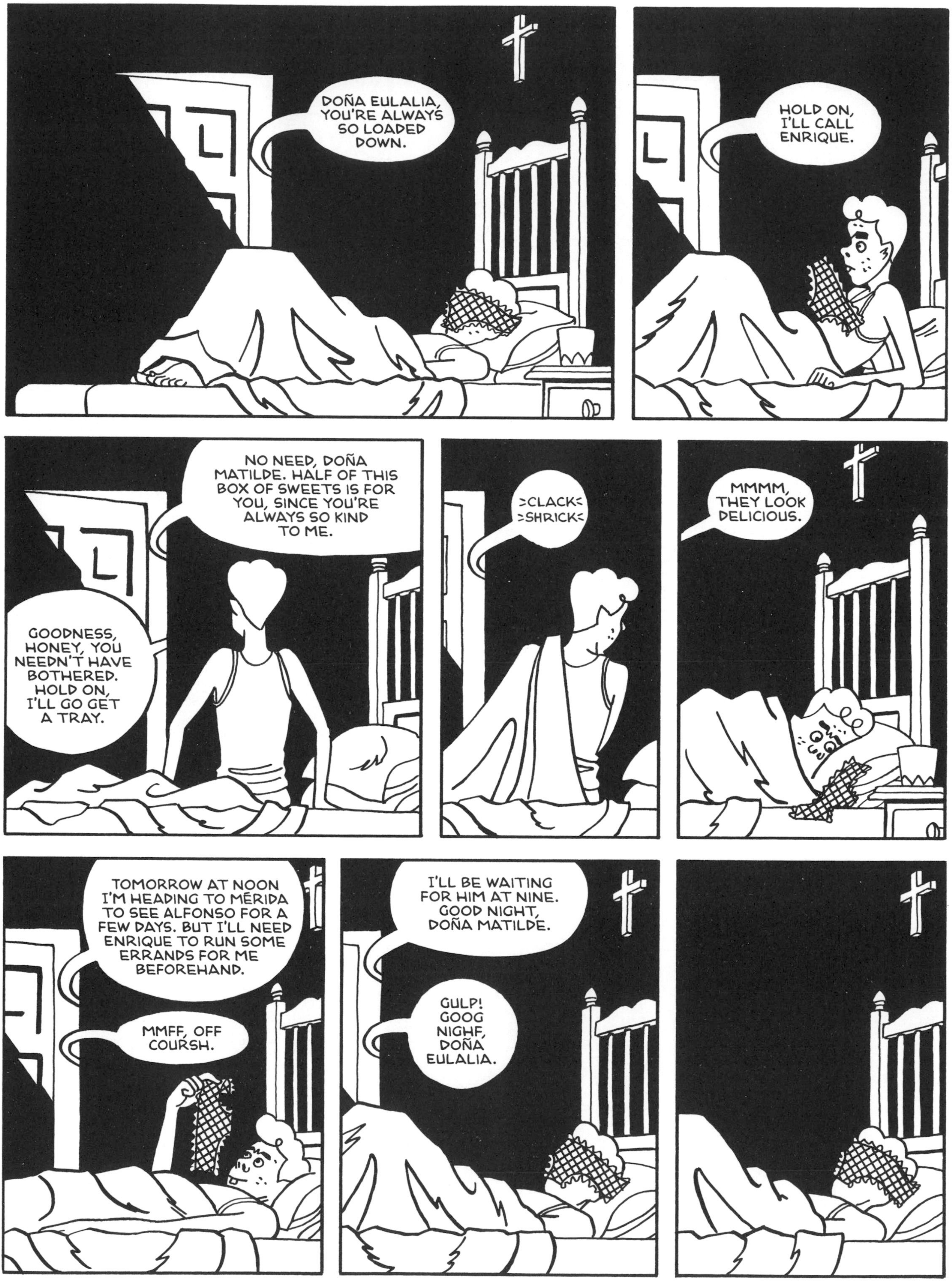
DOÑA EULALIA, YOU'RE ALWAYS SO LOADED DOWN.
HOLD ON, I'LL CALL ENRIQUE.
NO NEED, DOÑA MATILDE. HALF OF THIS BOX OF SWEETS IS FOR YOU, SINCE YOU'RE ALWAYS SO KIND TO ME.
GOODNESS, HONEY, YOU NEEDN'T HAVE BOTHERED. HOLD ON, I'LL GO GET A TRAY.
>CLACK<
>SHRICK<
MMMM, THEY LOOK DELICIOUS.
TOMORROW AT NOON I'M HEADING TO MÉRIDA TO SEE ALFONSO FOR A FEW DAYS. BUT I'LL NEED ENRIQUE TO RUN SOME ERRANDS FOR ME BEFOREHAND.
MMFF, OFF COURSH.
I'LL BE WAITING FOR HIM AT NINE. GOOD NIGHT, DOÑA MATILDE.
GULP! GOOG NIGHF, DOÑA EULALIA.

17
The Beginning of the End

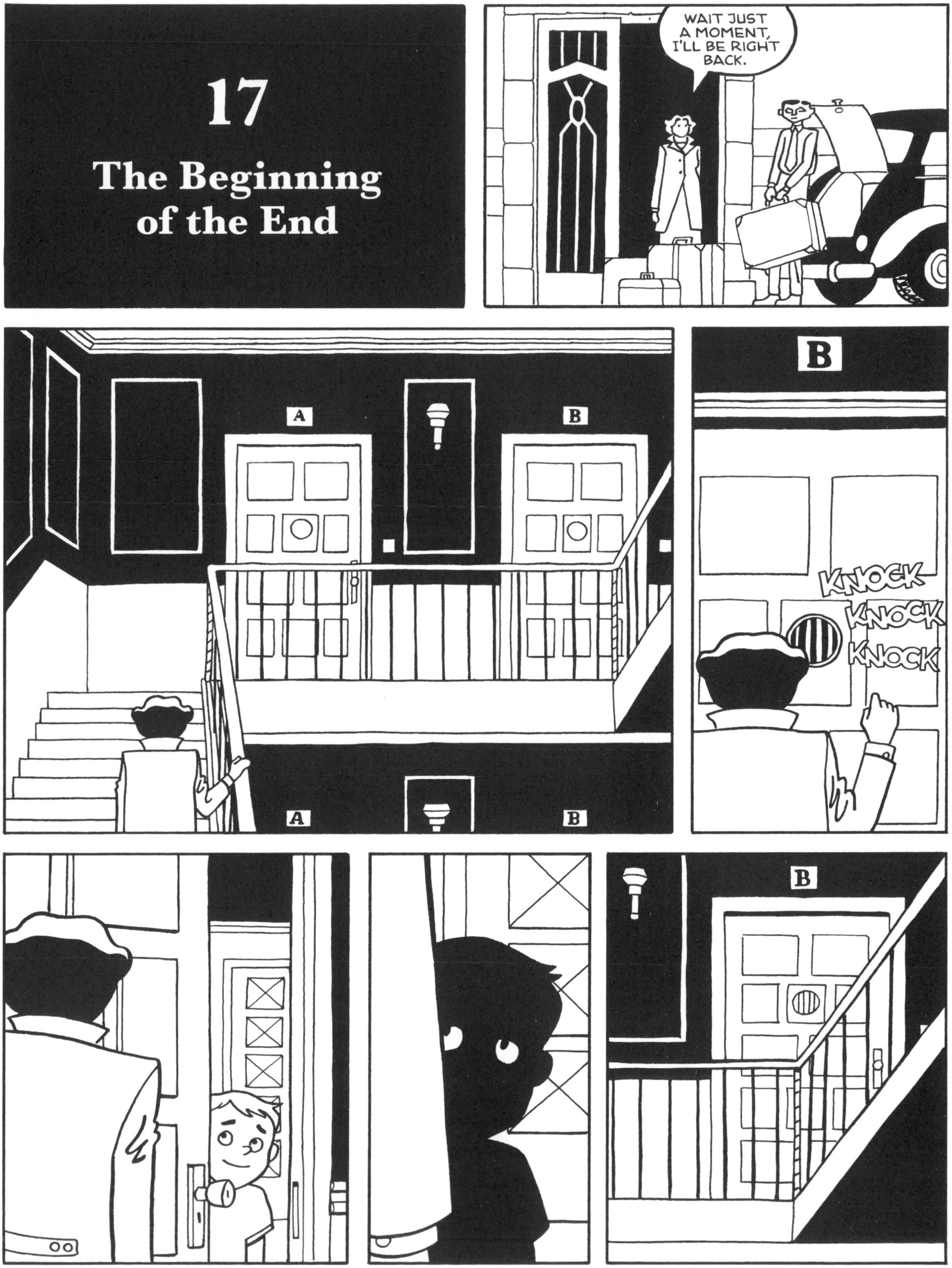
WAIT JUST A MOMENT, I'LL BE RIGHT BACK.
A
B
B
KNOCK
KNOCK
KNOCK
A
B
B

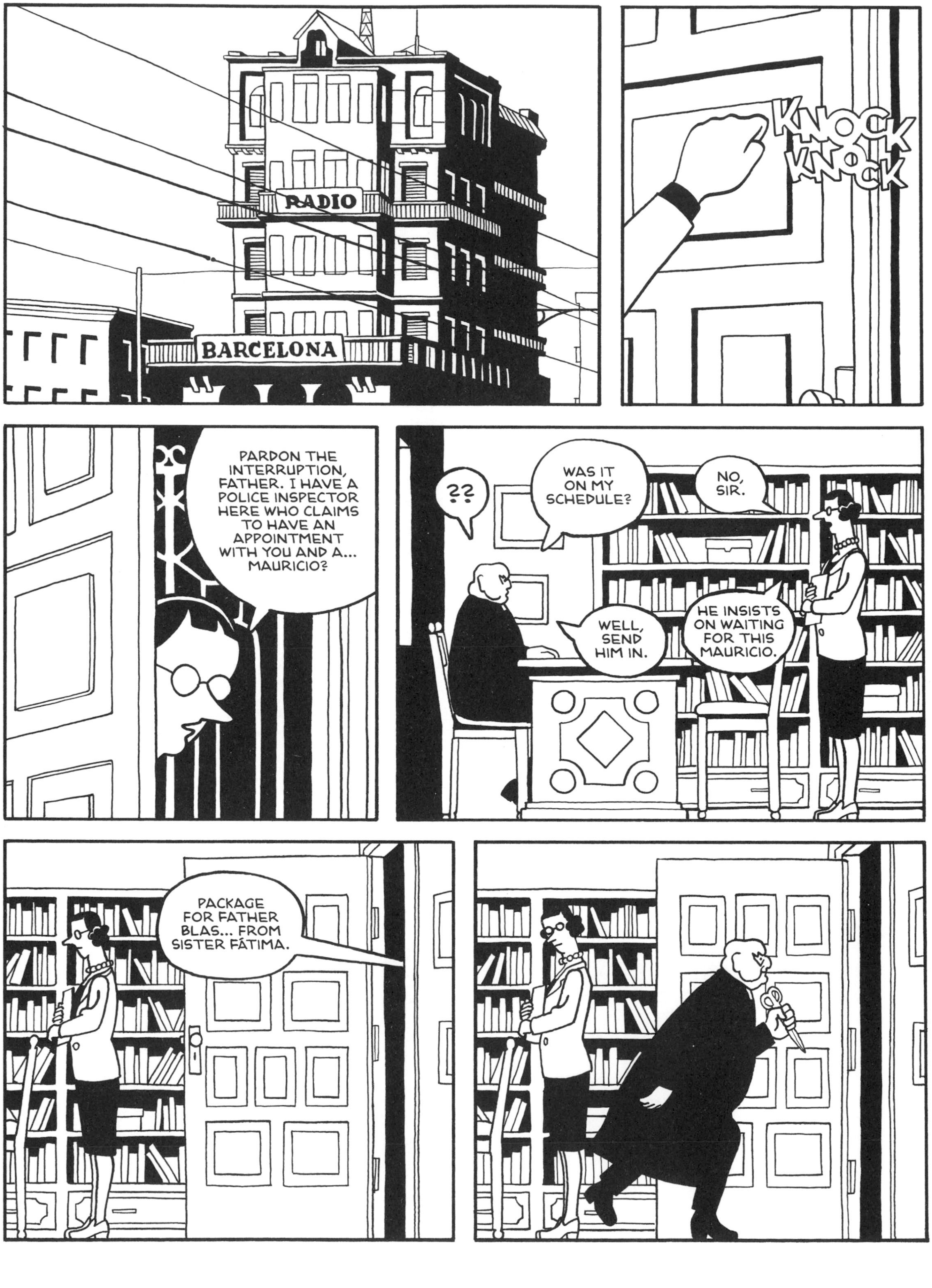
RADIO
BARCELONA
KNOCK KNOCK
PARDON THE INTERRUPTION, FATHER. I HAVE A POLICE INSPECTOR HERE WHO CLAIMS TO HAVE AN APPOINTMENT WITH YOU AND A... MAURICIO?
??
WAS IT ON MY SCHEDULE?
NO, SIR.
HE INSISTS ON WAITING FOR THIS MAURICIO.
WELL, SEND HIM IN.
PACKAGE FOR FATHER BLAS... FROM SISTER FÁTIMA.

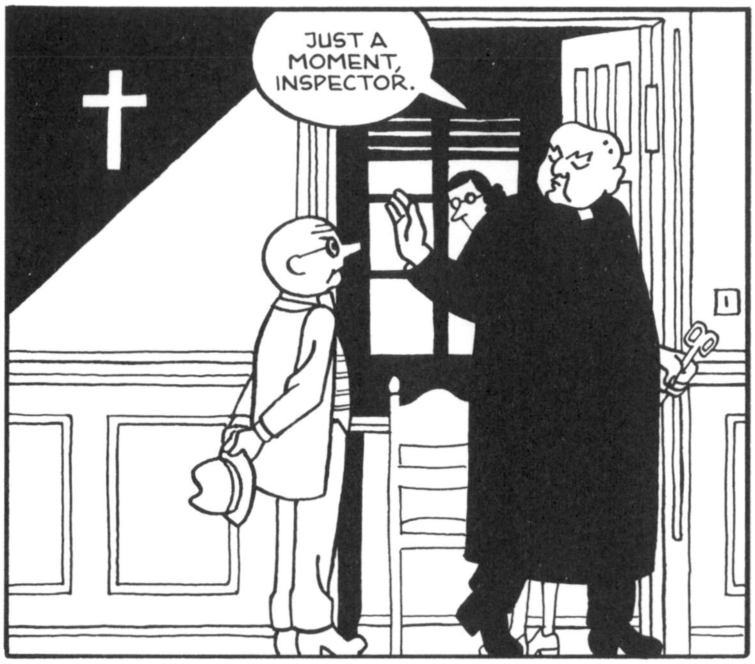
JUST A MOMENT, INSPECTOR.

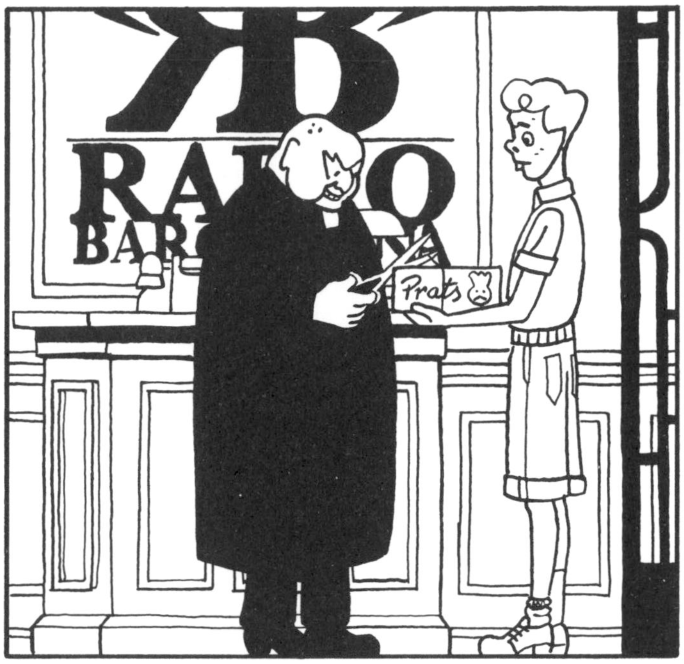
Prats

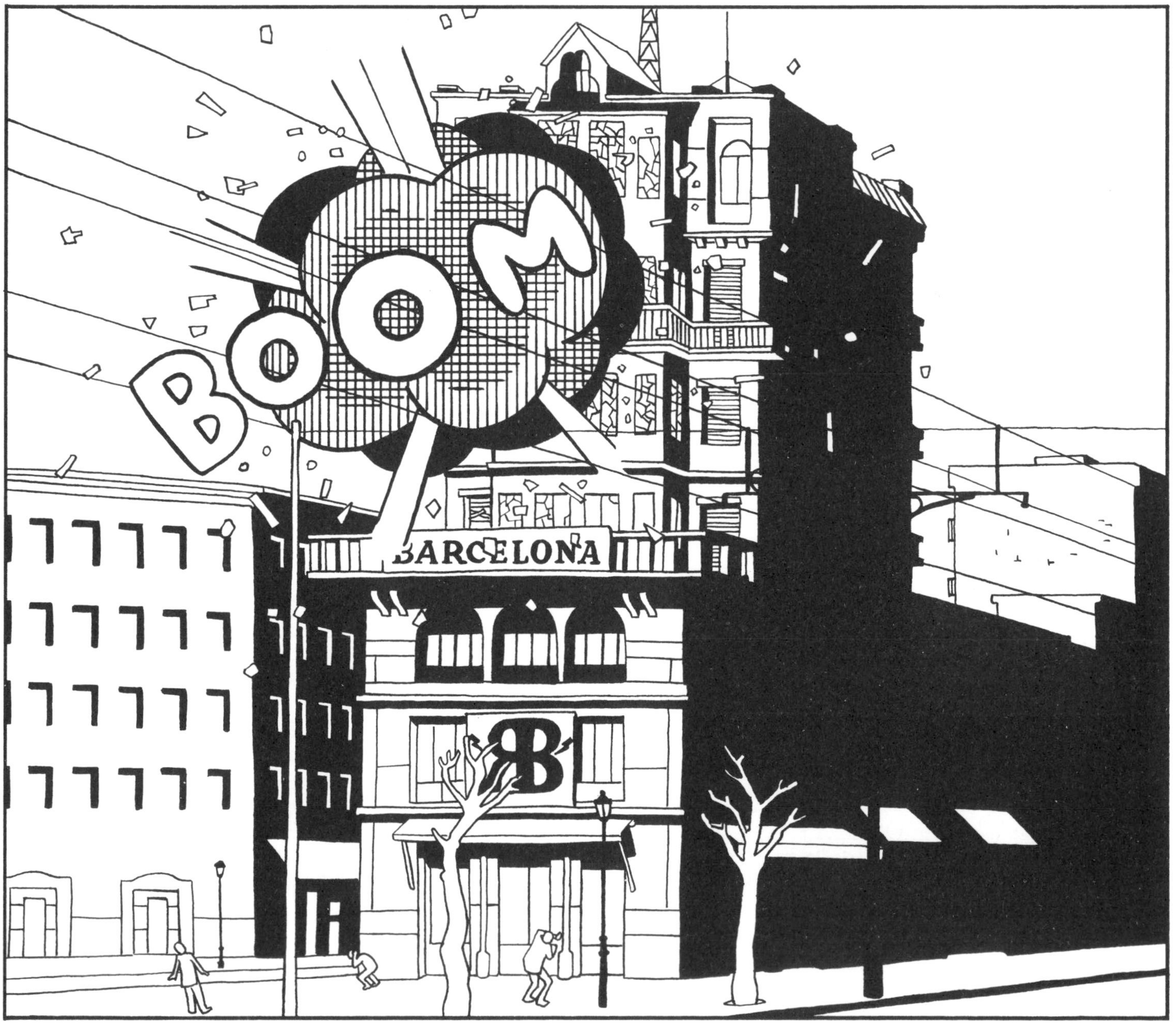
BOOM
BARCELONA

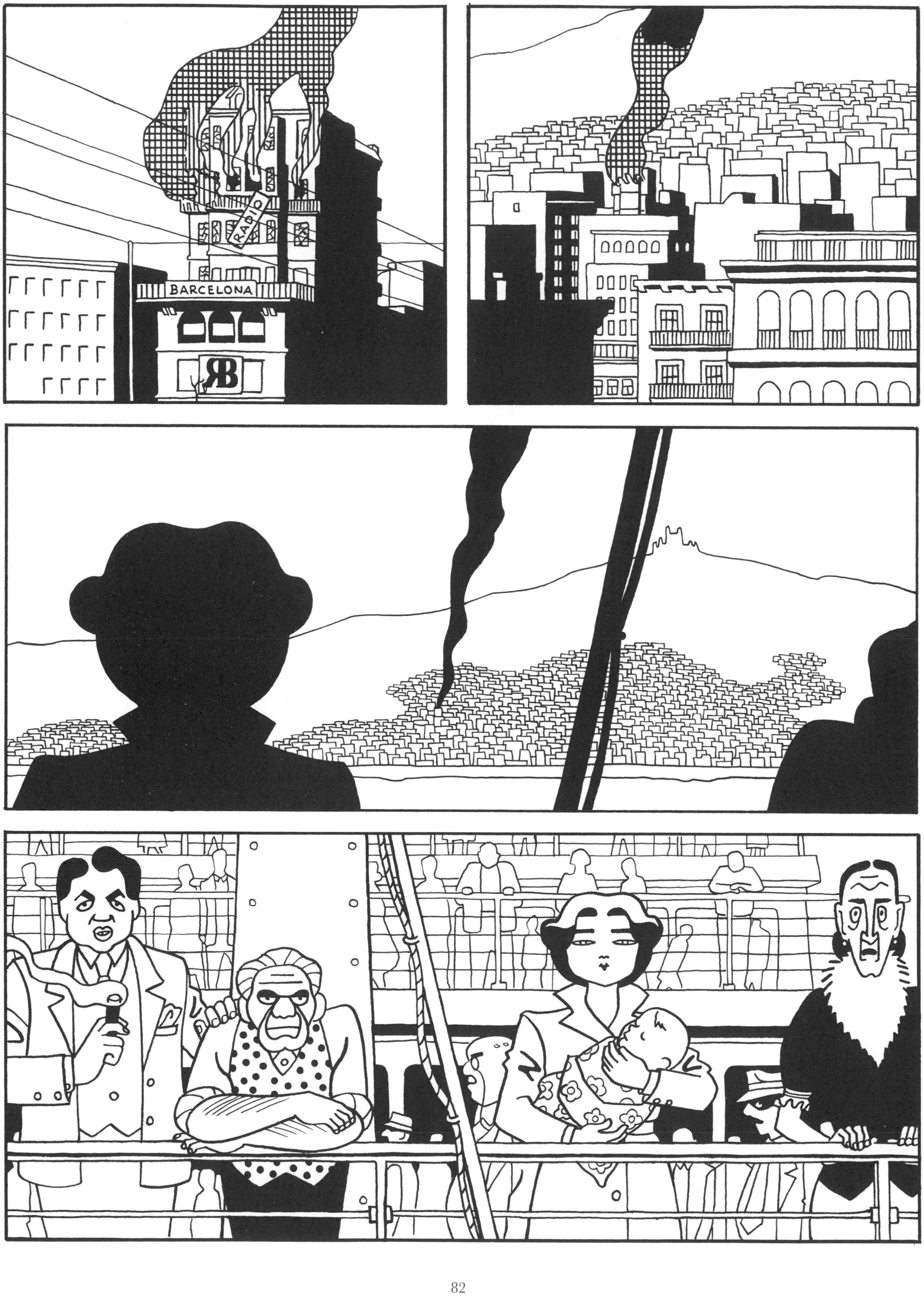
RADIO
BARCELONA
RB

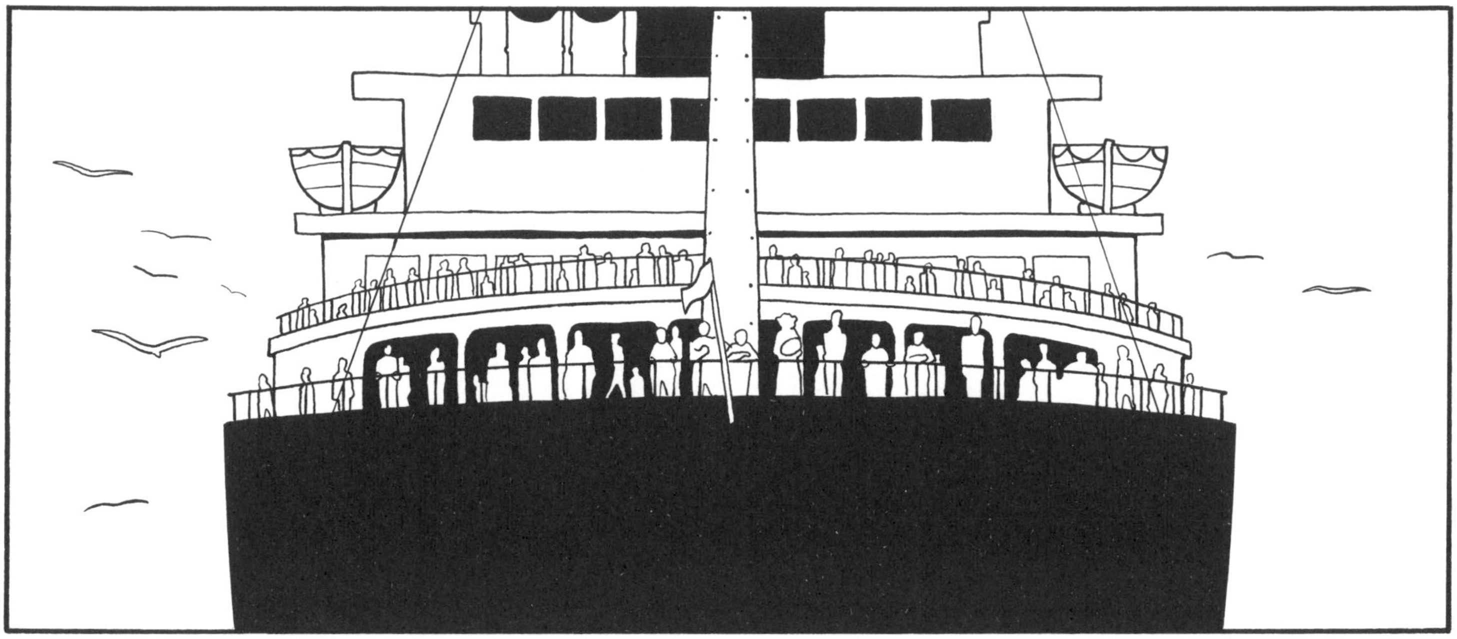

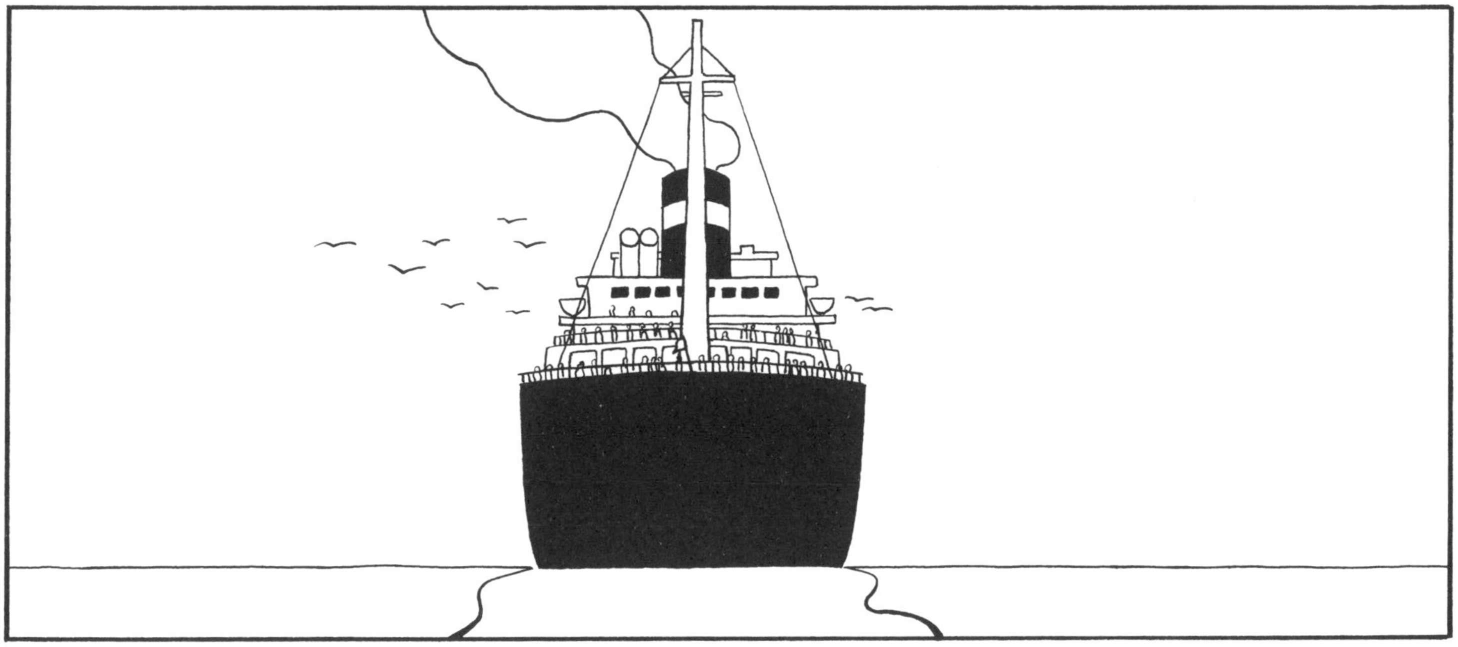

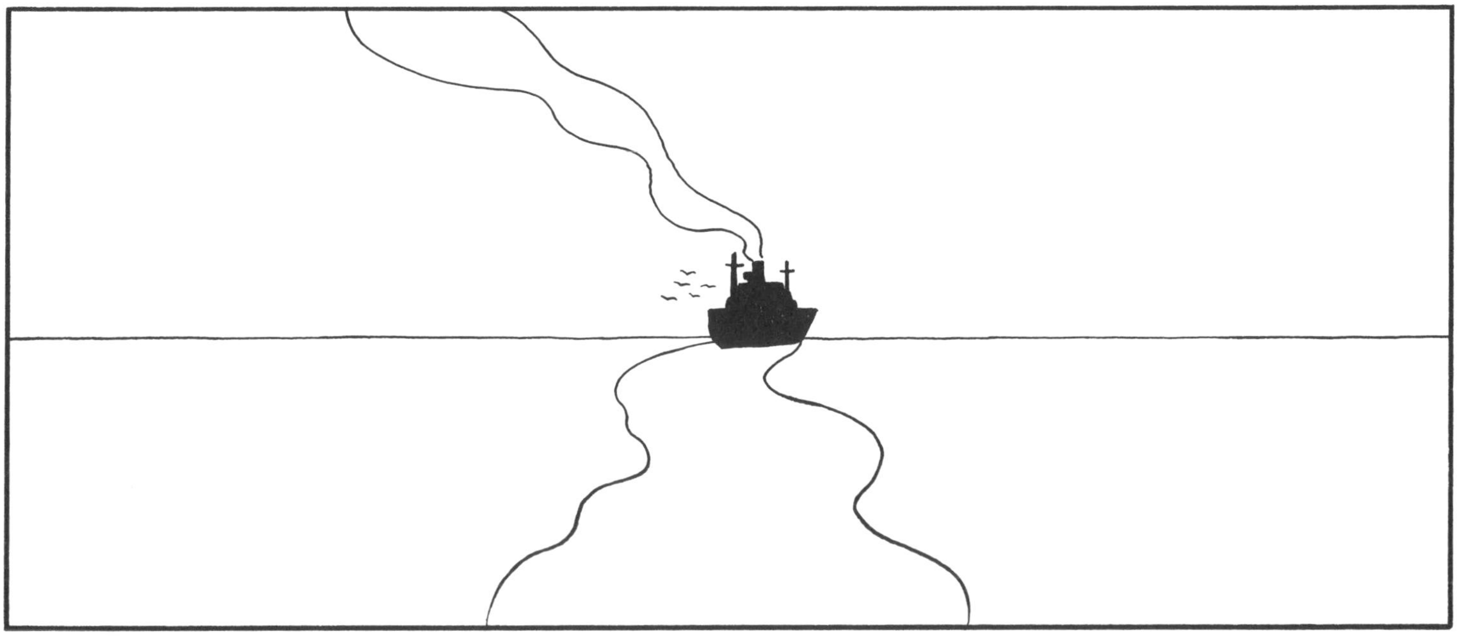

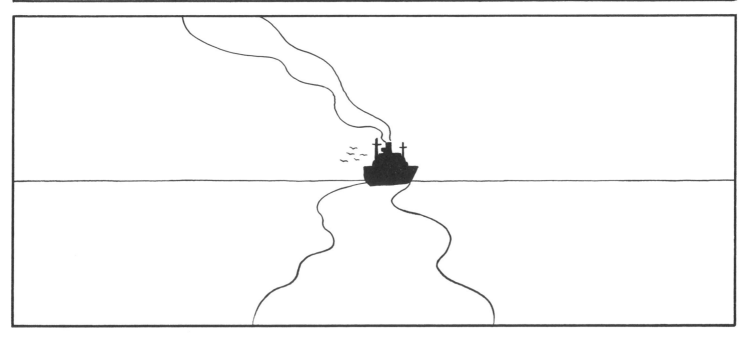

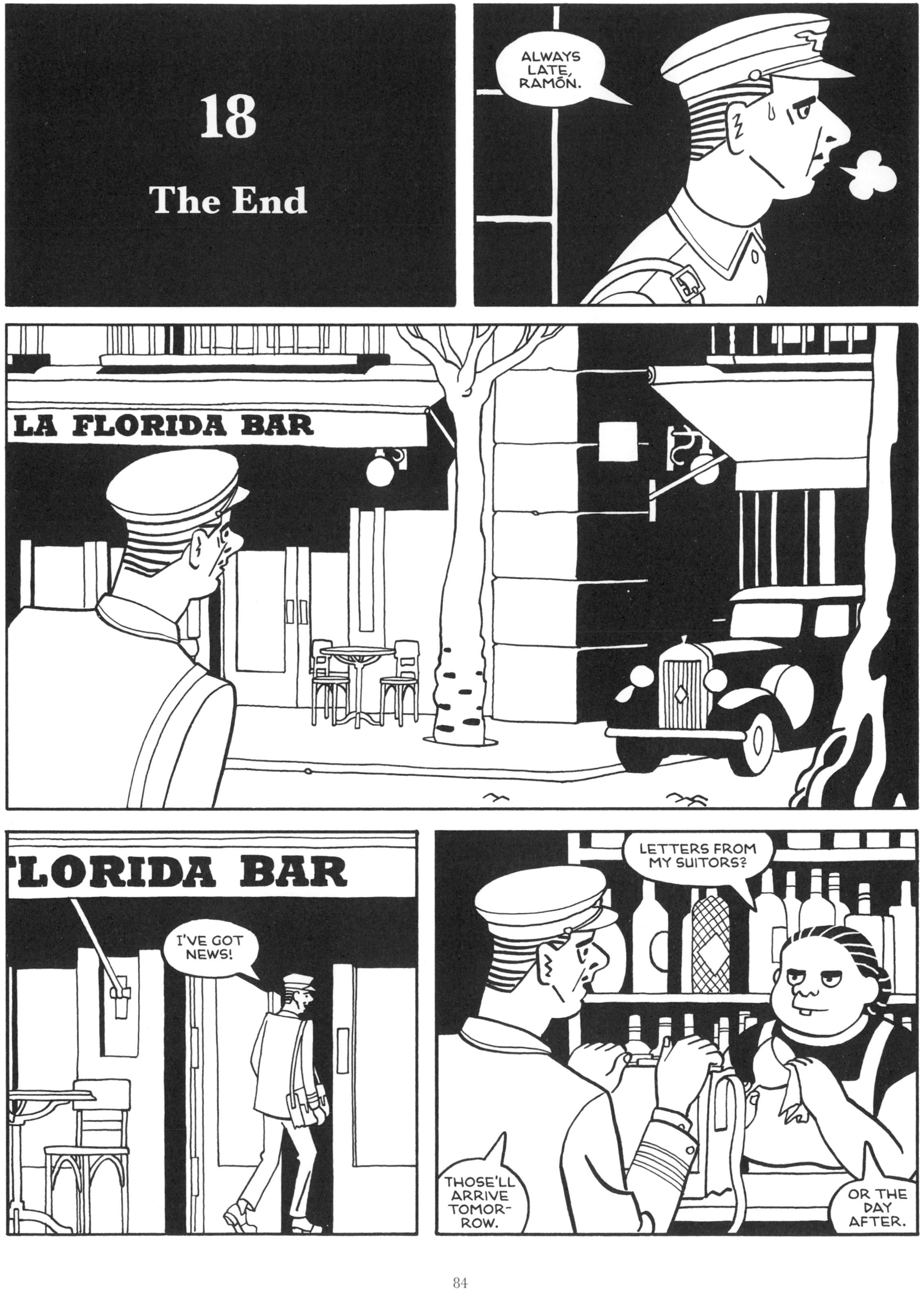
18
The End
ALWAYS LATE, RAMÓN.
LA FLORIDA BAR
FLORIDA BAR
I'VE GOT NEWS!
LETTERS FROM MY SUITORS?
THOSE'LL ARRIVE TOMOR-ROW.
OR THE DAY AFTER.

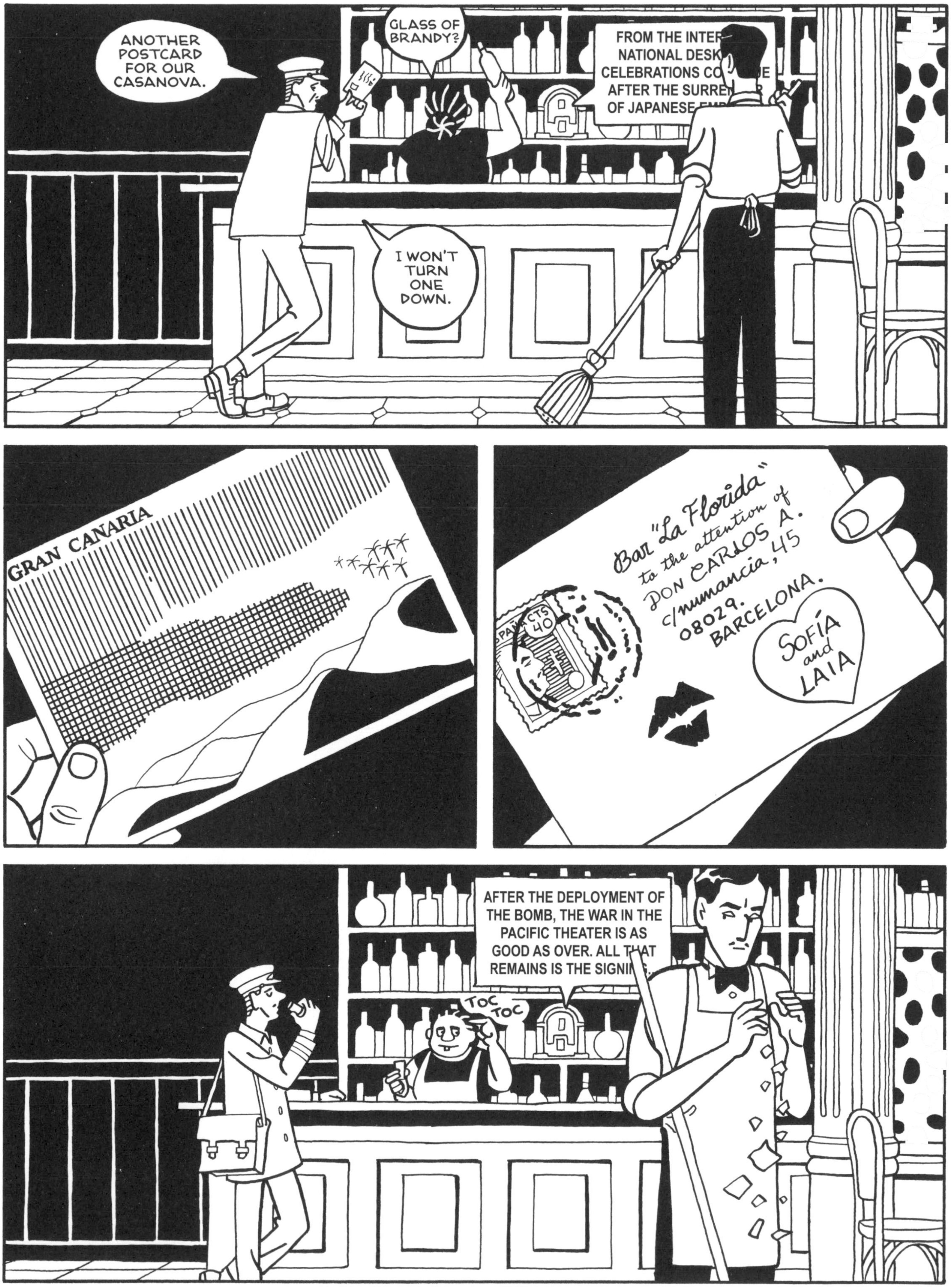
ANOTHER POSTCARD FOR OUR CASANOVA.
GLASS OF BRANDY?
FROM THE INTER- NATIONAL DESK CELEBRATIONS CO E AFTER THE SURRE OF JAPANESE
I WON'T TURN ONE DOWN.
GRAN CANARIA
Bar "La Florida" to the attention of DON CARLOS A. c/numancia, 45 08029. BARCELONA.
SPAIN CTS 40
SOFÍA and LAIA
AFTER THE DEPLOYMENT OF THE BOMB, THE WAR IN THE PACIFIC THEATER IS AS GOOD AS OVER. ALL THAT REMAINS IS THE SIGNIN
TOC TOC

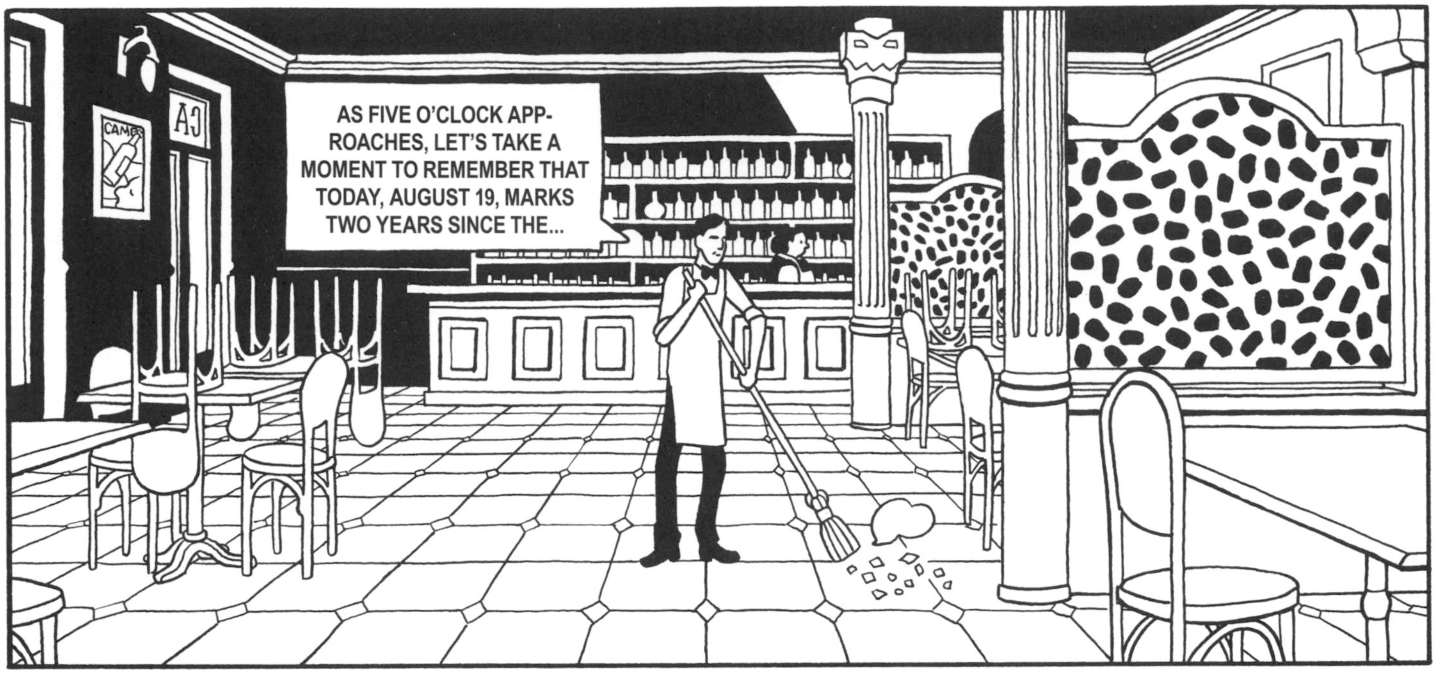
AS FIVE O'CLOCK APP-ROACHES, LET'S TAKE A MOMENT TO REMEMBER THAT TODAY, AUGUST 19, MARKS TWO YEARS SINCE THE...
CAMEO
CA

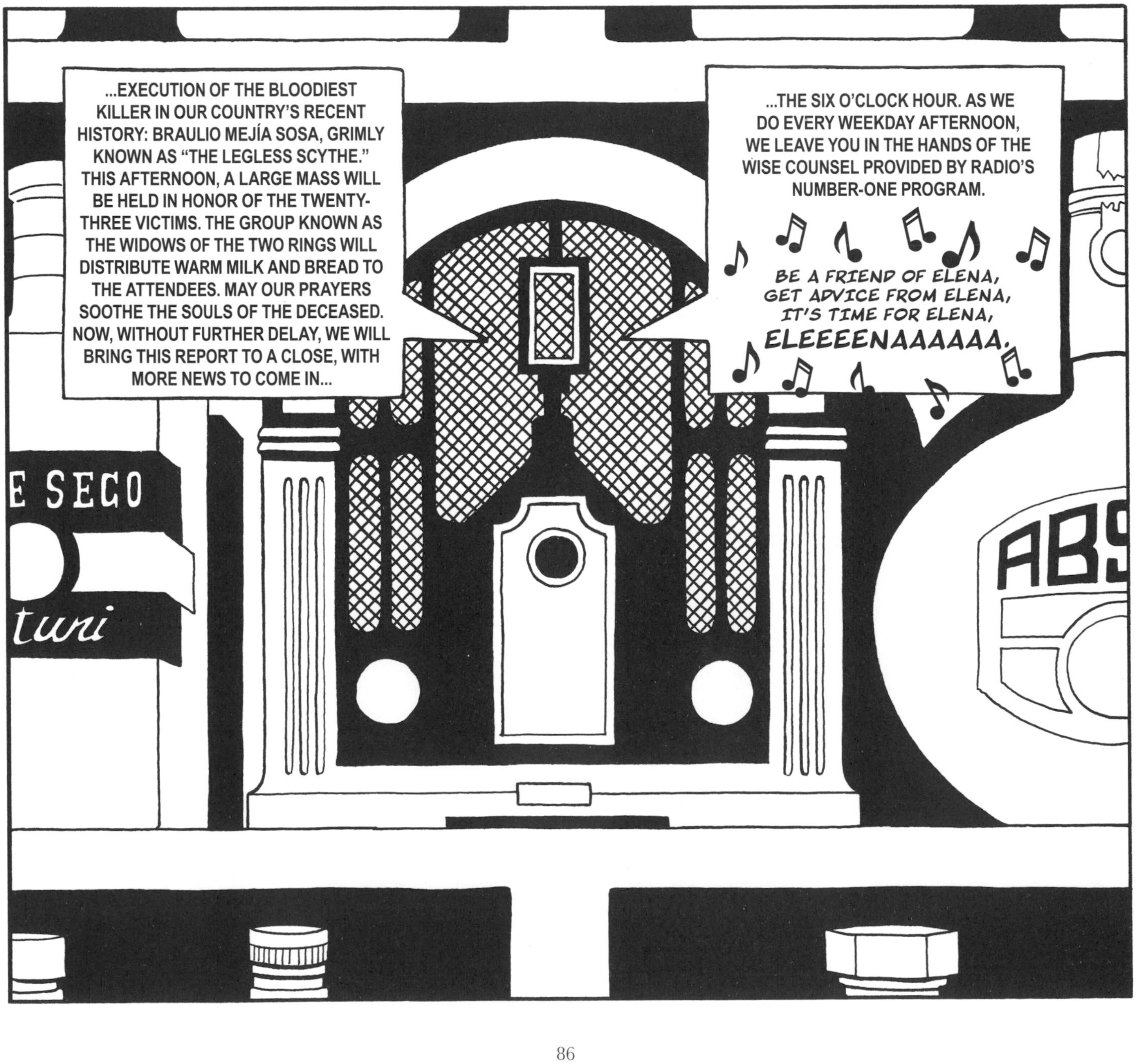
...EXECUTION OF THE BLOODIEST KILLER IN OUR COUNTRY'S RECENT HISTORY: BRAULIO MEJÍA SOSA, GRIMLY KNOWN AS "THE LEGLESS SCYTHE." THIS AFTERNOON, A LARGE MASS WILL BE HELD IN HONOR OF THE TWENTY-THREE VICTIMS. THE GROUP KNOWN AS THE WIDOWS OF THE TWO RINGS WILL DISTRIBUTE WARM MILK AND BREAD TO THE ATTENDEES. MAY OUR PRAYERS SOOTHE THE SOULS OF THE DECEASED. NOW, WITHOUT FURTHER DELAY, WE WILL BRING THIS REPORT TO A CLOSE, WITH MORE NEWS TO COME IN...
...THE SIX O'CLOCK HOUR. AS WE DO EVERY WEEKDAY AFTERNOON, WE LEAVE YOU IN THE HANDS OF THE WISE COUNSEL PROVIDED BY RADIO'S NUMBER-ONE PROGRAM.
BE A FRIEND OF ELENA, GET ADVICE FROM ELENA, IT'S TIME FOR ELENA, ELEEEENAAAAAA.
E SECO
turi
ABS

Epilogue

Every afternoon between 1947 and 1982, upon hearing the swelling melody of Victor Herbert's "Indian Summer" over the radio waves, Spanish households would drop what they were doing to listen to *El consultorio de Elena Francis*—a half-hour advice program with the largest audience of any radio show in Spain. Doña Elena, a matriarch with a wise voice and a soothing tone, would read letters from seven listeners and offer advice on a variety of topics including health, housekeeping, fashion, and especially beauty and relationship issues.

In contemplating this edition of my book, I thought it would be useful to give English-speaking readers some idea of the show's significant role in Spanish society. Fortunately, though the historical radio program provided inspiration for a major element of the plot, such knowledge is not essential for following the story. Nevertheless, I believe this information will enhance readers' understanding and aid them in contextualizing the characters and events.

The radio show itself merits sociological study. It shaped the mindset and habits of several generations of Spanish women. It was an effective indoctrination tool for the dictatorial Franco regime, signaling what womanhood meant for National Catholicism: "obedient girl, obliging wife, selfless mother." Of course, the program presented the version of Spain that the regime wished to depict—that's what the censors were for—but it also slipped in letters on racy topics such as domestic violence, infidelity, and homosexuality. These served as effective hooks for capturing listeners; people find it comforting to know that others have it worse than they do. In fact, *El consultorio de Elena Francis* could be considered the first forerunner of the reality show in Spain.

Doña Elena always gave the same advice: "Hang in there," "Marriage is sacred," "If he's unfaithful, it's because you're not doing enough," etc. It was the same advice the local priest might give, but the radio program offered the additional benefit of anonymity. Elena Francis was many women rolled into one: friend, confidant, spiritual guide, but also censor, judge, repressor. Her tone was maternal, and though she was sometimes indulgent and at other times quite stern, her infallibility and good judgment were indisputable. She was the kind of woman that all women aspired to be… and yet she never existed.

El consultorio de Elena Francis was one of the most successful and longest running promotional campaigns in the history of Spanish marketing. The creator of the program was the Instituto de Belleza Francis, a Catalonian cosmetics company that pushed its products by dressing up advertisements as advice. But what started as a few beauty tips developed into a portrait of Spain during the postwar period, the Franco era, and the transition from dictatorship to democracy. Behind Elena Francis was a group of scriptwriters, a couple of voice actresses, and a censor (usually a priest). They held that secret for nearly forty years.

The program also had a team that answered every letter, regardless of whether they were used on the air; that was one of the house rules. In 2007, while emptying out an old country house that had belonged to the owner of the Instituto de Belleza Francis, workers found hundreds of boxes full of paper, all of the letters received at the show. Cataloging them revealed the true nature of postwar Spanish society: poverty, violence, illiteracy, superstition, male chauvinism, repression, hunger, and fear. In the afternoons, Doña Elena would answer a few censor-selected letters; this was unquestionably a clever use of mass media by the Franco regime.

With the changes that took place with the democratic transition in 1978 and the rise of television, Elena Francis's program shut down. Nevertheless, this little-studied sociological phenomenon helps shed light on the roots of contemporary Spain.

The Process: Character Design

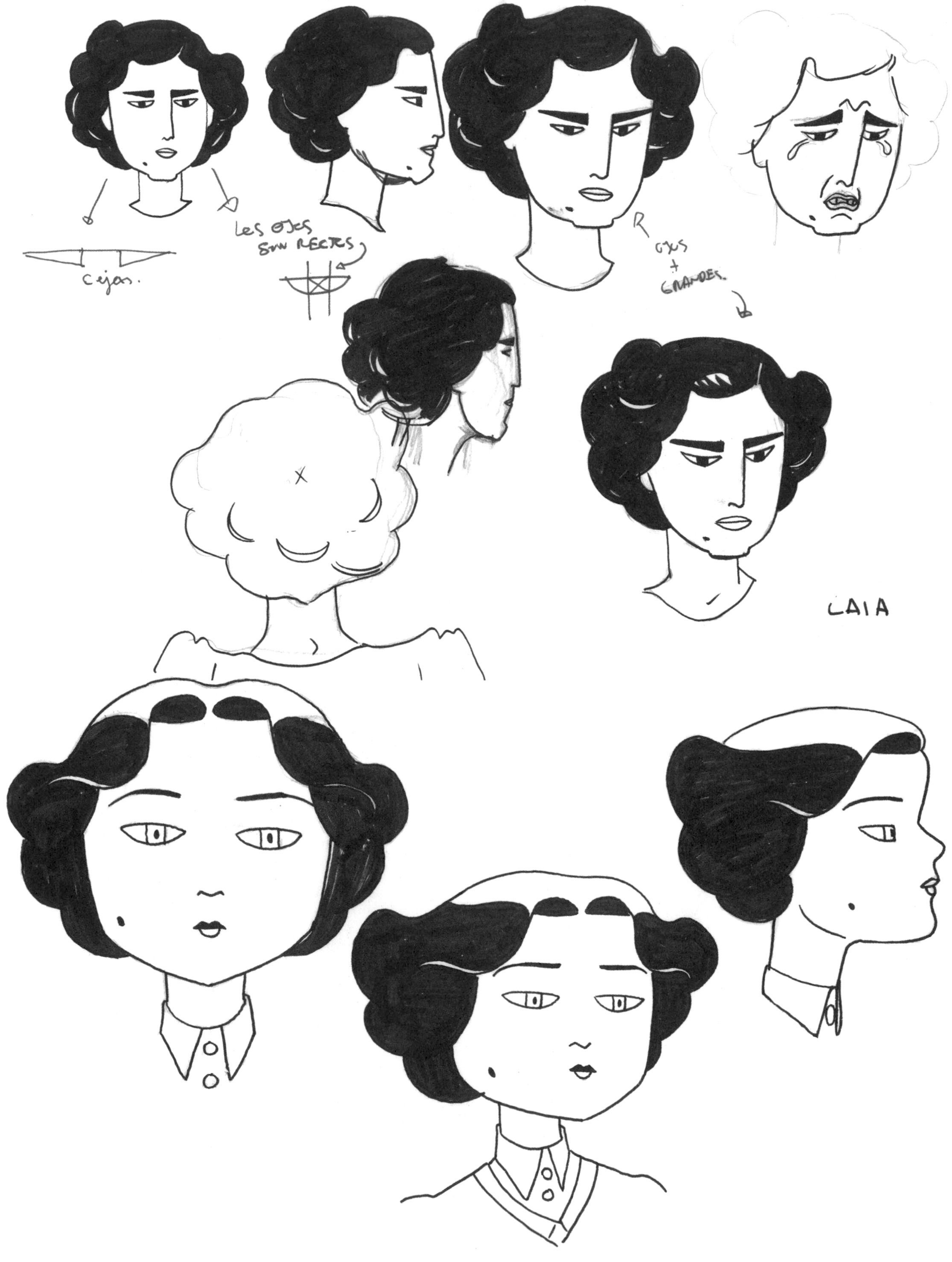
cejas.
LOS OJOS SON RECTOS
OJOS + GRANDES.
LAIA

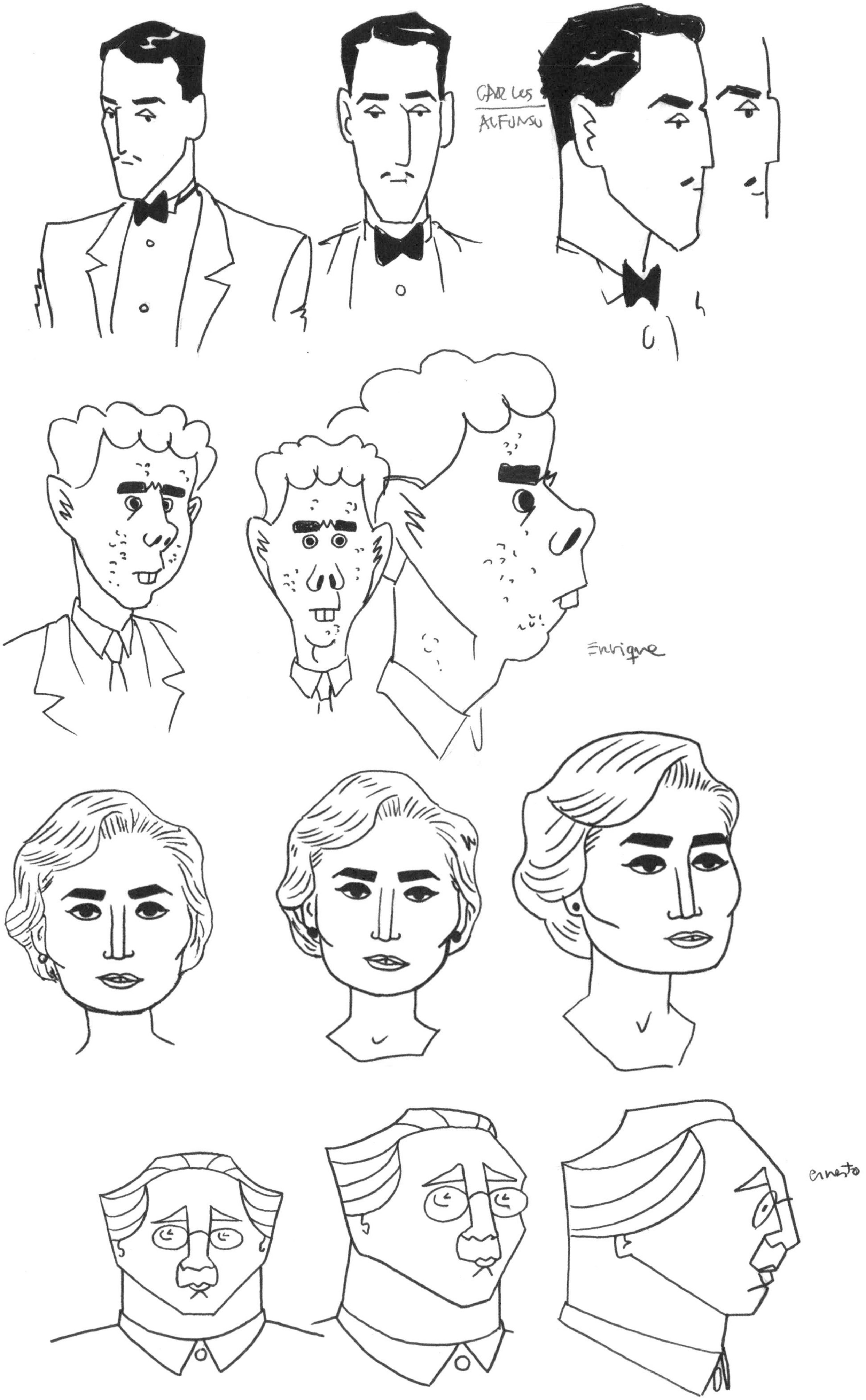
CARLES
ALFONSO
Enrique
ernesto

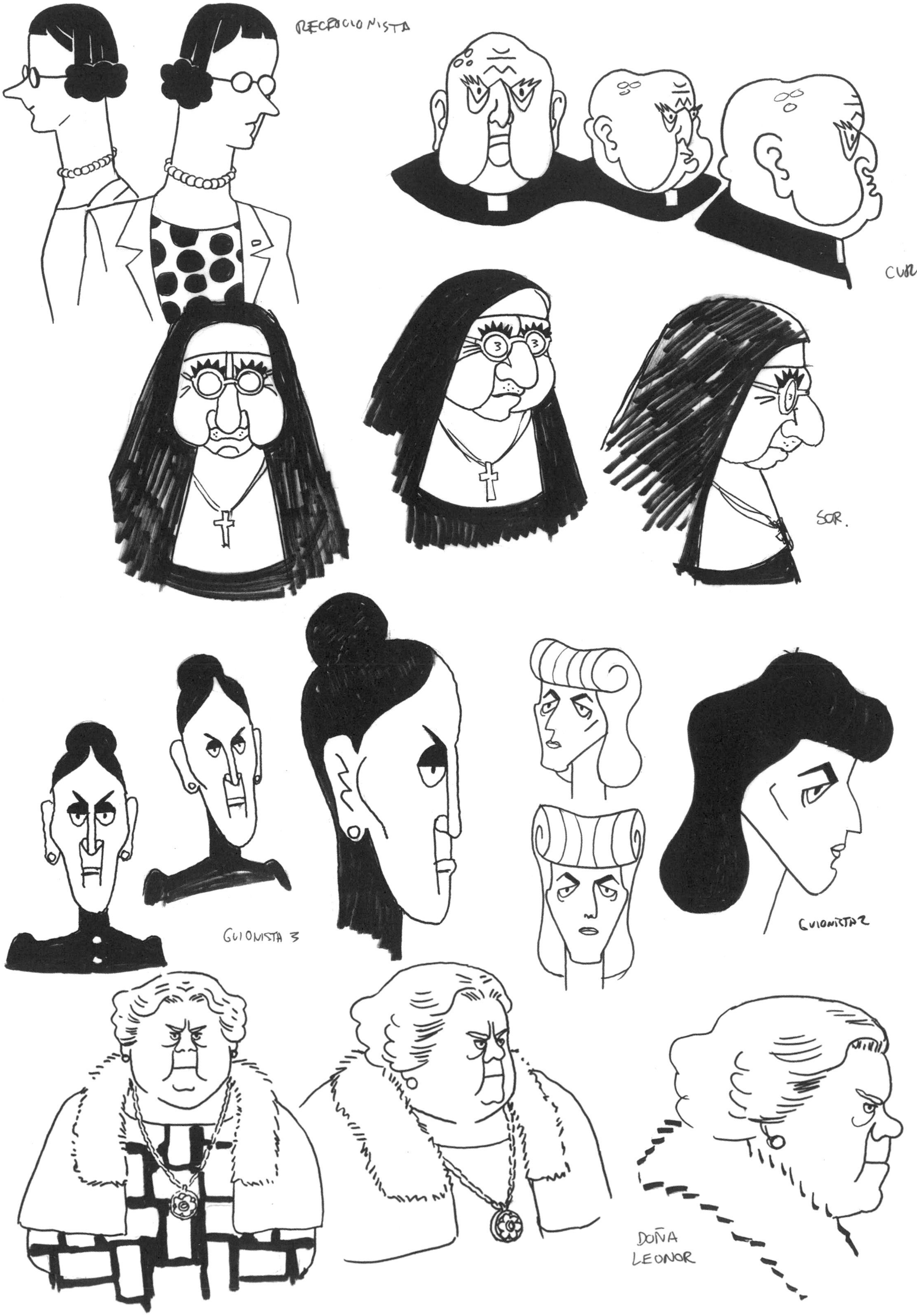
RECEPCIONISTA
CURA
SOR.
GUIONISTA 3
GUIONISTA 2
DOÑA
LEONOR

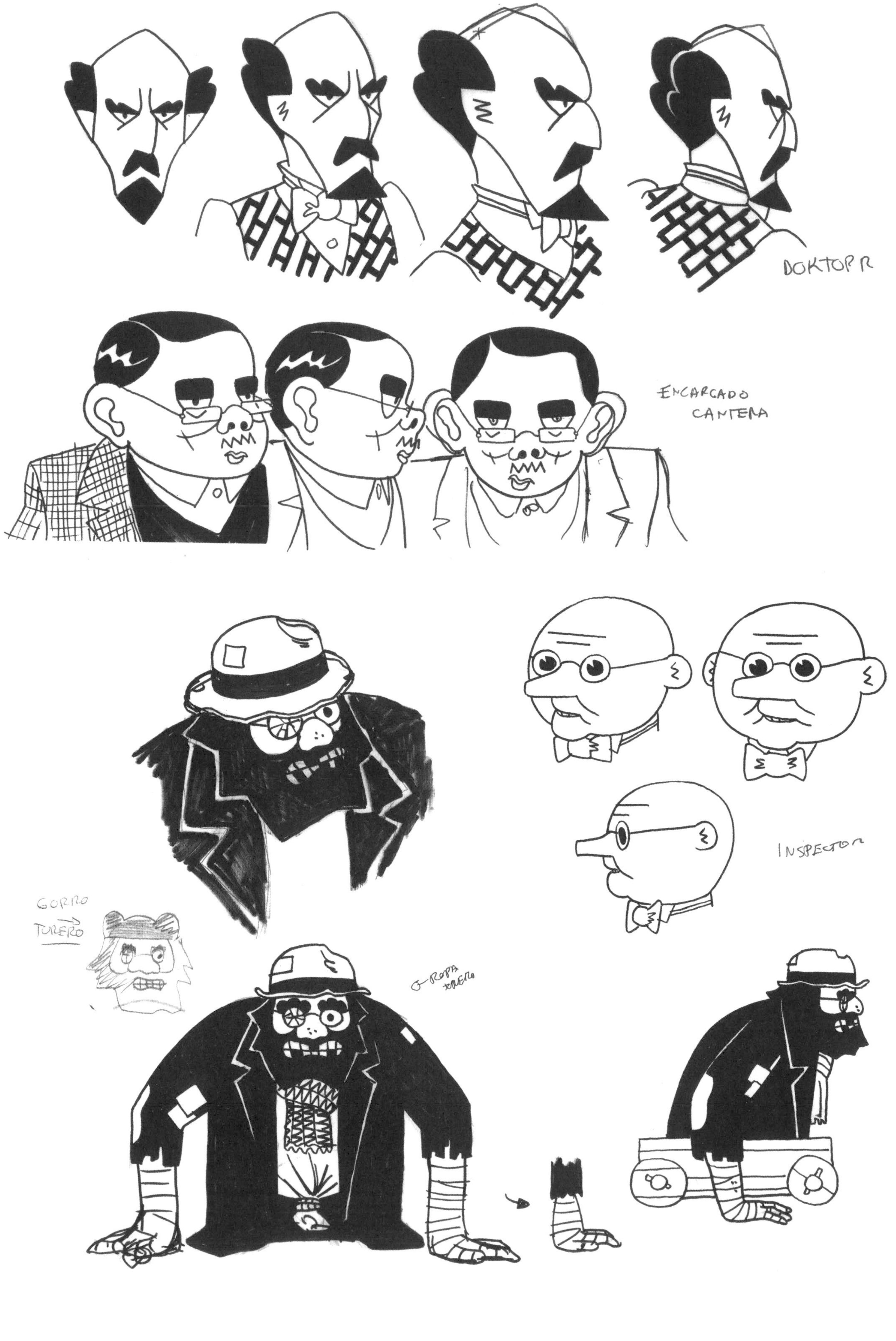
DOKTOR
ENCARGADO CANTERA
INSPECTOR
GORRO → TORERO
ROPA TORERO

RAYCO PULIDO (b. 1978) is a cartoonist and teacher from Telde, in the Canary Islands. In 2017, he won Spain's National Comics Award for *Lamia* (*Ghostwriter*). His other works include *Final Feliz* (with Hernán Migoya, 2004), *Sordo* (with David Muñoz, 2008), *Sin Título, 2008–2011* (2011), and *Nela* (2013).